FEDERALISM

Comparative Perspectives from India and Australia

FEDERALISM

Comparative Perspectives from India and Australia

edited by

IAN COPLAND and JOHN RICKARD

Published in association with
The National Centre for Australian Studies and
The Centre of South Asian Studies
Monash University
Melbourne

MANOHAR
1999

First published 1999

ISBN 81-7304-239-X

Published by
Ajay Kumar Jain for
Manohar Publishers & Distributors
2/6 Ansari Road, Daryaganj
New Delhi 110002

Lasertypeset by
A J Software Publishing Co. Pvt. Ltd.
305 Durga Chambers
1333 D.B. Gupta Road
Karol Bagh, New Delhi 110005

Printed at
Replika Press Pvt. Ltd.
Plot No. A-229, DSIDC Narela Indl. Park
Delhi 110040

Contents

Acknowledgements

This book grew out of an international conference held at Monash University in July 1996. The project-editors gratefully acknowledge the generous financial support of the Australia-India Council and the Commonwealth Department of Foreign Affairs and Trade.

Contributors

Dr Ian Copland and Professor John Rickard teach History at Monash University, Melbourne.

Professor Shibani Kinkar Chaube teaches Politics at Delhi University.

Professor H.P. Lee teaches Constitutional Law at Monash University, Melbourne.

Mr James A. Thomson works in the Crown Solicitor's Office, Perth.

Mr Robert Watt teaches Law at the University of Technology, Sydney.

Professor Beryl A. Radin teaches Public Administration and Policy at the State University of New York.

Professor Paul R. Brass teaches Politics at the University of Washington, Seattle. At the time of writing he was a Visiting Fellow at the National Centre for South Asian Studies, Melbourne.

Professor Zoya Hasan teaches Politics at Jawaharlal Nehru University, Delhi.

Dr Javeed Alam teaches History and Politics at the University of Himachal Pradesh, Simla. At the time of writing he was Visiting Fellow at the Centre for the Study of Developing Societies, Delhi.

Dr Suri Ratnapala teaches Law and is at present Associate Professor at the University of Queensland, Brisbane.

Dr Peter Mayer teaches Politics at the University of Adelaide.

Professor Stuart Macintyre teaches History at the University of Melbourne.

Professor Brian Galligan and Dr John Chesterman teach Public Policy at the University of Melbourne.

Professor John McLaren teaches Humanities at Victoria University, Melbourne.

The Honourable J.C. Bannon is a former Premier of South Australia. He now researches Politics at Flinders University, Adelaide.

Professor Bhajan S. Grewal teaches Business Studies at Victoria University, Melbourne.

Dr Rokkam S. Rao teaches Economics at the University of Andhra Pradesh, Visakhapatnam.

His Excellency G. Parthasarathy is a senior member of the Indian Foreign Service. At the time of writing he was High Commissioner to Australia.

Introduction

IAN COPLAND and JOHN RICKARD

Federal systems of government are common in the modern world, partly because federalism has often seemed an appropriate means of welding potentially incompatible communities into a nation state. Even as the English political tradition looked with disfavour on the idea of a written constitution, several federations, inscribed in constitutional texts, emerged from the disbanding of the empire. Yet, as we shall see, there are different kinds of federations, distinguished by different power-sharing arrangements between the federal centre and its constituent units. The Republic of India and the Commonwealth of Australia are two prominent members of this worldwide family.

In many respects, India and Australia stand in stark contrast to one another. India is home to over 900 million people, Australia to less than 18 million. Australia has one official language, India has thirteen. While Australia and India are both 'multicultural', in Australia this pluralism has not assumed territorial form (except very locally in big cities), whereas in India the constituent states of the Union all have distinct ethnic/cultural identities (so much so that some Marxist scholars reckon that India is a 'multinational' State). By and large, Australians live comfortably; many Indians, by contrast, struggle even to feed, clothe and house themselves adequately. Moreover the two countries achieved nationhood in very different circumstances. The federal compact in Australia was framed in a setting of relative peace; the Indian Constituent Assembly of 1946-50 deliberated against a background of partition, mass of migration, bloodshed, and the threat of war. Given their manifest societal and historical differences, it is not surprising that the two countries opted for rather different styles of federation; even so, the contrasts on paper are startling.

In Australia, the original balance of power in the Constitution lay clearly with the states which came together in 1901 to form the Commonwealth. The six 'contracting' states were prepared to give up to the Commonwealth powers over matters which seemed to them essentially national in scope, such as defence and communications, but they kept to themselves control over most of the administrative business of government, such as the delivery of education and public health. Broadly, 'residual' powers stayed with the states. What is more, they retained—in perpetuity—their own constitutions and boundaries. Constitutional amendment in Australia in the direction of further centralization is possible, but it is very difficult and has rarely succeeded; the most significant shifts of power to the Commonwealth have flowed from judicial interpretation. The Indian federation, on the other hand, treats its constituent states strictly as subordinate entities. One generic constitution, adopted unilaterally in 1950, applies to all the states. Residual powers are vested in the centre. The federal parliament can form new states out of existing ones, and can make laws on any subject, including subjects ostensibly reserved to the states, with the approval of two-thirds of its members. Unlike in Australia, the Upper House is not even notionally a 'States house'. Most important, the Indian Constitution gives the president (in effect, under the prevailing Westminster convention, the prime minister of the day) the right, in case of a local political deadlock, administrative breakdown or financial crisis, to sack a state government and run the state directly from the centre, through an appointed administrator, for a period of up to six months.[1] These provisions are so extreme, and so unusual, that some scholars question whether India is truly a federation.[2] We will return to this point later. Yet if the Indian Constitution is much more centralist than Australia's it is also, arguably, more democratic, in that it spells out the fundamental rights of its citizens. The Australian Constitution not only lacks a charter of civil rights but, as Brian Galligan and John Chesterman remind us, it did not for some decades even recognize a significant section of the population—the Aborigines—as full members of the body politic.

On the face of it Australia belongs at one end of the federal spectrum, India at the other. However, the political reality is not quite what the constitutional picture would suggest. In Australia, the years since federation have seen a steady, if somewhat surreptitious, increase in the Commonwealth government's authority over areas of public life that the founding fathers intended to be the preserve of the states. Much of this took place during the two World Wars, under the guise of the defence power, but more recently there have also been inroads under the Commonwealth's foreign affairs power, which has been construed by the High Court to include power over such areas as conservation and human rights where state policies conflict with Australia's international treaty obligations. James Thomson argues that there may be room in the Australian Constitution for still further federal penetration, specifically in regard to the amendment of state constitutions. Conversely, in India, the states exercise rather more power than is suggested by a narrow reading of the Constitution. While the Union maps out strategies and holds the purse-strings, much of the actual implementation of policy is carried out at the state level, which gives state governments and bureaucracies a lot of leverage and room for manoeuvre. Some Indian states have been known even to negotiate trade deals with foreign governments. Again, state governments are closer to the electors and to the local networks of patronage that are so integral to Indian politics. These networks cut across and transcend the formal layers of power. Thirdly, as in Australia, constitutional relations are mediated by the judiciary; but with the difference that the Indian Supreme Court, unlike the Australian High Court, has adopted a conservative stance toward federal power. As H.P. Lee, points out, today the power of 'President's Rule' is somewhat constrained by the willingness of the Court to judicially review proclamations issued under Article 356.

Hence the two federal systems are not as far apart as one might think. Moreover, contrary to popular opinion, there are several points of convergence. Both federations, unusually, emerged out of constitutional conventions elected by popular vote. At least one feature of the Indian federation—the Finance Commission—was borrowed directly from the Australian model. Although the Finance Commission and the Grants Commission operate rather differently, according to Bhajan Grewal there has been some discussion in India recently about modifying the Indian approach to grant distribution in ways that would 'bring the two countries' approaches closer'. In both federations there has been an incremental growth in central power at the expense of state powers. Australian and Indian state governments are equally strapped for cash under existing fiscal arrangements; and both (as Peter Mayer points out) have come to rely increasingly on gambling taxes to augment their revenues. Last but not least, as Shibani Chaube explains, the two federations bear the stamp of the British imperial experience that was common to both countries. But while the Indian federation stemmed from the dismantling of empire, Stuart Macintyre reminds us that in 1901 the Australian Constitution was hailed as evidence of maturity of the British Empire.

Given these illuminating parallels and contrasts, one would have thought that India and Australia represent a fertile field for comparative study. But Australian and Indian scholars in the humanities and social sciences do not meet regularly, and for the most part comparative work on the two countries, whether it be in the fields of English literature, or constitutional law, or colonial history, is conspicuously lacking. As for federalism, a quick search of the library catalogue unearthed only a handful of volumes relevant to our theme.[3] This symposium is a contribution to filling that gap. What do the sixteen essays that follow tell us about the workings of the Indian and Australian federations and, more generally, about the virtues and disadvantages of federalism as a governing system? Perhaps five main points emerge.

The first thing on which most of our contributors agree is that federations, to be successful, must broadly reflect the ethnic configuration of their constituent populations. They must, in John McLaren's words, mirror the sense of community that exists in the lived experience of their citizens. To be sure, most federal compacts are drawn up by lawyers and implemented by elite politicians. However federalism, as such, is not an artificial construct; it is, in Ronald Watts' phrase, a naturally recurring paradigm that has its roots in the face-to-face negotiations over territory of neighbouring communities.[4] As William S. Livingston wrote some years ago: 'The essence of federalism lies not in the constitutional or institutional structure but in the society itself. Federal government is a device by which the federal qualities of the society are articulated and protected.'[5]

Federalism is thus a logical system of government for diverse societies such as India; indeed many commentators would argue, with A.S. Narang, that it is the only possible form of government for that polyglot country.[6] True, one can argue about how well the current constitutional arrangements in India actually reflect the societal realities underneath, and at least one of our authors, Thomson, is somewhat sceptical in this regard; however it is hard to gainsay Suri Ratnapala's claim that, in comparison with countries like Sri Lanka and the former Soviet Union, India has done well in containing ethnic regionalism. One reason for this is doubtless the greater flexibility of the Indian federal system. However, as Australian case studies in this volume show, federalism is also appropriate for large, sparsely-populated countries where local communities are a long way from the seat of central power. Former South Australian Premier John Bannon makes this point forcefully. Federalism aids the cause of participatory democracy by enhancing community access to government and promoting governmental accountability to the voters.

The second point that emerges from this symposium is that federations are much more elaborate creations than we commonly take them to be. For one thing, federalism involves much more than a simple centre-state relationship. In both Australia and India, the division of powers is now a tripartite one, involving local as well as state governments. And it is one that is constantly in flux. In both countries state leaders are forever battling the encroachments of the centre, municipal bosses the tutelage of state local government and planning ministries. This tension is particularly acute when the contending governments are controlled by parties of different political complexion, or where, as happens frequently now in India, the state ruling party is a purely regional one dedicated to serving local interests. In the most recent Indian general election (1998) the Bharatiya Janata Party (BJP) went to the contest with sixteen political allies. At least six of them—the Akali Dal (Punjab), the Shiv Sena (Maharashtra), the Lok Shakti (Karnataka), the All-India Anna Dravida Munnetra Kazhagam (AIADMK) (Tamilnadu), the Telugu Desam Party (Andhra Pradesh), and the Haryana Vikas Party—are avowedly regional outfits, and the rest are effectively so being in the main confined in their support-base to one state. Altogether these parties won 73 seats and polled 11.2 per cent of the vote (up from 26 seats and four per cent in 1996). Moreover, as their reward for helping to get the BJP over the line, the allies demanded—and got—a number of senior portfolios in the new government. This cannot but add to their political clout at the centre.

Although Paul Brass' essay was written before the 1998 poll, its results amply confirm his judgement that regional parties are now entrenched in the Indian political scene. It remains to be seen, however, how effective this new 'party-federalism' proves in reversing the centralizing trends of recent decades. Thus, while neither the Indian nor Australian Constitutions recognize the existence of party politics, political parties are clearly an important element in the functioning of both federal systems. Another element whose importance is commonly overlooked is the bureaucracy. The bureaucrats who are responsible for implementing government policies are important players in their own right; but, as Beryl Radin explains in her study of the Indian Administrative Service (IAS), they can also be either a potential agency of federal power or a mediating, 'conflict-management instrument', depending on our vantage-point. Yet a third element is the judiciary, which Robert Watt sees as an important bulwark against the misuse of executive power at both federal and state levels.

The third conclusion suggested by this symposium builds on the previous one. Generally we tend to think of federalism as a vertical relationship between centre and region; but it is also about the way different regions interact with each other, in other words about the horizontal relationship between the several federal units. Ideally, perhaps, federations should be compacts of units that are more or less alike. However in the real world homogeneity over large areas is rare. Sometimes these regional differences are formally recognized in the Constitution, for example in the designation of less developed areas as 'territories' as opposed to 'states'. Both India and Australia observe this distinction. Again, special arrangements might be made for areas inhabited by tribal or aboriginal groups, such as the 'autonomous districts' within the states of north-east India described by Chaube. Generally, though, disparities between regions are a function of wealth rather than ethnicity, which begs the question of how far federations should strive to overcome them by redistributing tax revenues. Australians never had any doubt about the answer; indeed, several of the colonies would never have joined without the promise of federal compensation. But India (faced with far greater regional inequalities than Australia) has been much less assiduous and efficient in removing them. Far from becoming less, the economic gap between Indian states has widened over time. Nowadays rich Punjab meets over 90 per cent of its expenditure out of local revenues, whereas Assam, which gets a nominal royalty from the centre for its oil reserves, struggles to raise 40 per cent.[7] Mayer's analysis suggests that the gap is only going to increase. Something clearly needs to be done—and dividing up the pool more fairly on a per capita and needs basis would be a start. But, as Grewal warns, this expedient alone is unlikely to transform the growth rates of the weaker states.

The fourth theme that runs through this volume is that federations only work as well as they are allowed to by the federal and state politicians of the day. In India, and to a lesser extent Australia, there is a sense among academics and other commentators that too much power has been accrued in recent times by the federal centre. Tarun Bose, for example, reckons that the Indian states are now 'totally dependent upon and subservient to an omnipotent centre' in New Delhi;[8] while Narang thinks that the Indian states 'have been reduced to . . . glorified municipalities'.[9] As for the politicians, the West Bengal-based Communist Party of India (Marxist) (CPM) has been criticizing the fiscal provisions of the Indian Constitution for twenty years. More recently the Dravida Munnetra Kazhagam (DMK) Party of Tamilnadu added its voice, claiming that the special privileges enjoyed by Jammu and Kashmir (under the controversial Article 370) were threatening 'the very survival of a united India'.

The Australian federation too has its share of critics. Some see the states as ultimately dispensable, arguing, as one letter-writer to *The Australian* put it, that they be consigned to the 'dustbin of history'.[10] Traditionally, Australian centralists have tended to come from the Left; but recently the abolitionist cause has found favour among some on the radical Right, who associate the states with 'over-government' and see them as obstacles to the efficient management of the national economy.[11] On the other hand a socially conscious High Court has come under attack for its Mabo and Wik decisions which have, for the first time, not only recognized native title to land, but found that such title is not extinguished by pastoral leases. Some irate state governments, alarmed at what they see as an activist bench encroaching on a state preserve, have demanded a say in the appointment of High Court judges, a suggestion which the federal government, whatever its political persuasion, would be unlikely to find appealing.

However, in Australia the main complaints about federalism concern its fiscal aspects, in particular the inadequacy of the states' tax-base. This is a concern in India too, as Rokkam Rao demonstrates. But it is not the major one. There attention has been fixed primarily on the use—or misuse—of the presidential powers at the behest of a ruling party to unseat state governments controlled by political rivals. As Zoya Hasan notes, this strategy was honed to a fine art by the Congress (I) government of Indira Gandhi in the early 1970s; but other parties have not been slow to follow suit. In 1977 the incoming Janata coalition orchestrated the dismissal of nine incumbent Congress state governments; in 1980, the process was repeated in reverse. Altogether, since 1950, there have been over seventy cases of President's Rule. Lee is not alone in regarding this as a serious departure from the intentions of India's founding fathers. However, while many people would agree that the federal systems in both India and Australia are in dire need of overhaul, few would see any practicable alternative. Of our contributors, only Javeed Alam seems to have serious reservations about the system of federalism itself; and even he admits that there is no alternative in India's case short of 'continuous military deployment' to hold the country together by force—in the long-term certainly a hopeless prospect.

This leads on to the fifth and final point that emerges from this symposium: that the appeal of federalism in the modern world owes much to its capacity for evolution. As has been already observed, federations are constitutional expressions of geopolitical relationships, a systemic way of reconciling the contrary centripetal and centrifugal forces present in all societies. Although they appear to be fixed and stable, in fact they are always in disequilibrium, depending on which level—centre or region—is the more politically dominant. To paraphrase Iqbal Narain, federalism is constantly in the making.[12] Generally, socio-economic change has abetted the tide of centralization, but this need not always be the case. As Zoya Hasan points out, social movements in India over the past few decades, notably the rise of the Other Backward Castes (OBCs) have, if anything, bolstered the forces of regionalism. Likewise, political competition and economic development (in the more liberal environment of the 1990s) have strengthened the states as factors in the Indian polity. For the most part, as we have seen, the history of the Indian and Australian federations has been a history of progressive centralization, especially in the fiscal area.

Critics of this tendency—the 'states-rightists' in Australian parlance—

invariably point the finger at power-hungry federal politicians. And, as we noted earlier, they have a point at least in the case of Mrs Gandhi. The tendency of federations over time to become more centralist however owes much more to socio-economic change than it does to political conniving. With mass education, more standardized curricula, and greater access to the media, peoples' horizons become broader; parochialism (while not obliterated) is reduced. With modern communications technology, the reach of governmental agencies is greatly magnified, so that the need for intermediaries between state and people is lessened. With the advent of a global economy, there is pressure to break down local barriers to trade and investment. It is now fifty years since India's federation was established, almost a hundred years since the Australian Commonwealth was founded. Given the tumultuous changes that have occurred in the world in that time, we would expect the two federations to have evolved in significant ways; and so they have.

But have the Indian and Australian federations adapted successfully? Has the centralizing tendency been pushed too far? What are the prospects for further constitutional change?

In theory, as Ratnapala opines, it would be good if all federal systems could be left 'in a state of unimpeded flux'; if 'the process of spontaneous or natural federalism' could be allowed to regulate territorial distribution at any given moment. But this is, as he concedes, a practical impossibility. Instead, most federations have opted for regulated change, and both the Indian and Australian Constitutions contain mechanisms to provide for this (though, as we observed earlier, the Australian requirement for referring proposed changes to referenda makes the process slow and difficult). Moreover, the ruling parties of both countries have recognized the need for further structural adjustment. In the early 1970s the then Congress government appointed the Rajamannar Inquiry Committee to look into centre-state relations, and ten years later Mrs Gandhi gave retired Supreme Court judge R.S. Sarkaria a similar task; both committees agreed that the system had become unbalanced. Sarkaria's recommendations—essentially for a return to something like the compact of 1950—are described by G. Parthasarathy. To be sure, the Sarkaria report has been sitting on the table for a long time, but the BJP-led government elected in March 1998 has promised to implement it, at least in part, and Parthasarathy is hopeful that the next few years will see the enactment of significant reforms. Similar hopes have been aroused by the Australian Federal Convention held in late 1997 although it still remains to be seen whether Prime Minister Howard can resist pressure from his conservative colleagues to limit discussion in Parliament on reform to the issue of whether Australia should become a republic—an important question but not by any means the only, or even the most important, one that needs to be asked about the Australian federation.[13] However, some of the more interesting and helpful developments of recent years in the federal field in India and Australia have not involved constitutional change *per se*, but rather the establishment of mechanisms to promote better working relations between the several levels of government. In India a start in this respect was made with the setting up of the National Development Council. But this proved wooden and cumbersome, and in 1983 the chief ministers of the four southern states conclaved in Bangalore to explore better ways of coordinating their approach to New Delhi; since then, chief ministers conferences have become a regular feature of the Indian political calendar. The establishment of an Interstate Council under Article 263 (as recommended by the Sarkaria Commission) is another option currently under consideration. In Australia, too, 'executive federalism' has made significant strides over the last decade, its most notable achievement perhaps the creation of the Council of Australian Governments (COAG) in 1992. Bannon's paper gives an insider's view of the landmark 'leaders' meting' in Adelaide in 1991 which laid the groundwork for this initiative.[14]

The consensus in this volume is that federalism in India and Australia is still viable—but that some rethinking is necessary if the Constitutions of the two countries are to continue to reflect accurately their respective national goals and aspirations and meet the divergent needs of their pluralistic societies. Whether this will happen depends (as such things have always done) on political will.

Yet federalism itself is more flexible than the mere text of a Constitution might suggest; that has been its saving grace as a governing system. Insofar as federalism has often been embraced as a means of resolving political and regional tensions, it might be tempting to see the structures which emerge as having a transitional character—as if a federation might be a halfway house to some more complete union. Yet each federation soon acquires its own institutional force, its own political character and hegemonic culture. And the Constitution, as the source of nationhood, can itself become an icon. The challenge for future Indian and Australian governments is to design mechanisms for constitutional revision that permit us, quickly and efficiently, to make whatever structural adjustments may be necessary to bring the Grand Vision of the Constitution into line with the changing needs and concerns of ordinary citizens living in the everyday world of the city, the suburb, and the village.

NOTES

1. See, for example, Norman D. Palmer, *The Indian Political System* (London, 1961), pp. 95-6.
2. For example, Joyotpaul Chaudhuri and Ayesha Jalal. See Balveer Arora, Baladas Ghoshal and Joyotpaul Chaudhuri, *India's Beleaguered Federalism: the Pluralist Challenge* (Tempe, Arizona, 1992), p. 64; and Ayesha Jalal, *Democracy and Authoritarianism in South Asia: A Comparative and Historical Perspective* (Cambridge, 1995), p. 164. Chaudhuri prefers the term 'quasi-federal'.
3. For example, D. Basu, *Comparative Federalism* (Delhi, 1989); Bruce Grant, *Gods and Politicians* (London, 1982), pp. 155-69, 184-90; and J. Opo, *A Comparative Study of the Executive in Australia and India*, Ph.D. Thesis, 1970, University of London. Bruce Grant is a former Australian High Commissioner to India. I am indebted to James Thomson for these references.
4. R.L. Watts, 'Contemporary Views On Federalism', in B. de Villiers, *Evaluating Federal Systems* (Cape Town, 1994), as quoted by Ratnapala in this volume.
5. W.S. Livingston, *Federalism and Constitutional Change* (Oxford, 1956), p. 2.
6. A.S. Narang, *Ethnic Identities and Federalism* (Simla, 1995), p. 220.
7. Ibid.
8. Tarun Chandra Bose (ed.), *Indian Federalism: Problems and Issues* (Calcutta, 1987), p. 3.
9. Narang, *Ethnic Identities*, p. 151.
10. *The Australian*, 23 November 1995.
11. For a recent re-statement of the economic argument see John Nieuwenhuysen, 'The States Should Go', *The Age*, 21 April 1998.
12. Iqbal Narain in Bose, *Indian Federalism*, p. 23.
13. On the ambit of the Convention see the article by former Senator Sid Spindler, 'Convention Offers Opportunity to Renew Constitution', *The Age*, 1 April 1997.
14. See, however, the more recent appraisal of John Short, 'Closed Avenue Forces the States to Reroute', *The Australian*, 17 June 1997. Short believes that COAG is now 'effectively dead' as a forum for federal reform, at least for the duration of the Howard government.

1

Colonial Context of Regionalism: The Australian and Indian Experience

SHIBANI KINKAR CHAUBE

If we ignore the recent appearance of a number of small states on the world map, as a result of the dissolution of the Western empires and their successor trusteeship regimes, the modern states would generally appear to be large in size and complex in structure. Their societies are pluralistic, their authorities are hierarchical or federal.

A large state comes into being either through annexation or through union. Annexation involves force and hierarchy. Union involves volition and equality. Force is an attribute of authoritarianism, volition of democracy. The distinction between an empire and a federation is determined by the absence or presence of volition, though there could be intermediate regimes like the Canadian Federation of 1867 or the Austro-Hungarian Empire of 1869 (a federation literally means a contracted union).[1]

Pluralism may be expressed either in terms of territorial specificity or that of ethno-cultural specificity. Rigorous control of immigration has not allowed the coincidence of ethno-cultural specificities with territorial divisions in new societies like the USA and Australia, but in the older countries the coincidence is visible.

A major difference between the Indian federation and the United States federation (or, for that mater, the Canadian and the Australian federations) is that, although all of them have historical linkages with the British empire, the Indian federation belongs to the autochthons while the others are made up of immigrants even though they are all results of colonial conquest.[2]

The British rulers of India could not satisfactorily comprehend the socio-cultural complexities of the vast territory they had come to control, far less manage it neatly. In the first place they did not, or possibly could not, define the nature of their control over the territories. In the second place, they did not streamline the limits of their territorial control.

Technically, the British in the shape of East India Company was the *dewan* (revenue collector) of the Mughal ruler of India until 1857, and all Acts of British Parliament about India during that period pertained to the management of the Company and its Indian 'possessions'. Within this period the three Presidencies of Bengal, Bombay and Madras were merged under the control of the Governor of Bengal who was redesignated Governor-General by the Regulating Act, 1773. In 1833 the civil and military powers of the governors of Bombay and Madras were transferred to the governor-general. It was only by the Indian Councils Act of 1861 that legislative powers were returned to the governors. In 1870 the power to make regulation in backward tracts (the erstwhile 'non-regulation districts') was restored to the governor-general. It was within this framework that councils were created for assisting the governors and the governor-general in executive and legislative affairs. Gradually they were made responsive and, after diarchization, even responsible.

Deliberately or not, the British did not set any precise external limit to their power. By 1858, however, a more or less clear idea of India emerges in British pronouncements. The 1858 proclamation of Queen Victoria brought the East India Company's territorial possessions under her rule and such territories acquired the collective name of British India. The Queen, further, proclaimed to the 'Native Princes of India that all treaties and engagements with them by or under the authority of the Honourable East India Company are by us accepted and will be scrupulously maintained'.

Following this, the Interpretation Act of 1889 defined 'India' as 'British India together with any territories of any native prince or chief under the suzerainty of Her Majesty'. The status of the British Crown over the native princes, thus, legally came to be defined in terms of suzerainty (or, in political jargon, 'paramountcy').

The Indian Ocean and the French and Portuguese enclaves set the southern limit of the Indian empire, but the eastern, the northern and the north-eastern boundaries remained fluid. Annexation of Burma (Myanmar) in the east by 1883 brought British power almost face to face with the French colonies in South-East Asia but for the hilly buffer zone to the east of the Irawati valley. The Durand Line was drawn in the north-west only in 1902 and the McMahon Line in the north-east in 1914. Neither Afghanistan nor China accepted these borders and there remained an unadministered patch of territory to the north-west of British India that came to be designated, after 1935, as a tribal area. A similar tribal area was created in the east when Burma was separated from British India in 1937. And virtually the entire north-east frontier (tribal) tract, now constituting Arunachal Pradesh, was unadministered. Such 'tribal areas' constituted the twilight zone of the empire because they were inside India but outside British India or any native state and yet under the executive authority of the Governor-General.

Even the British Indian territories though were not uniformly administered. Normally, they were divided under two broad types, the governors' and the chief commissioners' provinces. Within the governors' provinces there were 'backward tracts' that, in 1935, were designated 'excluded' or 'partially excluded' areas. The exclusion was from the scope of the reforms. As a result, a wide variety of administrative and control patterns prevailed on the eve of the transfer of power.

British suzerainty over the 566 princely states took the form of different doses of 'political control' exercised by the Governor-General as the Viceroy, either directly or through the governors. For big states political officers were appointed. For small states sometimes neighbouring district officers of British India were assigned responsibility. In discharging his agency functions the governor exercised his discretion. Governors also exercised their discretion with regard to reserved subjects in the provinces as well as in the areas excluded from the reforms either totally or partially.

As in the princely states the territories in British India were not equally developed. The port towns of Calcutta, Bombay and Madras got the most attention in industrial and commercial development. Punjab got attention in development of irrigation. Railways and highways brought about a moderately integrated communication system. Mineral exploitation in middle India, tea plantations in the foothills of north-east India and coffee plantations in south India created enclaves of relative prosperity leading to immigration and urbanization. The economy of the country as a whole, however, was marked by great regional disparities.

The Indian federation was not just an inevitable consequence of the process of devolution of power. It was also a historical necessity—as even the British realized. They had annexed Indian territory at random and at different opportunities. They put such territories in uneven blocs first as presidencies and then as provinces, without attention to their ethno-cultural complexities. When they first sought to impart some rationality to the territorial arrangement they could only think of the religious division. The result was the partition of Bengal in 1905. The anti-partition agitation, dialectically, produced the linguistic (sub-) nationalism that became an article of faith with the Indian national movement. But administrative convenience and real politics demanded the reduction of the size of the Bengal Presidency. While the 1905 religious partition was undone in 1912, the new composite province of Bihar and Orissa was split in 1934.

The creation of Sind out of the Bombay Presidency in 1934 was an interesting example of the resolution of the dilemma between religion and politics. The Muslim League demanded its creation on the grounds that it was a Muslim-majority region. The Congress agreed to it on the ground of the distinctiveness of the Sindi language.

The British considered provincial autonomy as a means of managing religious communalism. The Indian National Congress saw it as an instrument of satisfying linguistic aspiration. It had provincialized its own organization in 1920 on the basis of language. The Cabinet Mission Plan of 1946 acknowledged only three major communities in India, the Hindu, the Muslim and the Sikh, and advocated a grouping plan which reversed the erstwhile British philosophy. The Congress was agreeable to a very high degree of provincial autonomy but not grouping. The irreconcilability of the Cabinet Mission, Muslim League and the Congress positions led to the partition of India on religious, communal lines even as there was a strong desire for the political unity of the new nation. The fact that India did not become a unitary state was due to the awareness of the existence of numerous cultural specificities.[3]

From 1905 Indian politics became the victim of the cross-cutting cleavage of religion and language, for undeniably the small Muslim elite of Bengal had largely welcomed the religious division of the Bengal Presidency (as was revealed by the hosting of the Muslim League's inaugural conference in 1906 by the Nawab of Dacca). In the south, where Muslim strength was almost negligible, linguistic (sub-) nationalism clashed with the administrative boundaries of the provinces as well as the political boundaries of the princely states of Hyderabad, Mysore, Travancore and Cochin. In the Bombay Presidency, where international finance capital was taking root, linguistic (sub-) nationalism was dormant in the British period. Bombay city remained cosmopolitan though Maharashtrian intellectual activities took roots in Poona (Pune).

The partition of India was the victory of the 'religious nationalism' of the Muslim League blessed by the administration. Yet, the irrationality of this victory was demonstrated within a quarter of a century when Pakistan was split by linguistic nationalism.

Although the Congress was committed to the linguistic re-organization of the provinces since 1930, the shock of partition and associated violence made its leaders hesitant. The Constituent Assembly postponed the decision but left scope for it in Article 3 of the Constitution. Half a decade after Independence the demand for the formation of Andhra Pradesh had to be conceded following the violent death of a veteran Congress leader, Potti Sriramalu. Even so the States Reorganization Commission (SRC) was lukewarm about a thorough reorganization on linguistic basis and the work was not completed till 1966.[4]

After 1966, however, linguistic movements were confined to demands for border adjustment as the broad reorganization had been completed. During this period a kind of anti-linguistic agitation—with stress on ethnic factors—developed, with a common grievance against 'exploitation' by the linguistic majorities in states. Thus, the reorganization of north-east India from 1963 to 1972 was the result of a protest against 'Assamese dominance'. None of the hill people had fought for their own language and most of the hill states, quite small in size, had several languages.[5] They happily adopted English as their official language. Recently, the Bodos of Assam and the Nepalese of the Darjeeling district of West Bengal were fighting for autonomy and citing their languages. But the Bodos are fragmented and scattered on the north bank of the Brahmaputra. On the other hand, the Nepalese of the Darjeeling hills do not unite with the Nepalese in Sikkim on their northern border even though they are an overwhelming majority there too.

Unsuccessful attempts have been made by the tribal groups in the middle Indian hills to develop common languages and scripts. In the most developed of such areas the tribes have ceased to predominate. But autonomy movements, existing essentially on ethnic slogans, occasionally assume regional facades by drafting non-tribal local residents.[6]

It is difficult to theorize on the precise role and impact of religion, language and ethnic affinity particularly if one takes into account the borderline languages. The SRC, for instance, turned down the case of Punjabi as a separate language and considered it a corrupt form of Hindi. According to Paul Brass Punjabi and Urdu are two languages which are heavily influenced by religious sentiments.[7] The cases of Maithili and Konkani are not affected by religion. But their distinctions flow from the fact that they are on the fringes of two major languages, in each case using distinct scripts.

It can only be said that the various autonomy movements are attempts at correcting the wrongs committed by the territorial arrangements of the British Raj. The operation of democracy, further, is throwing up successive ethno-cultural identities challenging the dictates of political economy. Even the Indian Left, which tried to make use of this process to its benefit, has been swept away by it. The advocacy in the 1940s for conceding the demands of 'Muslim nationalities' was thoroughly misunderstood. Its successful participation in the Samyukta Maharashtra and Mahagujarat Movements was forgotten by the new states. Partition of India strengthened communalism. Bifurcation of the Bombay province strengthened localism.

History and geography together have built the political mosaic of India. States are of different sizes and contain populations of different sizes. Though most of them are unilingual, the hills states in the north-east are multilingual. Structurally, however, there is much greater uniformity now than in the British days. Today there are only states and union territories with Delhi enjoying a somewhat intermediate status as the national capital territory.[8] Within some of the states in north-east India the autonomous districts have district councils enjoying a wide range of powers over local affairs and customary rights under the Sixth Schedule to the Constitution. In the rest of India the Fifth Schedule has provided unspecified powers and administrative machinery for the areas containing substantial tribal populations. Local self-government

(LSG) has recently been constitutionalized in the normally administered areas. But the difference between local self-government and full autonomy is that the former has no political identity while the latter has. The jurisdiction of a LSG is determined by mere administrative dictates while that of an autonomy is altered as well as created by political/constitutional decisions. There are, at the same time, ethno-cultural specificities of autonomies while the LSGs may be of a social nature.

There is significant political difference between autonomy and LSG. Pristine autonomy is ethno-cultural because the concept of the first family, first class or first tribe is central to it. The 'we'-'they' dichotomy restricts the admission of the outsider at least on equal terms. Rights of citizens are circumscribed by rights of groups. Thus the states are granted power to restrict public appointments on the basis of residence. Rights to purchase land are denied to outsiders by Jammu and Kashmir and the hill states of north-east India. Even immigration by 'outsiders' is restricted in several states. No LSG can impose such restrictions upon citizens. This in turn implies an authoritarian tendency among autonomies and a democratic tendency in LSG. When the Sixth Schedule to the Indian Constitution granted autonomous district councils to the hills of Assam, election of village councils was foiled in all hill districts except the Mizo. Since the 73rd Amendment several scheduled areas have been resisting elected panchayats. It is also known that many state governments are lukewarm to the 73rd Amendment because it would curtail their power of patronage to the LSGs if not cut into their funds.

The case of the Darjeeling Gorkha Hill Council provides an illustration of such a conflict. The council was formed a few years back as a local body with wide financial and administrative powers.[9] Its chairman, Mr Subhash Ghishing, is demanding central aid to this body to be directed straight to it without being routed through the Government of West Bengal. The Hill Council has so far refused to submit its accounts to state government audit.

On the other hand the Darjeeling Gorkha Hill Council has resisted the holding of local body elections which is mandatory under the 73rd and 74th Amendments to the Constitution. The Darjeeling Gorkha Hill Council was exempted only from the control of the municipal bodies and district panchayat.[10] The Constitution made exceptions for

Nagaland, Meghalaya and Mizoram as well as for the hill areas of Manipur where district councils, not under the Sixth Schedule but under an Act of Parliament, exist. It may be noted that under the 1950 Constitution the territories now covered by the states of Meghalaya, Mizoram and most of Nagaland were to have district councils. Because of Phizo's violent resistance, village development boards were set up in Nagaland. Village authorities and village councils were created in the two other areas through mixtures of elective and customary principles. Arunachal Pradesh had its panchayati raj through an election according to 'customary laws'. But the Arunachal Pradesh legislature has so far failed to pass any legislation on panchayat elections. An ordinance issued by the Governor simply says that the panchayats will be elected according to rules to be framed by the government.

While the urban centres of India, as elsewhere, tend to be multi-ethnic and multicultural, Indian villages are monolinguistic though not necessarily monoreligious. And 70 per cent of the Indian people live in villages. This pattern is modified in certain ways in respect of the tribal belts.

The tribal people constitute 7 per cent of the Indian population and they live in certain concentrations. But some of traditional tribal settlements have been infiltrated by non-tribal people who are generally seen as exploiters.

Tribal solidarity movements that have been developing since the 1940s achieved some success in north-east India because of certain geographically and politically favourable factors. In the central Indian hills their political aspiration for statehood has been thwarted by the overwhelming demographic and economic pressure of non-tribal groups. In peninsular India (Andhra Pradesh, Gujarat, Maharashtra and Kerala) they have adopted a peasant character and are fighting, occasionally with the support of political parties, for land. Only for Bihar have the central and the state governments agreed, in principle, on the creation of a Jharkhand Autonomous Council.

A broad cultural mapping of India today would show a Hindu-Hindi heartland of north India (UP, Bihar, Madhya Pradesh, Rajasthan and Haryana), a Hindu-non-Hindi inner periphery and a non-Hindu-non-Hindi outer periphery (Jammu & Kashmir, Punjab, most of the hill states of north-east India and parts of Sikkim and Kerala). The tribal people of central and peninsular India have fallen to the impact of this cultural layout. Their number is too small for attainment of territorial autonomy. Even in Jharkhand they are only one-third of the total population. However, as B.K. Roy Burman noted, tribes living at the borderlands of major civilizations have served the important dual role of bridge and buffer, maintaining civilization's continuity on the subcontinent.[11]

On the States Reorganization Commission, Sardar K.M.Panikkar suggested the division of big states like Uttar Pradesh (UP) into smaller ones for administrative convenience. The other two members did not agree. For quite a long time UP supplied the prime ministers of India and served as the bastion of the ruling party at the centre. During the 1970s, Chaudhury Charan Singh, a UP leader, and Jaya Prakash Narayan, a national level leader from Bihar with a socialist background, revived the proposal. It was noted at that time that a partition of UP between an eastern half and a western half would give a relative numerical dominance to certain particular castes. In recent years, after the introduction of reservation for OBCs in the state, an old demand for the creation of an Uttarakhand State in the upper-caste dominated hill districts of UP has become powerful. Similar caste-based demands have been raised on north-east India including West Bengal (Kamatapur/ Uttarakhand, Ujani Asom). The Maithili movement has been suspected to have upper caste backing. More than religion, but less than language, caste takes a regional pattern in India though on a smaller scale than both. A large-scale reorganization of UP (probably in three parts—the north, the east and the west) will suit administrative convenience. Extension of the same principle to north-east India will create more minuscule states economically dependent on central assistance.

Reorganizations have thus meant the creation of small states. Their heavy dependence on central assistance has functionally reduced their autonomy. Yet the ever-growing demand for such states indicates two features. In the first place, there is a growth of ethno-cultural particularism—a worldwide trend. Secondly, there is a rising aspiration of the ethnic elite for political power which, in turn, would mean political and administrative positions as well as governmental patronage. On the other hand, removal of their grievances against the 'majorities' brings in a new sense of integration at the national level.

After 1972 no reorganization of states has taken place. But the union territories are attaining full statehood one by one. This vertical movement in status illustrates the role of power in federal relations. Statehood means a full-scale state government with the powers allotted by the Seventh Schedule to the Constitution, a clear-cut autonomous space for the government, more funds, more political and administrative posts for the locals, more trade licenses and so on. The primary beneficiaries of these arrangements are regional literati. However, agriculture being a state subject, farmers have developed a stake in state politics particularly after the ushering in of the Green Revolution. Medium-sized states like Punjab, Haryana, Maharashtra and Karnataka, all products of state reorganization, have made great strides in agriculture. In large states like Uttar Pradesh, on the other hand, the Green Revolution accelerated regional disparity and strengthened the demand for smaller states.

But the crucial question is why the demands almost always seek legitimacy from the plea of regional disparity or internal colonialism. The colonial framework can provide some answer at least as far as India is concerned. The British brought under a common rule a vast territory that had never been under one government. They even rendered this territory a measure of economic integration. On the other hand, they intesified regional disparities by industrialization and spread of irrigation in select areas, ignoring the rest of the country. The total effect was a hierarchisation of the country's economy. It was not until independence that India could even think of removing regional disparity. The result was an endless number of allegations among regions as well as between the centre and the states.

A comparison between Australia and India will reveal more dissimilarities than similarities. Yet dissimilarities may be as instructive as similarities. The emergence of both federations out of the framework of British dominion probably was the major reason for Sir B.N. Rau examining, among others, the Australian governmental structure and suggesting a finance commission in line with the Commonwealth Grants Commission of Australia. This is as far as any similarity goes. Among the major dissimilarities is the headship of the two governments, one monarchical, another republican. Secondly, the Australian federation was born in the centripetal way, the Indian federation in the centrifugal way.

The differences are not symptomatic but caused by specific political circumstances. The Australian federation was the result of administrative union of the six British colonies and their territories on that continent, a process that had been completed in India by 1833. The federation also registered virtually total transfer of power from the Crown to the Australian Government (except the power over appeals). This was completed in India only by 1947 when the governor-general was granted unlimited power of assent on behalf of the British Crown in Parliament.

Until the end of the nineteenth century Australia was a continent and not a country. Its six colonies had grown up as colonial outposts supplying raw materials to Britain and receiving her excess population. The formation of the Commonwealth literally turned the sights of the colonies onto themselves. But the geography of Australia is such that the Commonwealth members could only look sideways and not inward. For 80 per cent of Australia's territory is arid or semi-arid. They could serve the colony economically (through mining and grazing) but not by hosting human settlement.

The weakening of Australia's links with England, particularly after World War II, has strengthened her national and regional orientation. Her major trade partners today are the United States of America, Japan, the United Kingdom, New Zealand, Korea and Germany, in that order. She is clearly carving out her immediate world at the southern half of the Indian Ocean-Pacific Ocean region.

Thanks to regulated immigration, Australia does not have an ethnic problem. Yet one feels that territory, which is the primary parameter of modern nationhood, offers a certain challenge to the nation-building programme of Australia. This feeling is based on the hypothesis that physical contact/proximity is a basic condition of community. For a state which is an extended community this contract must be continuous and multifaceted. Australia is a highly urban country with people tending to settle mainly in the urban centres at the coasts.

This discontinuity affected Australian government structures in the past. While six colonies united in a federation in 1901 and called themselves states, the Northern Territory was kept under exclusive control of South Australia till 1911. That year the Australian Capital Territory was created by the transfer of Canberra from New South Wales to the federal jurisdiction. The Northern Territory got limited self-government in 1978, the Australian Capital Territory a similar deal in 1988.

Australia's progress towards self-government is equally steady for the whole as well as for the parts. It will probably lead to the declaration of the country as a republic in the near future. The symbol of the British crown has so far served as a unifying force for the country even if vaguely. The removal of that symbol may necessitate the strengthening of other bonds including those of place. Australia's population geography does not contribute to such strengthening.

NOTES

1. Douglas Varney puts federation in the framework of popular sovereignty and sees federalism as an expression of pluralist democracy: 'In setting up a republic the Americans made a complete break with the notion of the monarch as sovereign. And in organising government on the basis of the separation of powers and limited government, they also did away with the idea of parliamentary sovereignty ... if none of the institutions of government could be sovereign, where was sovereignty to lie?'

   For Varney, who argues that the Americans, in 1787, consciously established a federal political system, 'popular sovereignty was an essential feature of federalism'. At the same time he concedes that 'the Americans were not proposing populism'. Their idea of popular sovereignty was republican and anti-feudal (Douglas Varney, 'Are all Federations Federal?' In Balveer Arora and Douglas Varney (eds.), *Multiple Identities in a Single State* (New Delhi, 1995), pp. 9-50 at pp. 30-1.
2. I have provided a summary of the process of British annexation of the Indian subcontinent in my *Colonialism, Freedom Struggle and Nationalism in India* (Delhi, 1996).
3. See Shibani Kinkar Chaube, 'Ethnicity and the Dynamics of Federalism in India' in Amal Mukhopadhyaya (ed.), *Political Miscellany*. (Calcutta, 1986), pp. 125-42, at pp. 125-7.
4. This contention has been put forward in my *Constituent Assembly of India: Springboard of Revolution* (New Delhi, 1973).
5. Shibani Kinkar Chaube, *Hill Politics in Northeast India* (Calcutta, 1973).
6. See K.S. Singh (ed.), *Tribal Movements in India*, Delhi, vol. 2.
7. Paul R. Brass, *Language, Religion and Politics in India* (Delhi, 1975), pp. 404-5.
8. Article 239AA of the Constitution of India inserted by the 69th Amendment in 1991. Delhi has been promised statehood by the new BJP government.
9. Article 243ZC(2) inserted by the 74th Amendment in 1992.
10. Article 243M(3) inserted by the 73rd Amendment in 1992.
11. B.K. Roy Burman, *Tribes in Perspective* (Delhi, 1994), pp. 81-2, 86-9.

2

Emergency Powers in Australian and Indian Federalism

H.P. LEE

'Does federalism have the potential to limit the oppressive powers of government?' Gillespie posed this question and responded to it as follows:

> If sovereignty were divided between rival levels of government, each with its own democratic franchise, it would set a major barrier to the concentration of political power in too few hands. First, federalism can limit government power to infringe rights, since it creates the possibility that a legislative wish to restrict liberties will lack the constitutional power, while the level of government that possesses the power lacks the desire. Second, the tortuous and legalistic decision making processes characteristic of federal systems limit the speed with which governments can act—even if their actions prove to be constitutional. Federalism helps enshrine the principle of 'due process', limiting arbitrary action by the state.[1]

Whether this response holds true when a national government seeks recourse to extraordinary powers to cope with extraordinary situations is the issue here. The experience in Australia and India may provide some pointers concerning the impact on centre-state relationships of invoking constitutionally entrenched emergency powers.

At the outset, a conspicuous difference between the Australian and Indian Constitutions should be noted. In Australia, the Commonwealth Constitution does not contain a comprehensive set of provisions relating to emergency powers. Hence there has not developed in its jurisprudence a corpus of principles regulating the exercise of these powers. In Australia the study of emergency powers is basically a study of a broad-spectrum of special powers which are located in some provisions of the Commonwealth Constitution and in various pieces of ordinary legislation enacted by the parliaments of the commonwealth and the states.

In terms of constitutionally entrenched emergency powers, the 'defence power' in Section 51(vi) of the Commonwealth Constitution empowers the Commonwealth Parliament to make laws, but subject to the Constitution, with respect to 'the naval and military defence of the Commonwealth and of the several states, and the control of the forces to execute and maintain the laws of the Commonwealth'. The defence powers can also operate in conjunction with other heads of powers, such as Section 51(xxxii) which empowers the Commonwealth Parliament to legislate with respect to the control of railways for the transportation for naval and military purposes, or Section 51(xxxix), the incidental power.

Section 114 of the Commonwealth Constitution provides that a state shall not, without the consent of the Commonwealth Parliament, raise or maintain any naval or military force. An obligation to protect the states is therefore reposed in the commonwealth. Section 119 thus provides: 'The Commonwealth shall protect every State against invasion and, on the application of the Executive Government of the State, against domestic violence.'[2]

In India, Part XVIII of the Constitution entitled 'Emergency Provisions', provides in Articles 352 to 360 detailed provisions regulating the use of extraordinary power (see Appendix I). Article 352 states that if the President is satisfied that a grave emergency exists whereby the security of India or of any part of the territory thereof is threatened, whether by war or external aggression or armed rebellion, he may, by proclamation, make a declaration to that effect in respect of the whole of India or of any such part of the territory thereof. The Explanation to Clause (1) of Article 352 indicates that there can be a resort to the Article even where the President is satisfied that there is 'imminent danger' of war, external aggression or armed rebellion. Article 353 deals with the effect of a proclamation of emergency. Thus while a proclamation is in operation, the executive power of the Union shall extend 'to the giving of directions to any state as to the manner in which the executive power thereof is to be exercised'. Furthermore, the power of the Parliament to make laws with respect to any matter shall include power to make laws conferring powers and imposing duties, or authorizing the conferring of powers and the imposition of duties, upon the Union or officers and authorities of the Union, 'notwithstanding that it is one which is not enumerated in the Union List'. The President is also empowered by Article 354 to direct that those provisions of the Constitution relating to the distribution of revenue between the Union and the states[3] shall cease to operate during the period of the emergency.

The equivalent of the Australian Section 119 is found in Article 355 of the Indian Constitution. It reposes a duty in the Union 'to protect every State against external aggression and internal disturbance'. Unlike Section 119, it also casts a duty to ensure that the government of every state is carried on in accordance with the provisions of the Constitution. The constitutional provision which has the greatest potential impact on the federal principle is Article 356. The Article states that if the President, on receipt of a report from the governor of a state or otherwise, 'is satisfied that a situation has arisen in which the government of the state cannot be carried on in accordance with the provisions of this Constitution', he is authorized to take action in the manner prescribed by the Article. Accordingly, the President may

(a) assume to himself all or any of the functions of the Government of the State and all or any of the powers vested in or exercisable by the Governor or any body or authority in the State other than the Legislature of the State;
(b) declare that the powers of the Legislature of the State shall be exercisable by or under the authority of Parliament;
(c) make such incidental and consequential provisions as appear to the President to be necessary or desirable for giving effect to the objects of the Proclamation, including provisions for suspending in whole or in part the operation of any provisions of the Constitution relation to any body or authority in the State.

The President is precluded by the proviso to Clause (1) of Article 356 from assuming to himself any of the powers vested in or exercizable by a High Court or to suspend in whole or in part the operation of any provisions of the Constitution relating to the High Courts.

An untrammelled use of Article 356 to deal with crises of 'failure of constitutional machinery in the states' can significantly erode the federal principle. This Article provides a startling contrast to the position in Australia.

Sawant J in *S.R. Bommai* v *Union of India*[4] said:

> The fact that during emergency and in certain other eventualities [the states'] powers are overridden or invaded by the Centre is not destructive of the essential federal nature of our Constitution. The invasion of power in such circumstances is not a normal feature of the Constitution. They are exceptions and have to be resorted to only occasionally to meet the exigencies of the special situations. The exceptions are not a rule.[5]

S. Ratnavel Pandian J in the same case highlighted the frequency of the resort to Article 356 in a period of 41 years leading up to 1991:

> [O]n 82 occasions the President's rule in States has been imposed by invoking or resorting to Article 356(1) and on 13 occasions the President's Rule has been imposed in Union Territories including erstwhile Union Territories which have become States under Section 51 of the Government of Union Territories Act, 1963. All total up to 95 times, of which on 23 occasions the assemblies were dissolved on the advice of the Chief Ministers or due to their resignations. It may be recalled that on 18 occasions the assemblies suspended were subsequently revived.[6]

In this paper I do not propose to canvas exhaustively the legal dimensions of the emergency powers provisions. The aim is to sketch some of the ramifications for the equilibrium of centre-state relations of invoking such powers.

The greatest emergency confronting any nation is war. As a pre-condition to the issuance of a proclamation of emergency, it does not pose difficult problems for the courts. The objective facts of a war situation can be judicially noticed by the courts. In the face of this type of emergency the judicial response has been to submerge the federal principle in the interests of national survival. In Australia, Isaacs J of the High Court in *Farey* v *Burvett*[7] said:

> A war imperilling our very existence, involving not the internal development of progress, but the array of the whole community in mortal combat with the common enemy, is a fact of such transcendent and dominating character as to take precedence over every other fact of life. It is the ultima ratio of the nation.[8]

Isaacs J, in referring to the use of the defence power in Section 51(vi) of the Commonwealth Constitution, added that '[i]ts limits . . . are bound only by the requirements of self-preservation'.[9]

The defence power in its most expansive scope has enabled the Commonwealth to impose 'extensive and detailed controls on the community of a kind that, in time of peace, would ordinarily be thought to fall under some other heads of legislative power and to have nothing significant to do with the defence power of the Commonwealth'.[10]

Later cases indicate that the dicta of Isaacs J was regarded as too sweeping and that in truth the defence power was subject to some limits. The defence power was, like the other heads of power in Section 51 of the Commonwealth Constitution, subject to the Constitution. Attempts by the Commonwealth to regulate the admission of students to universities or to prescribe standards for artificial lighting in factories were struck down by the High Court.

The broad consensus is that the defence power is purposive in nature. For a law of the Commonwealth Parliament to be validated under the defence power there must be established some 'real connection' between the law and the power. The purpose of the proposed law must be conducive to the efficient prosecution of war or the defence of the Commonwealth. The Court oversees the use of the power by construing its ambit by reference to the circumstances which enable the power to be called into play. By invoking a theme of a power which 'waxes and wanes' the court ensures that there is no flagrant abuse of it.

In contrast, the Indian Constitution in permitting a panoply of powers to be resorted to by the central government upon the proclamation of an emergency pursuant to Article 352 can provide a less than scrupulous government the opportunity to undermine the rule of law. The emergency proclaimed by the President at the instigation of Prime Minister Indira Gandhi in 1975 highlights the potential for abuse. This crisis has been extensively covered by many commentators and I shall refrain from repetition. Suffice it to say that the central government becomes an extremely powerful body if Article 352 is resorted to.

Consider, however, Article 356—this provision, which has no parallel in the Australian Constitution, poses a significant threat to federalism in India. I will turn the spotlight on the recent case of *Bommai*. The judicial exegesis by the Supreme Court of India on the scope of Article 356 casts some illumination on the role of the judiciary in reconciling the invocation of this Article and the federal principle.

Article 356 has serious implication for federalism in India. It is an Article which 'has a vital bearing on the democratic parliamentary form of government and the autonomy of the states under the federal Constitution'.[11] It is a power which if not properly supervised by the courts can lead to a situation whereby a central government can seek to undermine the governments of the states, particularly those that have fallen into the hands of political parties opposed to the one at the centre. A fundamental question to be resolved is whether the powers vested in the President under Article 356 are unfettered.

Bommai arose in the context of the removal of the governments and the dissolution of the legislative assemblies in six states. These actions were effected pursuant to a number of presidential proclamations: 21 April 1989 (Karnataka); 11 October 1991 (Meghalaya); 7 August 1988 (Nagaland); 15 December 1992 (Madhya Pradesh, Rajasthan and Himachal Pradesh).

In the case of the State of Karnataka, the Governor received nineteen letters from purported defectors causing the government to be deprived of majority support in the Legislative Assembly. The Governor sent a report to the President, referring to these nineteen letters and the inability of any other political party to form a government. On the next day, seven of the nineteen members wrote to the Governor claiming that their signatures had been procured by misrepresentation and reiterated their support for state government. Despite the offer by the chief minister to test his majority on the floor of the House, the Governor persisted in his view that the chief minister no longer commanded majority support and repeated his earlier request for intervention under Article 356(1). Sawant J levelled the following stinging attack on the actions of the Governor:

> We are of the view that this is a case where all canons of propriety were thrown to the wind and the undue haste made by the Governor in inviting the President to issue the Proclamation under Article 356(1) clearly smacked of mala fides. The Proclamation issued by the President on the basis of said report of the Governor and in the circumstances so obtaining, therefore, equally suffered from mala fides.[12]

In the case of the State of Meghalaya, the majority support of the chief minister was called into question. When the matter was put to a vote on the floor of the House, 30 members supported the motion and 27 voted against it. The Speaker, who had been elected the leader of the opposition group, refused to announce the result of the voting as, in his view, 5 of the supporters of the motion were disqualified from voting (purportedly under anti-defection legislation). The Speaker persisted in this view despite the claims by these 5 members that they were independent members of the Legislative Assembly. There was protracted politicking leading up to a presidential proclamation. Again, Sawant J pronounced:

> The unflattering episode shows in unmistakable terms the Governor's unnecessary anxiety to dismiss the Ministry and dissolve the Assembly and also his failure as a constitutional functionary to realise the binding legal consequences of and give effect to the orders of this Court. What is worse, the Union Council of Ministers also chose to give advice to the President to issue the Proclamation on the material in question.... [P]rima facie, the material before the President was not only irrational but motivated by factual and legal mala fides.[13]

In Nagaland, 13 members of the ruling party in the Legislative Assembly left the party to form their own new party. One of them claimed sufficient support to form the government. The Governor sent a report to the President on the developments, expressing his fear that if the state of affairs was allowed to continue, it would affect the stability of the State. In the meanwhile, the chief minister tendered his resignation to the Governor and recommended the imposition of presidential rule. A proclamation was accordingly made.

In the case of Madhya Pradesh, Rajasthan and Himachal Pradesh, the proclamation pursuant to Article 356(1) was effected upon the reports of the governors in the wake of the demolition of the Babri Masjid at Ayodhya in December 1992.

The judgements of the members of the Supreme Court underlined the judicial concern with an unfettered exercise of powers pursuant to Article 356. First of all, there was strong endorsement of federalism as an 'essential' or 'basic' feature of the Indian Constitution. The Supreme Court also warned that the powers conferred by Article 356 should be used 'very sparingly' per Pandian J,[14] per Ahmadi J,[15] per Ramaswamy J,[16] or 'as a last measure' per Sawant and Kuldip Singh JJ[17] or 'with circumspection' per Ramaswamy J.[18]

In holding the proclamations pertaining to the states of Karnataka, Meghalaya and Nagaland to be unconstitutional, the judges were at pains to point out that the use of Article 356 to oust a state government simply because it was of a different political complexion from the party controlling the central government would amount to a mala fide exercise of power. Ahmadi J described it very vividly:

The mere defeat of the ruling party at the Centre cannot by itself, without anything more, entitle the newly elected party which comes to power at the Centre to advise the President to dissolve the Assemblies of those States where the party in power is other than the one in power at the Centre. Merely because a different political party is elected to power at the Centre, even if with a thumping majority, is no ground to hold that 'a situation has arisen in which the Government of the State cannot be carried on in accordance with the provisions of this Constitution', which is the requirement for the exercise of power under Art. 356(1) of the Constitution.[19]

The fundamental issue both for Australia and India is whether a proclamation by the head of state is a justiciable issue. The power is often conditioned on the 'satisfaction' of the head of state which amounts to the exercise of a very subjective discretion. The issue can create tension between the judiciary and the executive arm of government. Thus Lord MacDermott, delivering the reasons for the Privy Council's decision in the Malaysian case of *Stephen Kalong Ningkan* v *The Government of Malaysia*[20] said:

Whether a Proclamation under statutory powers by the Supreme Head of the Federation can be challenged before the courts on some or any grounds is a constitutional question of far-reaching importance which, on the present state of the authorities, remains unsettled and debatable.[21]

Until 1981, it would have been inconceivable for the Australian courts to judicially review the validity of a vice-regal proclamation. In the early 1917 case of *Duncan* v *Theodore*,[22] Isaacs and Powers JJ had said that it was 'not open to impute mala fides with respect to the issue of a royal Proclamation, which is the act of the King himself or his representative'.[23] Referring to *Duncan* v *Theodore*, Dixon J in *Australian Communist Party* v *Commonwealth*[24] also declared: 'The good faith of any of his Acts as representative of the Crown cannot be questioned in a Court of Law'.[25] In the same case, Fullager J supported this stand: 'It is not open to impute mala fides with respect to an act of the King himself or his representative. . . .'[26] Dixon J elaborated:

[T]he expression by the Governor-General in Council of the result in a properly framed declaration is conclusive. In the case of the Governor-General in

Council, it is not possible to go behind such an executive act done in due form of law and impugn its validity upon the ground that the decision upon which it is founded has been reached improperly, whether because extraneous considerations were taken into account or because there was misconception of the meaning or application, as a court would view it, of the statutory description of the matters of which the Governor-General in Council should be satisfied or because of some other supposed miscarriage. The prerogative writs do not lie to the Governor-General.[27]

In 1981, the High Court in *Toohey* exploded the doctrine of vice-regal immunity in relation to the exercise of statutory discretions vested in a vice-regal representative. In consequence, there can be judicial review of the exercise of a statutory discretion by a vice-regal representative, at least in relation to the grounds of improper purpose or mala fide.

The Indian Supreme Court in *Bommai* has indicated that a proclamation issued pursuant to Article 356(1) is not immune from judicial review. B.P. Jeevan Reddy J said, 'The Supreme court or the High Court can strike down the proclamation if it is found to be mala fide or based on wholly irrelevant or extraneous grounds.'[28]

Sawant, Kuldip Singh and Pandian JJ were of the view that the exercise of power by the President under Article 356(1) to issue a Proclamation is subject to judicial review 'at least to the extent of examining whether the conditions precedent to the issuance of the Proclamation have been satisfied or not'. This was elaborated as follows:

> This examination will necessarily involve the scrutiny as to whether there existed material for the satisfaction of the President that a situation had arisen in which the Government of the State could not be carried on in accordance with the provision of the Constitution. . . [T]he material in question has to be such as would induce a reasonable man to come to the conclusion in question. . . . Hence, it is not the personal whim, wish, view or opinion or the ipse dixit of the President de hors the material but a legitimate inference drawn from the material placed before him which is relevant for the purpose. . . . Although, therefore, the sufficiency or otherwise of the material cannot be questioned, the legitimacy of inference drawn from such material is certainly open to judicial review.[29]

The justiciability of a proclamation issued under Article 356(1) was also supported by J.S. Verma and Yogeshwar Dayal JJ, and, on the ground of mala fide, by Ahmadi J.

When the federal systems of Australia and India are contrasted, the conspicuous presence of Article 356 considerably weakens the centre-state equilibrium under the Indian Constitution. In many instances, the resort to Article 356 had been actuated by political considerations. However, the use of that Article has been slightly constrained by the willingness of the Supreme Court, as a result of *Bommai*, to engage in some form of judicial review in relation to the validity of a proclamation issued pursuant to Article 356. In Australia too, as a result of the *Toohey* decision, there is also a greater awareness on the part of the judiciary to ensure that abuse of executive powers cannot be shielded absolutely from judicial scrutiny.

NOTES

1. J. Gillespie, 'New Foundations', in J. Brett, J. Gillespie and M. Goot (eds.), *Development in Australian Politics* (Sydney, 1994), pp. 60, 69.
2. See also *Defence Act* 1903 (Cth), Sec. 51. See generally H.P. Lee, *Emergency Powers* (Sydney, 1984), pp. 200-7.
3. Articles 268 and 269.
4. AIR 1994 SC, p. 1918.
5. Ibid., p. 1979.
6. Ibid., p. 1943.
7. (1916) 21 CLR, p. 433.
8. Ibid., p. 453.
9. Ibid.
10. David Derham, 'The Defence Power' in Else-Mitchell (ed.), *Essays on the Australian Constitution*, 2nd edn., 1961, p. 157.
11. AIR 1994 SC, p. 1958.
12. Ibid., p. 1988.
13. Ibid., pp. 1990-1
14. Ibid., p. 1943.
15. Ibid., p. 1955.
16. Ibid., p. 2045.
17. Ibid., p. 1983.
18. Ibid., p. 2035.
19. Ibid., p. 1953.
20. (1958) 2 MLJ, p. 238.
21. Ibid., p. 242.
22. (1917) 23 CLR, p. 510.
23. Ibid., p. 544.

24. (1951) 83 CLR, p. 1.
25. Ibid., p. 179.
26. Ibid., p. 257.
27. Ibid., p. 179.
28. Ibid., pp. 2112-13.
29. Ibid., pp. 1969-70.

3

Australian and Indian State Constitutional Law: Some Comparative Perspectives

JAMES A. THOMSON

Within a larger panorama—the Australian[1] and Indian[2] Constitutions and comparative exegesis of their premises, provisions, powers and structure—some constituent fragments—Australian and Indian states, their constitutions[3] and comparisons[4]—can be uncovered. Despite differences, similarities emerge. From both directions obvious examples can be garnered. Differences include: an Indian republic while Australia remains a constitutional monarchy; quantitatively many more words and provisions in the Indian, compared with the Australian, Constitutions; and enactment by the United Kingdom Parliament of Australian, but not Indian, Constitutions. Similarities encompass a history containing a British interlude;[5] written constitutions with a system of parliamentary responsible government; and courts which exercise the power of judicial review to declare legislation, executive acts and constitutional amendments unconstitutional.

Such forays into comparative constitutional law[6] might assist discernment of potential possibilities in the language and structures of written constitutions. Different and, perhaps, better legal arguments, reasons and theories can be revealed to assess and deal with familiar or novel problems. Of course, perennial factors—context, circumstances and conditions exultant, for example, during the drafting and adoption of constitutions—always remain. Combined, these two themes—comparative perspectives and local uniqueness—reinforce a major premise: the contingent, not reified, nature of constitutions.

India

Except for Jammu & Kashmir,[7] one constitution, embodied in the Indian Constitution,[8] encompasses all Indian states.[9] Indeed, at least to some extent, even Jammu & Kashmir complies with this 'incorporation' framework. Specific power, which has been utilized, is contained in the Indian Constitution to apply, by Presidential order with the concurrence of and in consultation with Jammu & Kashmir's government or Constituent Assembly, provisions of the Indian Constitution to this state.[10] Textually,[11] the possibility remains open that this gradual 'incorporation' process will culminate in Jammu & Kashmir relinquishing their state constitution[12] and, like other states, utilizing the 'state' constitution in the Indian Constitution.[13]

Historical circumstances provide an explanation for this incorporation of a single 'state' constitution into the Indian Constitution. United Kingdom legislation[14] from at least 1772 to 1950[15] provided the constitutional structures for Indian governments. Examples include: the East India Company Act 1772 (UK);[16] Government of India Acts 1800, 1833, 1853, 1854, 1858, 1859, 1861, 1865, 1869, 1870, 1911, 1912, 1915, 1916, 1919, and 1935;[17] and Indian Councils Acts 1861, 1869, 1871, 1874, 1892, 1904, 1907 and 1909.[18] British India, other than princely or Indian states[19] and tribal and special areas,[20] was divided into provinces[21] and this legislation established legislative, executive and judicial aspects of the provincial and central governments. Gradually, governmental power devolved from Britain to the provinces and to the central government. That transfer involved not only a shifting of power but also a movement, albeit slowly, from appointed British officials to nominated and elected Indian personnel who were vested with and could exercise power.[22] Federal demarcations, as to provincial and central powers, emerged more clearly with the Government of India Acts of 1915, 1916 and 1919.[23] By 1921, when the 1919 Act became operative, this United Kingdom legislation encompassed a governor-general; governors; lieutenant-governors; an Indian legislature (consisting of the governor-general and the Council of State and Legislative Assembly); local provincial legislatures (consisting of the governor and nominated or elected members); demarcation (including the capacity of governor-general in council to classify as central, provincial, transferred or reserved subjects) of matters in respect of which the Indian and provincial legislatures could make laws; and a judicial system.[24] Again, building upon this structure,[25] the Government of India Act 1935[26] incorporated central—a federal executive and legislative—and provincial institutions, procedures and powers together with a division—federal, concurrent and provincial lists—of legislative powers, and a court system.[27] Also, the 1935 Act provided for Indian princely states to be included within this federal legislative structure. However, prior to independence, that was not achieved.[28]

Despite this lacuna and the characterization by Indian nationalists of the 1935 Act as a 'slave constitution' and 'charter of bondage',[29] it became the model for the Indian Constitution.[30]

Four further circumstances explain the emergence, from the Constituent Assembly,[31] of a 'state' constitution within the Indian Constitution. First, 'the provinces of India were already members of a federal union during the framing period', 1946-9, of the Constitution.[32] Secondly, a standard form 'state' constitution had been created by United Kingdom legislation and was operational.[33] Thirdly, there was virtually no impetus to create separate constitutions for all or some provinces. Instead the British Cabinet Mission reported in 1946 that

> India was to remain one state, but the power of the Central Government would be confined to foreign affairs, communications, and defence. The provinces would be grouped into three regions [one] . . . Muslim [a second]. . . Hindu . . . and in the third the [Muslim and Hindu] population . . . would be nearly equal. The provincial representatives to the All-India Constituent Assembly . . . would meet in three group assemblies to frame constitutions for their component provinces and, if desired, for their group as well. . . . When all this was done [they] would return . . . to the All-India Assembly to draft the national constitution.[34]

On 30 April 1947 the Constituent Assembly established a committee to 'report on . . . the principles of a model provincial constitution'.[35] That committee 'prepared [a] model constitution . . . for the provinces'.[36] Indeed, '[t]he most singular aspect of the drafting of the federal provisions was the relative absence of conflict between the "centralizers" and the "provincialists". . . . In the Constituent Assembly . . . Allegiance to provincial governments was muted.'[37] Thus, the antecedent United Kingdom legislative model—for one 'state' constitution within the Indian Constitution—was easily adopted. Fourth, there was the position of princely states.[38]

Total absorption of the Princely States into the Indian constitutional structure, which occupied the decade between the announcement of the Cabinet Mission Plan on 16 May 1946 and States Reorganization in 1956, was very largely accomplished during the life-span of the Constituent Assembly. At the beginning of this period the Princely States were in no way part of the Union . . . . Yet by the time the Constitution was inaugurated [on 26 January 1950], few distinctions remained between the former Princely States and the other states of the Union, previously the provinces of British India. . . . The [Constituent] Assembly [in 1948] found itself confronted by the problem of constitutions for the States. The Covenants [between the Indian government and princely states] establishing the relationship between the Union and the various States and Unions of States, laid down that the States and Unions could convene their own constituent assemblies and frame their own constitutions. By the autumn of 1948, however, few constituent assemblies had been formed, and those functioning lacked direction. On 25 October 1948, P. Govinda . . . moved . . . that the [Constituent] Assembly set up a committee to prepare a model constitution for the State constituent assemblies to follow. Although several Assembly members opposed this [because] . . . there should be no such constituent assemblies and the States should use the Constitution drafted for the provinces, the [Constituent] Assembly . . . favoured the idea. . . . The [Rau] committee reported [in March 1948] that its model constitution varied little from that already framed for the provinces. The only major difference . . . was that the State legislatures were empowered to amend their Constitution, whereas the provincial legislatures were denied constituent powers in relation to any of the provisions of the Indian Constitution.

With the rapid pace of events, this plan, too, became outmoded. A conference of the Prime Ministers of the States and Union of States with officials of the [Indian] States Ministry decided on 19 May 1949 that constituent assemblies in the various States and Unions should not frame their own constitutions on the basis of the [Rau] model . . . but that a constitution for all the States and Unions should be included in a special chapter of the [Indian] Constitution. Rau's model was presumably to be used for this purpose. The legislatures of the States were to continue to have constituent powers under the arrangement, however. . . . By October [1949], this scheme had . . . become outdated. The [Constituent] Assembly adopted . . . Article 238 of the [Indian] Constitution . . . which applied, with certain minor exceptions, the constitution of the provinces to the States. . . . Patel summed up the reasons behind this change. 'As . . . the States come closer to the Centre . . . it was realised that the idea of separate constitutions being framed for the different constituent units of the Indian Union was a legacy of the Rulers' polity and that in a people's polity there was no scope for variegated constitutional patterns.'[39]

Therefore, the princely territories (except Jammu and Kashmir) were brought into the Indian Federation and Constitution and placed, as far as possible, on the same basis as the former provinces (which now became states). Integration of both categories was achieved by the Constitution (7th Amendment) Act, 1956.[40]

AUSTRALIA

'[V]ariegated constitutional patterns'[41] prevail in Australian states.[42] Each state has its own constitution.[43] Therefore in Australia there are six state constitutions. From this perspective, the contrast between Indian and Australian states is stark. Without constitutional amendments, can that dichotomy be softened or even eliminated? Four possibilities emerge. First, Australian state constitutions share several virtually identical features. For example, state legislative power is generally conferred in terms of the peace, order and good government of the state.[44] One consequence of such textual similarity is that judicial interpretation of one state constitution can apply to and govern provisions in other state constitutions.[45] Thus uniformity can characterize such aspects of Australian state constitutional law. Amendment powers and procedures, including the existence of manner and form provisions, may be another example.[46] Secondly, Australian states have been governed by the same constitutional legislation. An example is the Colonial Laws Validity Act, 1865 (UK).[47] Currently, the Australia Acts, 1986 (UK & Clth)[48] render to all states the same constitutional powers and limitations.[49] Thirdly, some provisions in the Australian Constitution—either by granting power or imposing prohibitions—apply directly to states.[50] Classic examples include grants of state legislative power,[51] state executive power to issue writs for senate elections,[52] state executive and parliamentary power to appoint senators[53] and express[54] prohibitions on imposing customs and excise duties,[55] interference with interstate trade and commerce,[56] raising defence forces or taxing Commonwealth property,[57] making currency[58] and discriminating against residents of other states.[59] Fourthly, there is Section 106 of the Australian Constitution:[60]

> The Constitution of each State of the Commonwealth [of Australia] shall, subject to this Constitution, continue as at the establishment of the Commonwealth, or as at the admission or establishment of the State, as the case may be, until altered in accordance with the Constitution of the State.

Some hints emerge in early drafts of the Australian Constitution[61] and in the 1891 Constitutional Convention debates[62] that a constitution for all the States or, at least, some major aspects—legislative, executive and amendment powers—of a 'state' constitution would be incorporated into the Australian Constitution. However, the possibility of such incorporation quickly dissipated and only remnants, such as Section 106, remain.[63]

What is the scope and effect of Section 106? Is it merely an interpretative guide, a constitutional prohibition, or the statement of a truism?[64] Does Section 106 accomplish something more, for example a substantive relationship between Section 106 (and, consequently, the Australian Constitution) and state constitutions? On the latter, several suggestions have been postulated. Immediately after Federation, an incorporation thesis was advanced:

> [I]t may be argued that the Constitutions of the States are incorporated into the new [Australian] Constitution, and should be read as if they formed parts or chapters of the new Constitution. The whole of the details of State Government . . . may be considered as . . . provided by and elaborated in the Federal Constitution.[65]

On this view, unlike the Indian incorporation, several state constitutions inhere in the Australian Constitution. Without proceeding that far, another interpretation envisages Section 106 as converting colonies into a new constitutional entity: states; conferring constitutions, (albeit their pre-1901 colonial constitution), on states; providing the basis from which states derived their existence; and sustaining the continuing existence of state constitutions.[66] Narrower is the proposition that as a matter of 'language' Section 106 recognizes that state constitutions continue to be operative, but does not 'effect that continuance itself'.[67] The basic norm of state constitutions is not Section 106 and no substantive relationship exists. Consequently, the foundation or legal efficacy of state constitutions resides elsewhere—perhaps in United Kingdom parliamentary sovereignty[68] or else in the Australian people.[69]

To resolve these Australian conundrums assume, especially because of emerging judicial support,[70] that the Australian Constitution, especially via Section 106, provides the constitutional sustenance for state Constitutions. What results ensue?

Some Consequences

Being anchored in national constitutions does not obviate an obvious difference between Indian and Australian state constitutions. India's incorporation model precludes, in relation to state constitutional law, the classic benefits of federalism: tolerance and encouragement of difference, diversity and experimentation between states.[71] Lost is an opportunity to ameliorate stultifying uniformity.[72] The Australian hybrid model—fragments of state constitutional powers, prohibitions and structures specified in the Australian Constitution[73] and a federal constitutional foundation for separate state constitutions[74]—enables more prosaic state constitutions to flourish.[75]

Adumbration of a single[76] state constitution within the Indian Constitution has another obvious consequence: *ipso facto* state constitutional law is federal constitutional law. Again, the Australian situation is more ambiguous. If the relationship between the Australian Constitution, for example via Section 106, and state constitutions is something more than mere recognition and continuation,[77] Australian state constitutional law will also be federalised,[78] with two possible outcomes. First, issues arising under or involving state constitutions will be matters within federal jurisdiction and, therefore, in Australia's dual—federal and state—court system[79] subject to Commonwealth laws regulating federal jurisdiction with the potential to confine state constitutional law litigation to the Federal Court and High Court of Australia.[80] Secondly, this conversion—state into federal constitutional law—may protect or render immune state constitutions from Commonwealth or Union action. From this perspective in an Australian context, Section 106 may be a general limitation (in addition to implied federalism prohibitions[81]) on Commonwealth power.[82] Even so, not all Commonwealth legislation which, for example, directly amends state constitutions,[83] may succumb to this barrier.[84] However, to the extent that Commonwealth power is vulnerable, manipulation of this state protection could occur. Of course, that may depend upon two factors: what can be encompassed by Section 106's terminology—'[t]he Constitution of each State'[85]—and the ability of state parliaments or other entities[86] to amend state constitutions, for example, to bring matters within the purview of Section 106.

Does a similar situation—protection of the 'state' constitution from

Union power—also prevail in India? In contrast to Australia, where a referendum (not Commonwealth legislation[87]) is required to amend the Constitution,[88] the 'Parliament', pursuant to Article 368, 'may in exercise of its constituent power amend' the Constitution.[89] What limits *vis-a-vis* the 'state' constitution, restrict this power?[90] Two procedural limits are embodied in Article 368: first, the requirement that all amendments obtain 'a majority of the total membership of [each] House [of Parliament] and [at least] two-thirds of the members of [each] House present and voting' and the President's assent; second, ratification by resolutions passed by 'not less than one-half of the States' legislatures for amendments to state executive power in Article 162 and to High Courts in the states. One substantive limit—the 'basic structure' doctrine[91]—may also curtail the ability of the Indian Parliament to amend the 'state' constitution.[92]

Similarly, are Australian state constitutions, albeit by a Commonwealth Bill approved by requisite majorities at a referendum,[93] exposed to such amendments? Even advocates of a minimal substantive state constitution-Section 106 relationship[94] respond affirmatively.[95] For example:

State constitutions can be amended pursuant to section 128 [of the Australian Constitution] because [s. 128] [impliedly] authorizes amendment of section 106 wherein [State constitutions] are incorporated .... Republican government could, therefore, be introduced into a State by a referendum under section 128, even against the wishes of the electors of that State.[96]

Assume no such relationship existed.[97] Does Section 128 suffice to authorize amendments to or interfere with state constitutions? Again, an affirmative answer can be advanced.[98]

The starting point ... must be that section 106 is expressed as being subject to the remainder of the [Australian] Constitution, which includes section 128. Section 128 allows the [Australian] Constitution to be 'altered'. What limitation could be put forward as preventing the document from being 'altered' in a manner which produced an inconsistency between [the Australian Constitution] and the Constitution of a State? Were this ... to occur, would not the [Australian] Constitution as amended take priority over the State Constitution?[99]

State Executive Power

Is state executive power immune from such vulnerability? Some procedural protection is offered by the Indian Constitution.[100] Added to the scope under Article 368 for textual amendments,[101] a plethora of provisions have, directly and indirectly, the capacity to place state executive power under the President's auspices or Indian Government's control. Examples include presidential appointment of state governors (Article 155); governors' tenure during presidential pleasure (Article 156(1)); presidential assent or veto of state legislature's bills (Articles 31(4), 200, 201, 254(2), 304); and presidential proclamations, for example, to vest in the President all state government functions and state governors' powers (Article 356).[102] Use and abuse of these provisions has enabled a massive transfer—virtually the removal—of executive power from states to the central government.[103]

Occasionally evidence emerges that the Australian government does 'participate' in the appointment of State governors.[104] Potentially more far-reaching is Section 2 of the Australian Constitution:[105]

A Governor-General appointed by the Queen shall be Her Majesty's representative in the Commonwealth, and shall have and may exercise in the Commonwealth during the Queen's pleasure, but subject to this constitution, such powers and functions of the Queen as Her Majesty may be pleased to assign to him.

It has been suggested that

[section 2] must refer solely to [the Queen's] prerogatives with respect to the States. . . . [T]he Queen could assign to the Governor-General her functions in respect of the States, whereupon, as s. 106 of the Constitution may indeed require, they would probably be exercisable only on the advice of State Ministers. . . . It is not suggested . . . that the powers of the *Governors* could be transferred to the Governor-General under s. 2, but there is no apparent reason why the same person could not be appointed the [Queen's] representative in both the Commonwealth and one or more States; after all, State Governors now act as Administrators of the Commonwealth in the absence of the Governor-General. . . . The States . . . oppose the transfer to the Governor-General of the Queen's powers in respect of the States . . . and . . . State legislation seeking to entrench . . . the role of the Queen and the United Kingdom government in the State's constitutional structure might be thought to present some obstacles . . . to such a transfer of Royal powers. . . . But these provisions, obliging the Governor to obey royal Instructions . . . , neither prevent the Queen from assigning her powers to the Governor-General, nor oblige the Governor to ignore any instructions of the Governor-General exercising such assigned powers. . . .[106]

No such Section 2 assignment has, as yet, been made. However, Section 7 of the Australia Acts 1986 (Clth & U.K.) mandates, except for a governor's appointment and termination, that 'all powers and functions of Her Majesty in respect of a State are exercisable only by the Governor of a State'. Consequently, are there 'powers and functions of the Queen' in respect of a State—other than appointment and dismissal of governors—that still exist for assignment by the sovereign to the Governor-General under Section 2?[107] A negative answer has been proffered:

[There has been] speculation that section 2 might still have some practical effect if the powers and functions of the Queen referred to [in s. 2] related to her 'powers and functions' in respect of the States. However, the possibility of the Queen assigning to the Governor-General under section 2 some of her powers in respect of the States has been largely, although perhaps not completely, forclosed by section 7 of the *Australia Acts* 1986 (Commonwealth and United Kingdom). Accordingly, for all practical purposes, the second part of section 2 of the Constitution can now be regarded as entirely obsolete.[108]

Even so, the power remains: obsolescence does not constitute a constitutional amendment.[109] Especially with regard to appointment and dismissal powers potentially assignable to the Governor-General, the Indian experience cannot be discarded.

Other lessons from the Indian Constitution and experience may also be relevant and useful, particularly in the context of Australia's development from a constitutional monarchy to a republic.[110] First, where in federal republics there is essentially a parliamentary executive, rather than an executive presidency form of government, only India retains state and national components 'headed by a separate, largely ceremonial officer—the president of India . . . and State governors appointed by the president'.[111] That is not emulated, for example, in Austria and Germany where there is a national president but no equivalent office in *Land* governments.[112] If Australia and Australian states changed to a republic while retaining their parliamentary executives, the Indian model appears to conform to traditional Australian gubernatorial arrangements. Secondly, there is the 1956 Indian innovation of states sharing the same governor. By expressly indicating that nothing in Article 153 'prevent[s] the appointment of the same person as Governor of two or more States' the Indian Constitution provides more than implicit constitutional recognition for that arrangement.[113] If Australian states anticipate that cost, budgetary burdens or lack of suitable appointees[114] might present problems, their occurrence could be ameliorated by replicating the Indian Constitution.

Other comparative facets, such as the territorial integrity and vulnerability of states,[115] can also be enlightening. For Australia and India the reason is obvious. Exploring their vast differences and prominent similarities would reveal defects, alternatives and, perhaps more importantly, possibilities inherent in state constitutional arrangements. Within the Australian and Indian federations, these adventures and discoveries ought to be nurtured, not neglected.

NOTES

1. Commonwealth of Australia Constitution Act 1900 (UK) (operative 1 January 1901). See generally J. La Nauze, *The Making of the Australian Constitution* (1972); R. Lumb and G. Moens (eds.), *The Constitution of the Commonwealth of Australia: Annotated* (5th edn., 1995); L. Zines, *The High Court and the Constitution* (4th edn., 1997).
2. Constitution of India (adopted by the Constituent Assembly on 26 November 1949 when, by virtue of Article 394, some Articles came into effect with the remainder operative from 26 January 1950). See generally G. Austin, *The Indian Constitution: Cornerstone of a Nation* (1966); B. Rau, *The Framing of India's Constitution* (5 vols. 1965-71); B. Rau, *India's Constitution in the Making* (1960); H. Seervai, *Constitutional Law of India: A Critical Commentary*, 3rd edn., vol. 1 (1983) and vol. 2 (1984); D. Basu, *Shorter Constitution of India* (11th edn., 1994).
3. For Australia see Constitution Act 1902 (NSW), Constitution Act 1975 (Vic.), Constitution Act 1867 (Qld), Constitution Act Amendment Act 1896 (Qd), Constitution Acts Amendment Act 1971 (Qld), Constitution Act 1934 (SA), Constitution Act 1934 (Tas.), Constitution Act 1889 (WA) and Constitution Acts Amendment Act 1899 (WA). However, 'State Constitution Acts do not contain all those statutory provisions which could properly be described as constitutional'. Lumb, 'Methods of Alteration of State Constitutions in the United States and Australia' (1982) 13 *Fed. L.R. 1*, 10. See also Australia Acts 1986 (Clth and UK). See generally R. Lumb, *The Constitutions of the Australian States* (5th edn., 1991); and P. Hanks, *Australian Constitutional Law: Materials and Commentary* (5th edn., 1994). For India see Part VI (Articles 152-237) of the Indian Constitution; Constitution of Jammu & Kashmir (reproduced in A. Anand, *The Constitution of Jammu & Kashmir,*

pp. 357-445 (2nd edn., 1995). See generally W. Lee-Warner, *The Native States of India* (1910); P. Masaldan, *Evolution of Provincial Autonomy in India, 1858-1950* (1953); R. Coupland, *Report on the Constitutional Problem in India* (1943); B. Prasad, *The Origins of Provincial Autonomy: Being a History of the Relations between the Central Government and the Provincial Governments in British India from 1860 to 1919* (1941); N. Varadachariar, *Indian States in the Federation* (1936); H. Singh, *The Indian States: A Study of their Constitutional Position* (1949); V. Menon, *The Story of the Integration of the Indian States* (1956); *White Paper on Indian States* (rev. edn., 1950); S. Dash, *The Constitution of India: A Comparative Study* (1968), pp. 50-67; A. Prasad, *Centre and State Powers under Indian Federalism* (1981); C. Pal, *State Autonomy in Indian Federation: Emerging Trends* (1981).

4. See, for example, 'State Constitutional Law: Some Comparative Perspectives' (1989) 20 *Rutgers LJ* 1059.
5. Australia: 26 January 1788 (Governor Philip arrived at Botany Bay) to 3 March 1986 [Australia Acts (Clth & UK) operative 5.00 a.m. Greenwich mean time]. See generally A. Atkinson, *The Europeans in Australia: A History* (1997); C.M.H. Clark, *A History of Australia* (1962-81) (5 vols.). For India, see generally V. Smith, *Oxford History of India* (4th edn. by P. Spear, 1981); A. Keith, *A Constitutional History of India 1600-1935* (1936); S. Sharma, *A Constitutional History of India, 1765 to 1954* (1955); A. Gledhill, *The Republic of India: The Development of its Laws and Constitution* (1964).
6. See, for example, Thomson, 'Comparative Constitutional Law' (1989) 6 *Arizona J Int'l & Comp L* 22; Thomson, 'American and Australian Constitutions: Continuing Adventures in Comparative Constitutional Law' (1997) 30 *John Marshall L Rev* 627.
7. See Anand, supra note 3. See also infra notes 10-13.
8. See especially Part VI (Articles 152-237—'The States') of the Indian Constitution. See generally supra note 3 (literature on Indian states). For somewhat similar examples of State constitutions incorporated in national constitutions see Thomson, supra note 4, pp. 1072-3 (Nigeria, Camaro Island, Pakistan, United Arab Emirates).
9. Similarly for India's Union territories. See Seervai, supra note 2, pp. 173-83 (vol. 1).
10. Indian Constitution Article 370(1)(d) & (2); Constitution (Application to Jammu & Kashmir Order, 1954 (C.O. 48) (reproduced, with amendments, in Anand, supra note 3, pp. 447-66). See generally idem, pp. 124-5, 128-241. That 1954 Order 'deals only with the [c]onstitutional position of the State of Jammu & Kashmir within the framework of the Indian Constitution . . . [and its] effect . . . has been to bring the position prevailing in the State more at par with the rest of [India] . . . ' idem, pp. 165, 166.
11. See, for example title of Article 370 ('*Temporary* provisions') (emphasis added); Article 370(3) ('this article shall cease to be operative').

12. Reproduced in Anand, supra note 3, pp. 357-445.
13. Idem, pp. 130-1 (suggesting that Article 370 contains 'the power to finalise the constitutional relationship between [Jammu and Kashmir] and the Union of India' and that Article 370 is not 'capable of being abrogated, modified or replaced unilaterally'). See also Part XX of the 1954 Order (supra note 16) which adds proviso to Article 368(2) stipulating that an amendment to the Indian Constitution (including Article 370) does not 'have effect in relation to the State of Jammu and Kashmir unless applied by [Presidential order under article 370(1)]', pp. 461-2. Similarly, Part 1 of the 1954 Order adds a proviso to Article 3 to protect the territorial integrity of Jammu & Kashmir, pp. 105-6, 166-9, 451.
14. Prior to 'British settlement' see supra note 10 (references). During British occupation (1765-1947) Indians drafted, for example, 'a Constitution of India Bill' 1895. W. Morris, 'The Politics of the Indian Constitution (1950)', in V. Bogdanor (ed.), *Constitutions in Democratic Politics* (1988), pp. 128, 131
15. East India Company Act 1772 (UK) (13 Geo. 3, c. 63); Indian Independence Act 1947 (UK) (providing that, after 14 August 1947, the government of India, until the Indian Constituent Assembly otherwise provided, was to be 'in accordance with the Government of India Act, 1935'). See also infra note 31 ('Indian Parliament').
16. 13 Geo. 3, c. 63. On the East India Company's activities in India, see H. Furber, *John Company at Work: A Study of European Expansion in India in the Late Eighteenth Century* (1940, rpt. 1970); P. J. Marshall, *Bengal: The British Bridgehead Eastern India 1740-1828* (1987); C.A. Bayly, *Indian Society and the Making of the British Empire* (1988); M.H. Fisher (ed.), *The Politics of the British Annexation of India 1757-1857* (1993).
17. See 39 & 40 Geo. 3, c. 79 (1800); 3 & 4 Will. 4, c. 85 (1833); 16 &17 Vict., c. 95 (1853); 17 & 18 Vict., c. 77 (1854); 21 & 22 Vict., c. 106 (1858); 22 & 23 Vict., c. 41 (1859); 25 & 26 Vit., c. 67 (1861); 28 & 29 Vict., 17 (1865); 32 & 33 Vict., c. 97 (1869); 33 & 34 Vict., c. 3 (1870); 1 & 2 Geo. 5, c. 25 (1911); 2 & 3 Geo. 5, c. 6 (1912); 5 &6 Geo 5, c. 61 (1915); 6 & 7 Geo. 5, c. 37 (1916); 9 & 10 Geo. 5, c. 101 (1919); 25 & 26 Geo. 5, c. 42 (1935). See generally Keith, supra note 5; Gledhill, supra note 5.
18. See 24 & 25 Vict., c. 17 (1861); 32 & 33 Vict. c. 98 (1869); 34 & 35 Vict., c. 34 (1871); 37 & 38 Vict., c. 91 (1874); 55 & 56 Vict., c. 14 (1892); 4 Edw. 7, c. 26 (1904); 7 Edw. 7, c. 35 (1907); 9 Edw. 7, c. 4 (1909).
19. These states (despite British settlement) were ruled by Indian princes and, under the British Crown's suzerainty, only formally surrendered to British authority matters concerning external relations, interstate disputes, currency and defence. Estimates of their number vary from 550 to over 600. Geographically, these states constituted about third of India and included about one quarter of its population. Before 1947, only a few States possessed written constitutions underpinned by statute (e.g. Mysore, Hyderabad,

Travancore, Baroda, Gwalior). This was due to change with the establishment of voluntary unions of states [e.g. in Gujarat (Saurashtra) and the Deccan]. Gandhi approved the Constitution of the Deccan Union. But Patel and the States Department made it known that they disapproved of these princely unions (perhaps, because such unions might have pre-empted the nationalists' own constitutional design) and no such unions eventuated. See generally, Austin, supra note 2, pp. 243-54 ('Extending the [Indian] Constitution to the Princely States'); J. Manor, *Political Change in an Indian State: Mysore 1917-1955* (1977); R. J. Moore, *Escape From Empire: The Attlee Government and the Indian Problem* (1983); A.K. Neogy, *The Paramount Power and the Princely States of India 1858-1881* (1979); R. Jeffrey (ed.), *People, Princes and Paramount Power: Society and Politics in the Indian Princely States* (1978); and I. Copland, *The Princes of India in the End-Game of Empire, 1917-47* (1997); See also supra note 3 (references); infra note 26; text accompanying infra note 39.

20. See, for example, M. Galanter, *Competing Equalities: Law and the Backward Classes in India* (1984), pp. 147-53.
21. Two provincial categories existed: full provinces having (British) governors or lieutenant-governors and chief commissioner's provinces administered by the central government.
22. For example, for a period of time '[t]he central government [in India] was run from London by the Secretary of State for India assisted by a Council of Advisors'. Pal, supra note 3, p. 112. See, for example, Part 1 (Secs. 1-18) (Home Government) of the Government of India Act 1915 (UK). 'No matter how substantial the devolution of authority to the provinces under the 1919 Government of India Act or how apparently federal the provisions of the 1935 Act, or to what extent Indians held office in either the federal or provincial governments, power was centralized and always in British hands.' Austin, supra note 2, pp. 188-9.
23. See supra note 17. On the 1919 Act's antecedents see *Report on Indian Constitutional Reform* (*Cmd. 9109*) (1918).
24. See, for example, Grewal, supra note 19, pp. 4-9 (legislative and fiscal aspects and operation of 1919 Act).
25. On the 1935 Act's antecedents see *Report of the Indian Statutory Commission (Cmd. 3568-9)* (1930); *Proceedings of the Round Table Conference (3 sessions) (Cmd. 3778, 3997, 4238)* (1931-2); *Report of the Joint Committee on Indian Constitutional Reform (H.C. 51)* (1934); Gledhill, supra note 5, pp. 25-6.
26. Provisions in this Act relating to the Federal Legislature (consisting of the British Crown, the Council of States and House of Assembly) did not become operative because the 'princes ... could never agree on their representation in the [Council of States]' as stipulated in Sec. 18(2) & (3) and the First Schedule. T. Leonard, 'Federalism in India', in W. Livingston (ed.), *Federalism*

in the Commonwealth: A Biographical Commentary (1963), p. 106. However, the 1935 Act 'worked relatively smoothly in the provinces during ... 1937-42'. Idem, p. 107. See also supra note 15 'The problem of bringing the Princely States into an Indian federation, [was] bequeathed to the [Constituent] Assembly and the Union Government by the departing British. ... For over one hundred years before [1947 Indian] independence these States had ... a special relationship with the Paramount Power. Their treaties with the British had left [States] a good deal of internal autonomy—glorified by the ruling Princes into "sovereignty". ... [T]hey clung ... to the manifestations of their "sovereignty". As a result, the 1935 Act provided only that the States could accede to the [Indian] federation if they so desired. The negotiations concerning the terms of accession were to be undertaken with each State separately by the Viceroy. ... Initiated in 1937, on the coming into force of the 1935 Act, these negotiations dragged on until the [1939 Second World] War, with the result that none of the Princely States became members of the [Indian] federation'. Austin, supra note 2, p. 245 [footnote omitted]. See also text accompanying infra notes 39, 40.

27. See generally Gledhill, supra note 5, pp. 26-41; Grewal, supra note 19, pp. 9-14; W. Morris, supra note 14, p. 130, p. 149 n 2; Leonard, supra note 25, pp. 102-6 (bibliographical commentary).
28. See supra note 26. As to the post-1947 accession of princely states to the Indian Union see supra note 26 and infra notes 39, 40.
29. W. Morris, supra note 14, p. 130.
30. See, fore example, p. 130 ('model'); Austin, supra note 2, p. 328 ('debt to the 1935 Act ... very great'). But note V. Patel's 26 November 1949 statement to the Constituent Assembly: 'Unlike the scheme of 1935 our new Constitution is not an alliance between democracies and dynasties, but a real Union of the Indian people based on the basic concept of the sovereignty of the people'. Austin, supra note 2, p. 254. For other influences see Tripathi, 'Perspectives on the American Constitutional Influence on the Constitution of India', in L. Beer (ed.), *Constitutionalism in Asia: Asian Views of the American Influence* (1979); S. Sorabjee, 'Equality in the United States and India', in L. Henkin and A. Rosenthal (eds.), *Constitutionalism and Rights: The Influence of the United States Constitution Abroad* (1990); Charles, 'American Influence on the Indian Constitution: Focus on Equal Protection of the Laws' (1986) 17 *Columbia Human Rights LJ* 193.
31. Convened on 9 December 1946, it adopted the Indian Constitution on 26 November 1949. See generally Austin, supra note 2. 'The Constituent Assembly was in its second aspect ... a part of the government, [because]. . . the Constituent Assembly (Legislative) was the Indian Parliament'. Idem at 15. See also supra note 15 (1935 Act).
32. Austin, supra note 2, p. 192. That is, '[t]he [Indian] Federation was not the

result of an agreement by the states to join in a federation' and, therefore, secession was not constitutional; Idem, p. 192 (quoting B. Ambedkar's speech to Constituent Assembly).

33. See supra note 24 ('working relatively smoothly').
34. Austin, supra note 2, p. 5. This Plan was publicly released on 16 May 1946. See generally idem, pp. 3-8. [It became 'outmoded' on 15 August 1947 with the Indian Independence Act 1947 (UK) coming 'into effect'.] See also idem, p. 190 (Second Report of the Constituent Assembly's Union Powers Committee).
35. Rau, supra note 2, p. 141. See also idem, pp. 141-52 ('A Model Provincial Constitution').
36. Austin, supra note 2, p. 34 (footnote omitted).
37. Idem, pp. 186, 191. Compare Pal, supra note 3, p. 27 ('some . . . Constituent Assembly [members] were staunch supporters of Provincial autonomy and their [Assembly] speeches . . . complain[ed] against providing . . . excessive powers to the Centre').
38. See note 19.
39. Austin, supra note 2, p. 243, pp. 251-2 (footnotes omitted including Report of the Committee on a Model Constitution for Indian Provinces (dated about 21 March 1949). See also idem, pp. 243-54 (how princely states were persuaded to join the Union of India); Watts, supra note 19, p. 18 ('combination of persuasion, cajolery, bribery, and the threat of military power' to induce princely states 'to accede to the Union'). 'By Independence Day [15 August 1947], all the [Princely] States, excepting Hyderabad, Kashmir, Junagadh, and two insignificant ones, had joined the Union, ceding as a minimum their authority over Defence, communications, and Foreign Affairs'. Austin, supra note 2, p. 250.
40. Repealing Part VII (Article 238) of the Indian Constitution (removing references in the Constitution to the former princely states).
41. See text accompanying supra note 39.
42. See supra note 3.
43. But note Thomson, 'State Constitutional Law: Gathering the Fragments', (1985) 16 *U. West. Aust. LR*, 92 (myriad of documents comprising a state constitution); Lumb, 'Methods . . .', supra note 3.
44. See, for example, Lumb, *The Constitutions*, supra note 3, p. 84 (text of state constitutions).
45. See, for example, *Pearce* v. *Florenca* (1976), 135 CLR 507 (W.A. Constitution); *Union Steamship Co* v. *King* (1988) 166 CLR 213 (N.S.W. Constitution).
46. See, for example, Carney, 'An Overview of Manner and Form in Australia' (1988) 5 *Qld U. Tech LJ* 69; Goldsworthy, 'Manner and Form in the Australian States' (1987) 16 *Melb ULR* 403; Goldsworthy, 'The "Principle of Ranasinghe": A Reply to H.P. Lee' (1992) 15 *UNSW LJ* 540.
47. 28 & 29 Vict., c. 63. See generally, D. Swinfen, *Imperial Control of Colonial*

Legislation 1812-1865: A Study of British Policy Towards Colonial Legislative Powers, pp. 167-83 (1970); Campbell, 'Colonial Legislation and the Laws of England' (1965) 22 *U Tas L R* 148. See also Australian Colonies Act, 1861 (UK) 24 & 25 Vict., c. 44; Australian Constitutions Act, 1850 (No. 2) (UK) 13 & 14 Vict., c. 59.

48. See supra note 7.
49. But see Sec. 13 (Queensland); sec. 14 (WA).
50. Thomson, supra note 43, p. 92 (Australian Constitution 'does . . . in fundamental ways, affect, shape and interact with state constitutional powers, structures and institutions').
51. Aust. Const. Sec. 7 para 2; Sec. 9.
52. Aust. Const. Sec. 12. See generally Lumb and Moens, supra note 1, pp. 66-8; G. Sawer, *Federation Under Strain: Australia 1972-1975,* (1977), pp. 229-33.
53. Aust. Const. Sec. 15. See generally, Thomson, 'Casual Senate Vacancies: Section 15's Continuing Conundrums' (1992) 3 *Pub LR* 149.
54. For implied federalism and free speech limitations see, for example, *Commonwealth* v *Cigamatic Pty Ltd.* (1962) 108 CLR 372; Zines, supra note 1, pp. 353-72, 384, 389-91; *Stephens* v *Western Australian Newspapers* (1994) 184 CLR 211.
55. Aust. Const. Sec. 90. See generally Lumb and Moens, supra note 1, pp. 438-52.
56. Aust. Const. Sec. 92. See generally Lumb and Moens, supra note 1, pp. 453-77, 573-98.
57. Aust. Const. Sec. 114. See generally Lumb and Moens, supra note 1, pp. 527-30.
58. Aust. Const. Sec. 115. See generally Lumb and Moens, supra note 1, p. 531.
59. Aust. Const. Sec. 117. See generally Lumb and Moens, supra note 1, pp. 540-3.
60. See generally Lumb and Moens supra note 1, pp. 499-507; Zines, supra note 1, pp. 336-41. For possible interpretations of 'Constitution of each State' see idem, pp. 291-2; *McGinty* v *Western Australia* (1996) 70 ALJR 200, 256-7 (Gummow, J). See also G. Craven, *The Convention Debates: 1891-1898: Commentaries, Indices and Guide,* 561-2 (1986) (prior Sec. 106 drafts and debates at the 1891 and 1897-8 Constitutional Conventions). See also Aust. Const. Sec. 107 ('Every power . . . ').
61. See, for example, Part VI ('Provincial Constitutions') (Clauses 67-81) of A Bill for the Federation of the Australasian Colonies (February 1891) (drafted by A.I. Clark) [reproduced in (1958) 32 ALJ 67, 73]; Parts X ('Provincial Constitutions—Executive Power'), XI ('Local Parliaments') and XIII ('Powers of Local Parliaments') of A Bill for an Act for the Union of the Australasian Colonies (26 February 1891) (drafted by C. C. Kingston) (reproduced in

S. Griffith, *Successive Stages of the Constitution of the Commonwealth of Australia*, pp. 46, 57, 60 (1891) (Dixson Library, NSW) (Ms. Q. 198) (CY Reel 221). See also draft Bills (including Clark's) worked on, from 23-6 March 1891, by S. Griffith and the Drafting Committee—Griffith, Kingston and Clark—pp. 26, 27, 39-41 (alterations to Clark's draft), pp. 63, 64, 82, 86-7 (alterations on draft sent to Printer on 24 March), pp. 91, 92, 109-10 ('Chapter V The States' of 26 March draft). For a discussion see La Nauze, supra note 1, pp. 48-50, 57. On 18 March 1891 the Constitution Convention adopted resolutions (1) and (6): 'That the powers and privileges and territorial rights of the several existing Colonies shall remain intact, except in respect to such surrenders as may be agreed upon as necessary and incidental to the power and authority of the National Federal Government' and 'That provision should be made in the Federal Constitution which will enable each State to make such amendments in its Constitution as may be necessary for the purposes of the Federation'. *Official Report of the National Australasian Convention Debates*, pp. 99-500 (1891). See idem, pp. 477-95 (discussing 6th Resolution including differences of view as to whether and, if so, how and the extent to which the Australian Constitution should include a 'state' constitution or deal with existing colonial (state) constitutions).

62. See, for example, La Nauze, supra note 1, p. 45 (concluding that the 1891 'Convention had not been arranged for the purpose of imposing ... internal reforms upon individual colonies'). See also supra note 61 (6th Resolution).
63. See generally Aust. Const. Chapter V 'The States'.
64. See, for example, Thomson, 'Are State Courts Invulnerable?: Some Preliminary Notes' (1990) 20 *UWA LR*, pp. 61, 66-7 (discussing those possibilities); Zines, supra note 1, pp. 336-40 (Sec. 106 as a limitation on Commonwealth legislative power).
65. J. Quick and R. Garran, *The Annotated Constitution of the Australian Commonwealth*, p. 930 (1901). Compare the suggestion that Sec. 106 effects an 'importation' of some (for example, implied freedom of political communication), but not other (for example, implications of equality of voting power) aspects 'of the Australian Constitution into State Constitutions'. *McGinty* v *Western Australia* supra note 60, p. 228 (Toohey, J).
66. See, for example, McGinty supra note 60, p. 206 (Brennan, CJ), 227 (Toohey, J). See generally Douglas, 'The Western Australian Constitution: Its Source of Authority and Relationship with Section 109 of the Australian Constitution' (1990) *20 UWA LR* 340.
67. Craven, 'A Few Fragments of State Constitutional Law' (1990) 20 *UWA LR* 353, 371. For discussion of whether state constitutions 'are part of the Commonwealth Constitution' see G. Winterton, *Monarchy to Republic: Australian Republican Government* 141 (1994) (suggesting that the 'view' that 'section 106 is the source of authority of State constitutions ... is questionable [b]ut, even if State Constitutions do not legally derive from the

Commonwealth Constitution ... they are incorporated within it by virtue of section 106') (footnotes omitted).

68. *Western Australia* v *Wilsmore* [1981] WAR 179, 183-4 (Burt, C J) (United Kingdom legislation 'sole source of authority' for state constitutions). See, for example, Zines, supra note 1, p. 341. But see Douglas, supra note 66, pp. 348-9 (discussing and criticizing view that Sec. 106 continues, but is not the source of state constitutions). Of course, if the Australian Constitution (and, therefore, Sec. 106) derives its authority from the United Kingdom, then, on either view, state constitutions ultimately rest on British parliamentary sovereignty. Thomson, supra note 43, pp. 92-3 ('opposing views coincide').

69. Especially if residual state-United Kingdom constitutional links have been severed, albeit by the Australia Acts 1986 (Clth and UK). For state constitutions see Thomson, supra note 43, p. 93; Thomson, 'The Australia Acts: A State Constitutional Law Perspective' (1990) 20 *U. West. LR* 409, pp. 412-14. For the Australian Constitution see Lindell, 'Why is Australia's Constitution Binding? The Reasons in 1900 and Now, and the Effect of Independence' (1986) 16 *Federal LR* 29; *Australian Capital Television* v *Commonwealth* (1992) 177 CLR 106, 138 (Mason, CJ) ('Australia Act 1986 (UK) marked the end of the legal sovereignty of the Imperial Parliament and recognized that ultimate sovereignty resided in the Australian people'); Zines, supra note 1, pp. 393-97; Zines, 'The Sovereignty of the People', in M. Coper and G. Williams (eds.), *Power, Parliament and the People* 91 (1997). Other possible sources of authority include the Australia Acts 1986 (Clth and UK) and a 'constituent' legislative power. Douglas, supra note 66, pp. 350-1; McGinty, supra note 60, at 278 (Gummow, J) ('binding effect of Sec. 73 [of W.A. Constitution] derived from Sec. 6 of the *Australia Acts*').

70. See McGinty, supra note 60, pp. 206, 227 (citing earlier cases).

71. For example, Justice Brandeis envisaged a 'federal system [where] a single courageous state may, if its citizens choose, serve as a laboratory; and try novel social and economic experiments without risk to the rest of the country'. *New State Ice Co.* v *Liebmann* (1932) 285 U.S. 262, 311. See for example, Steiner, 'A Progressive Creed: The Experimental Federalism of Justice Brandeis' (1983) 2 *Yale L & Pol. R* 1. Justice Holmes referred to 'the making of social experiments ... in the insulated chambers afforded by the several states'. *Truax* v *Corrigan* (1921) 257 U.S. 312, 344. See generally F. Frankfurter, *The Public and its Government* (1930), pp. 48-51.

72. Of course, in relation to India, Justices Cardozo's view—that the United States Constitution 'was framed upon the theory that the peoples of the several states must sink or swim together, and that in the long run prosperity and salvation are in union and not division'—is apposite. *Baldwin* v *G.A.F. Seelig Inc.* (1935) 294 U.S. 511, 523.

73. See supra notes, pp. 50-9.

74. See supra notes, pp. 60-70.
75. But see text accompanying supra notes 44-5 ('uniformity' and 'virtually identical features').
76. But note the Constitution of Jammu & Kashmir and its relationship (via Article 370) with the Indian Constitution. See text accompanying supra notes, pp. 7-13.
77. See text accompanying supra note 65.
78. See generally *Final Report of the Constitutional Commission* (1988) (vol. 1), pp. 68-72.
79. See, for example, J. Crawford, *Australian Courts of Law* (3rd edn., 1993); *BP Australia Ltd* v *Amann Aviation Pty Ltd* (1996) 137 ALR 447 (cross vesting scheme) (special leave to appeal to High Court granted).
80. Aust. const. Secs. 76(i), 77 (i) and (ii).
81. See supra note 54.
82. For a discussion and preference for implied federalism limitations see Zines, supra note 1, pp. 336-40.
83. See, for example, Australia Act 1986 (Clth) Secs. 13 (Qld Constitution), 14 (WA Constitution).
84. '[T]he words "subject to this Constitution" in Sec. 106 . . . are apposite for ensuring that where fulfilment of the purpose of a Commonwealth power requires interference with State constitutional rules, the Commonwealth has the power to do so . . . '. Zines, supra note 1, p. 340 (referring to the defence power [Sec. 51(vi) and Sec. 51 (xxxviii) of Aust. Const.]). See also Douglas, supra note 66, pp. 343-7 [relationship between Secs. 51 (vi), (xxxviii) and 106]; Thomson, supra note 64 (similar); Winterton, supra note 67, p. 142 [utilization of sec. 51 (xxxviii) legislation to avoid state manner and form requirements].
85. See supra note 60 ('possible interpretations').
86. See, for example, Sec. 73(2) of Constitution Act 1889 (WA) (referendum).
87. For possibilities inherent in Aust. Const. Sec. 51 (xxxvi) see, for example, Thomson, 'Altering the Constitution: Some Aspects of Section 128' (1983) 13 *Federal LR* 323 n. 4(i); Thomson, 'History, Justices and the High Court: An Institutional Perspective' (1995) 1 *Aust. J Legal Hist,* pp. 281, 304, n. 92 [relationship between Sec. 51 (xxxvi) and Sec. 96]. '[A] large number of provisions in the [Australian] Constitution ... leave to the [Commonwealth] Parliament the power of altering the actual constitutional provisions'. Attorney General (Clth); ex rel *McKinlay* v *Commonwealth* (1975) 135 CLR 1, 25 (Barwick, CJ).
88. Aust. Const. Sec. 128. See generally Lumb and Moens, supra note 1, pp. 36, 567-2.
89. Indian Const. art. 368. See Generally S. Sathe, *Constitutional Amendments 1950-1988: Law and Politics* (1989); Aikman, 'The Debate on the Amendment of the Indian Constitution' (1978) 9 *Vic U Wellington LR* 357; Rudolph and

Rudolph, 'Judicial Review versus Parliamentary Sovereignty: The Struggle over Stateness in India' (1981) 29 *J Clth & Comp. Politics* 231; Morgan, 'The Indian "Essential Features" Case' (1981) 30 *Int & Comp L Q* 307; Sudarshan, 'In Quest of State: Politics and Judiciary in India' (1990) 28 *J Clth & Comp. Politics* 44. Compare *Boland* v *Hughes* (1988) 83 ALR 673, 674-5 (Mason, J) (Australian constitutional amendments be declared unconstitutional by the Australian High Court).

90. In relation to Jammu & Kashmir see supra note 13.
91. For examples of constitutional amendments infringing the Constitution's basic structure and, therefore, beyond Article 368 amendments power, see, *Kesavananda Bharathi* v *Kerala*, AIR 1973 SC 1461; *Minerva Mills* v *Union of India*, AIR 1980 SC 1789.
92. For discussion of the basic structure limitation's nature and scope see Sathe, supra note 19, pp. 68-94.
93. Aust. Const. Sec. 128. See supra note 88.
94. See, for example, supra note 67 (Winterton's 'incorporation' theory).
95. But see Thomson, 'Altering the Constitution', supra note 87, p. 337 (reasons for a negative response).
96. Winterton, supra note 67, pp. 141-2. See also Quick and Garran, supra note 21, p. 990 ('amending power ... extends to the structure and functions of [state] Governments'); Douglas, supra note 66, pp. 351-2 (same); Thomson, supra note 93, pp. 337-8. But compare supra note 101.
97. See text accompanying supra note 70.
98. See, for example, Thomson, 'Altering the Constitution', supra note 87, p. 338 (arguments and examples).
99. Craven, supra note 67, pp. 371-2.
100. See text following supra note 90.
101. See supra notes 89, 90, 92.
102. See generally *Bommai* v *Union of India* AIR 1994 SC 1918.
103. See generally *President's Rule in the States and Union Territories* (5th edn., 1991); S.C. Arora, *President's Rule in Indian States (A Study of Punjab)* (1990).
104. See, for example, Hanks, supra note 7, p. 302 (1976 refusal to reappoint old Governor). Do provisions such as Aust. Const. Secs. 12 and 15 (see text accompanying supra notes 58 and 59) give the Australian government a constitutional interest in the appointment of state governors?
105. See generally G. Winterton, *Parliament, the Executive and the Governor-General: A Constitutional Analysis* (1983), pp. 51-2, 245-6; Final Report, supra note 78, pp. 342-3; Report of the Advisory Committee on Executive Government (June 1987), pp. 56-7.
106. Winterton, supra note 105, pp. 52-246 (footnotes omitted) (emphasis in original).
107. See, for example, Thomson, 'The Australia Acts', supra note 69, p. 425.
108. Report, supra note 105, p. 57.

109. Compare, e.g. Aust. Const. Secs. 59, 74. See Lumb and Moens, supra note 1, p. 333 (characterizing Sec. 59 as 'a dead letter' and 'inoperative'); Thomson, 'Appointing Australian High Court Justices: Some Constitutional Conundrums', in H.P. Lee and G. Winterton (eds.), *Australian Constitutional Perspectives,* p. 251, n. 1 (1992) (contrasting views of Sec. 74).
110. See, for example, Winterton, supra note 67.
111. Idem, pp. 105-6.
112. See idem, p. 106.
113. Indian Constitution, Article 153.
114. Compare the situation in WA from June 1931 to October 1948 when there was no state Governor. Boyce, 'Governor and Parliament', in D. Black (ed.), *The House on the Hill: A History of the Parliament of Western Australia 1832-1990,* (1991), pp. 265, 272-4.
115. For Australia, see Aust. Const. Secs. 111, 123; Lumb and Moens, supra note 1, pp. 525-6, 561-2. For India see Indian Constitution, Article 3; Pal, supra note 3, p. 29 (concluding that 'in view of . . . Article 3 . . . India is an indestructible union of destructible states').

4

Judicial Appointments within a Federal Structure

ROBERT WATT

The status that is given to the independence of the judiciary in the common law world can never be overestimated. It is the definitive factor separating a democracy from a totalitarian state. In Australia, at least in the federal judicial structure, it can be used both formally as a precept of constitutional law to ensure the separation of functions of government, as well as informally via standing orders of the Parliament to ensure that members do not intrude into the domain of the court while litigation is in progress. It may be narrowly construed, for example, to ensure that members of the judiciary do not sit on Royal Commissions or other executive non-judicial tribunals and thus be too close to the executive arm of government, or it may be widely interpreted, to ensure that adverse comments about the judiciary are suppressed in the name of maintaining public confidence in the judicial function. And while these precepts will apply to either a unitary or a federal system, in the latter the very nature of the task of the highest court—as a constitutional court establishing parameters of governmental power—requires strict observance.

At the heart of judicial independence is the desire to ensure that the judiciary are guaranteed the right to function without fear of retribution or sanction. Yet in much of the literature the selection of the judiciary is seldom mentioned in the context of the independence which it subsequently enjoys. It is a rule of faith that the selection process will yield those most highly qualified and suitable for the judicial function.

In Australia appointments to the High Court and other federal courts are made under Section 7 of the Constitution by the Governor-General in Council. Thus legally the Governor-General must act with the advice of the federal Executive Council. In constitutional terms the will of the government is so exercised. However, there has been for much of the time since Federation in 1901, at least from when the High Court was established in 1903, a tension in the appointment of High Court justices. The settlement of *inter se* questions between the Commonwealth and the states was left in the hands of the High Court[1] in the belief that the problems and special conceptions of federalism would be very familiar.[2] As early as 1912 the question of a potential judicial appointee favouring the Commonwealth or the states was one which could cause serious political and constitutional tumult.[3] Over the years political allegiance has raised the same issue, insofar as the Australian Labor Party for much of that time has had as a plank the centralization of power in the hands of the Commonwealth. This has always made the federal relationship extremely important in arguing against political appointments, at least in those courts in Australia that can decide *inter se* matters.

Yet over the last decade, at least two phenomena have brought the judicial selection process once more before the public. The first is the recognition that certain groups in society, most notably women,[4] and some ethnic groups, are not adequately represented in the judiciary in anywhere near the numbers that they 'ought' to be. The second, applying particularly to the High Court of Australia, has been the perception that the Court is adopting a greater political role. This particular perception has been assisted by the reading of a number of implied freedoms into the Australian Constitution, most notably the implied freedom of free political speech. In 1992 the Court in *Australian Capital Television Pty Ltd* v *Commonwealth*[5] struck down legislation enacted by the Australian Parliament that would have restricted political advertising. The reason given was that the Constitution was always to be interpreted 'to protect and promote individual liberty'. This particular decision had the effect of not only labelling the Court as 'activist'; it was seen, with the help of media editors, as a blatantly 'political' stance.

However, there has been a third development which may well have played a role in changing perceptions of the judiciary. The recently retired Chief Justice of the High Court, Sir Anthony Mason, appeared in the last few years to go out of his way, as Chief Justice, to court publicity—to expose the general public to the nature of the judicial process. In doing so he was prepared to defend the 'law-making role' of the Court, rather than hiding behind the facade of merely interpreting the law. Sir Anthony is not alone in this. There is a new breed of judges who are not content to remain closeted behind the closed doors of their courts.

The debate has been joined. More and more people are asking: what indeed should be the role of the judge in the political environment? This development is being reinforced in the law schools by the work of critical legal studies exponents which makes clear the political nature of all judicial decisions. Public interest in this debate has been heightened by the need to make a number of new appointments to the High Court in the last two years. To paraphrase one commentator, the choice for the executive would be between a 'black-letter' lawyer or a 'rainbow-hued' judicial innovator. However, whatever the ultimate appointment, the process has clearly been called into question.

Traditionally the process at both federal and state levels, in the absence of formal statutory process, other than to consult with state Attorneys-General in the selection of High Court appointments,[6] has been for the executive to choose, in the vast majority of cases, from the leaders of the Bar. The results are clearly apparent: the vast majority are males of Anglo-Saxon or Celtic background. Indeed when we add a non-government school education to the equation, we find that 90 per cent of all of the federal judiciary fit into this narrow band. With their Bar background, we find here a fertile field (or is it a stagnant pond?) for the development of conservatism. Gone are the days when our judges were viewed as 'living oracles',[7] but failure to recognize the innate political nature of past appointments leaves both women and ethnic groups unhappy with the present system.

Apart from these considerations, are there other reasons for examining alternate models for judicial appointment? Even in the United Kingdom, the tradition of appointing only highly qualified persons to judicial posts has been made clear only since Clement Atlee's premiership in 1946. As has been noted, 'its continuance relies [*only*] on the precarious base of convention'.[8] Again, in Canada, there was such an outcry over a blatant political appointment in 1984 that it has been suggested as one of the likely reasons for the government's subsequent defeat. Certainly it brought home to Canadians the need for finding better methods of appointing the judiciary.[9]

Our constitutional problem is the way we have traditionally treated the judiciary as a single entity without attempting to isolate the various tasks undertaken in the judicial process—especially in a federal system. This has put tremendous strain upon various aspects associated with the judiciary, including isolating questions relating to its independence from executive interference—in all of its manifestations.

This has led to strange results in one particular area where in the federal arena and some states, most notably Victoria, members of the Bench are either constitutionally unable[10] to accept appointment to Royal Commissions or unwilling,[11] and in other states regularly provide such services to the executive.[12]

Yet with respect to appointments, three problems are critical: (1) what should be the choice of selection criteria for the judiciary? (2) what should be the process of selection? (3) what should be the method of accountability, applicable in all other public sectors, of judges?

There is no doubting that in the selection of judges, merit should be the principal consideration.[13] But the manifestation of merit is complex.

Thus legal skills, including knowledge of the law and intellectual capacity, may well be in higher demand in the appellate court than, say, in the lower community courts found particularly in the states and territories of Australia.

Advocacy skills, *per se*, will be essential for some judges and less so for others. But even here, what is included in advocacy skills will be subject to debate. In one list[14] it included not only oral communication skills and knowledge of evidentiary rules, but also forensic and analytical abilities as well. From a list of personal qualities there may be some more in demand for judges acting in some capacities than for others. While integrity and high moral character would be essential for all, sympathy, charity and patience would be in higher demand in a court of first instance than in the appellate court.

The selection and publication of criteria is not, however, the principal problem. For many, the principal problem will be how such information is gathered, with the related problem of the application of natural justice rules in protecting the rights of prospective candidates. How can an individual answer critics and any specific adverse comments made during the process if we continue to adopt a selection process which is, to say the least, arbitrary?[15] In all systems of our model—at least England,

India and Australia—there is no doubt consultation. But the requirement of consultation and the width that is takes appears to vary widely.

In both the Australian and Indian Constitutions there is the requirement of consultation, in the former only for High Court appointments, in the latter for both the Supreme Court and the State High Courts. In Australia, this is a relatively recent addition. Until its inclusion in Section 6 of the *High Court of Australia Act 1979*, the appointment of new members of the Court was made by the Governor-General upon advice of the federal Executive Council. It was a political decision. In 1975, the New South Wales Parliament established a select committee to examine the question of judicial appointments to the High Court. It called for submissions and indeed in its Report[16] are the opinions of a number of the foremost academics of the day, together with the views of the legal societies.

During the next four years this momentum continued, including being raised at the Australian Constitutional Conventions in Melbourne in 1975 and Perth in 1978. It was finally included in the 1979 Act. Was this the correct decision? Should there be more than 'mere' consultation? The matter came up once more at the Australian Constitutional Convention in 1985,[17] and was further considered by the Constitutional Commission in 1988,[18] particularly by the Advisory Committee.[19] Separating appointments to the federal Courts from appointments to the High Court, that committee noted the alternatives that were possible. Possible models have also been raised in the more recent *Discussion Paper on Judicial Appointments*, 1993.[20] These include:

(a) Popular election of judges;
(b) Legislative ratification of judicial appointments;
(c) Establishment of a commission to recommend suitable appointees to the Government; and
(d) Retaining the present model but requiring consultation in all appointments.

We may well add a fifth, a model that reflects the Indian requirement that:

(e) Pursuant to Section 124(2) of the Indian Constitution, every judge of the Supreme Court shall be appointed by the President after consultation with such of the judges of the Supreme Court and of the State High Courts as may be deemed necessary. In the case of a judge other than the Chief Justice, the Chief Justice of India shall always be consulted.

The use of popular elections has never received wide acclaim in jurisdictions with close associations to ours.[21] Yet in the United States, certainly at state level, it has been used widely since they were introduced in Mississippi in 1832. Indeed at one period, at the beginning of the Civil War, 24 of the then 34 states had an elected judiciary, while today, only eight states use *partisan* elections for the selection of appellate and general jurisdiction trial courts.[22] Most of this group use elections for retention purposes as well.[23] While for most of this period the judicial elections were low-key affairs, conducted with civility and dignity, and relatively inexpensive, in the recent past this has changed considerably. Over the last fifteen years, the Texas judicial elections have been extensively studied and show dramatic changes in respect of political interference and rising costs.[24] However, another twelve states use *non-partisan* elections in the selection of judges.[25] Seen as removing the political element, the value according to advocates is that it retains public accountability.[26] It has also tended to avoid some of the excesses found in the partisan elections.[27]

Legislative ratification has the distinction of being used in the United States for the appointment of all federal judges, including those on the Supreme Court. But with the spotlight occasionally being focused upon a hapless individual, this may not be high praise at all. Few who witnessed the events surrounding the nomination and subsequent ratification hearings surrounding the appointment of Clarence Thomas in 1991, and before that the pressures on Douglas Ginsburg and Robert Bork to withdraw from consideration, have any illusions of the downside of such a procedure. For a while Canada toyed with the idea,[28] but once rejected, support quickly subsided.[29] If such a method were used in Australia, it would logically fall upon the Senate to conduct the hearing, and, like the United States, it would surely have to be a committee of that body. The one body that exists is the Senate Standing Committee on Legal and Constitutional Affairs. Would it work in Australia? Are there any reasons for rejecting the views of some Canadian critics of their own scheme that 'the process might become too politicised and deter good prospects from allowing their names to be put forward for consideration'.[30] The Constitutional Commissioners noted the US model and the Swiss situation, which allows for the appointment of federal judges by its federal Parliament, but clearly and without qualification rejected the model. They concluded that, apart from questioning executive decisions within the Parliament, any further control would erode public confidence, particularly as 'there would be little confidence that they would be acting as independent scrutineers of a candidate's qualities'.[31] It has been suggested that if it were a two-thirds majority of senators present and voting, this would ensure at least bipartisan support for a successful candidate.[32]

It is the establishment of a commission which has attracted the most support by those who favour change.[33] Its advantages are compelling: it would be seen as an answer to the charges of secrecy in the selection process; it would enhance the independence claim; it would provide a stronger guarantee of scrutiny, together with a measure of protection against political or capricious appointments. When the selection criteria specifically make it clear that diversity is to be a factor to be taken into account, this model appears to be able to cope adequately. Thus the disadvantages tend to be associated with little choice: the best people on the body, there may be a decline in the confidence of the process, and it may well be costly and cumbersome. However, practically all the disadvantages would be solved by the creation of the 'correct' body. The composition of such a body would always be debatable but its success would depend upon the right balance. Practically all suggestions are for such a commission to include some members from outside the profession.[34]

Following on from the adoption of the Westminster model, the government is responsible for the selection of the judiciary and it becomes an act for which it must take political responsibility. Yet without a great deal of change, there are ways that this approach can be adapted to serve additional policy aims, particularly with respect to diversity. It may be well to advertise and to seek expressions of public interest; likewise, to open up additional sources from which the selection process may be sought. Thus the civil service and academia may well provide fertile grounds from which the selection may be made.[35]

In India the President consults the judiciary. This has the distinct advantage of allowing non-partisan appointments. It would probably allow the most effective groups of observers to choose the most meritorious candidate—particularly if the previous discussed criteria are utilized. There is built into the model the idea that judges know the best qualities that make a good judge and are best qualified to assess whether any particular person possesses those qualities.[36] Indeed it has been one of the cornerstones of a number of plans in the United States, known generally as the 'merit' plan of selection that involve peer review and critique.[37]

Yet a major problem is that if the field from which the judiciary will be chosen is sufficiently restricted, coupled with the conservative nature of those involved in advising on the appointment, there is a real likelihood of extreme conservatism being perpetuated. Indeed, in his submission to the New South Wales Parliamentary Committee, Professor Nygh noted the verdict of an American commentator on the Prince's Privy Purse Case, that India had acquired a Bench that was out of touch with current politics.[38]

A group of eleven men, only one who had ever had any contact with electoral politics, and all of whom were highly educated, well-to-do men of late middle age who had been little involved in the independence movement, overturned an action by the executive branch in an area of extreme political sensitivity. The men intervened in a relationship which their institution had not sought to regulate previously and they did so in spite of the provision which had been used before to defer any dispute settlement to the parties themselves. The avowed aim of the executive in this instance was supported by a large segment of the populace and certainly by a large majority of the elected legislature. The Court's decision, while heralded by many, also resulted in significant opposition to the Court as an institution, and various calls were made to change the composition of the institution and to change the rules under which the institution operated. Further, by basing its jurisdiction upon a conclusion as to the character of the princes' rights, the Court circumscribed any future settlement of the dispute between the parties.

Professor Nygh places *Golak Nath* v *Punjab*[39] in much the same category—a 'dangerous step taken by the Court'. He concludes: 'This assertion of power by the Supreme Court has been greeted by Indian commentators with much hostility and could eventually give rise to a political reaction which might well endanger the future of the Court.'[40]

But what of political influence? In the process of judicial appointment, executive influence can be extremely subtle. In the appointment of the puisne judge it would probably be safe to say that Indian judicial appointments were neither more nor less political than in other common law jurisdictions. Governments take many factors into account when making an appointment to the highest constitutional court and generally the Indian government is no different. In Australia a conservative government in 1964 appointed Garfield Barwick, then Attorney-General, to the position of Chief Justice. The Labor Government in 1975 appointed its Attorney-General, Lionel Murphy, to the same Court. Over the years there had been many other appointments of persons from politics. The only problem which could caused concern (it has not as yet arisen in Australia nor the United States, but has in India) is the non-appointment of ad hoc or temporary judges. Particularly during the Emergency period in India there were serious charges made against the New Delhi government. It was said, for example, that they had ordered that temporary judges were not to be appointed to fill positions where incumbent judges had given judgements against the government. This would seem to indicate that as a general rule temporary judges should not be appointed, nor should there be a strong tradition of appointing from lower courts to fill positions on higher courts. Yet that is exactly what is happening in the United States as Presidents are able to more safely judge the voting pattern of a prospective Supreme Court appointment from the ranks of the circuit courts. Few recent appointments have been made outside this field. The question must be raised: is that desirable?

However, it is in the appointment of the Chief Justices that there have been the most extraordinary accusations of political intrusion. These are mostly associated with the breach of the convention not to appoint the next most senior judge. Notwithstanding that the Indian Law Commission in 1958[41] recommended that the seniority convention be dropped in favour of the appointment of the best qualified, the latter procedure was not followed until 1973. Justice Ray was elevated to the position over three more senior judges—Justice J.M. Shelat, Justice K.S. Hegde and Justice A.N. Grover. The judges who were by-passed resigned in protest. A storm of protest followed with a number of leading Indian jurists publicly accusing the government of Mrs Gandhi of acting in this way because the recent rulings of the three had displeased the government.[42] The 'supersession' matter was not closed with this one example. In 1977, in the dying days of the Congress government, Justice M.H. Beg was elevated to the position of Chief Justice over Justice H.R. Khanna. Once more the accepted reason was that he was being punished for his dissenting judgement in the *Habeas Corpus* case.[43]

There is one other area, peculiar to the Indian legal system, that has been the subject of a great deal of disquiet and is related to the independence issue. This is the fact that under the Indian Constitution judges of the state High Courts can be transferred between Courts. There is considerable scope for removing a judge by reappointing him or her if the decisions being handed down are not to the government's liking. In June 1976 there was a wholesale move with sixteen judges being transferred. One judge, Justice S.H. Seth of the Gujarat High Court, challenged the presidential order transferring him to the Andhra Pradesh High Court and the matter was finally determined in the Supreme Court.[44] By a margin of three to two, it was held that transfers could be made notwithstanding an absence of consent, but that they could only be on the basis of public interest and not as a punitive measure. The majority noted that although the requirements of the process of 'consultation' are not clear-cut, they do require the Chief Justice to be aware of all the facts, and to express his opinion on nothing less than a full consideration of the facts.[45] Bhagwati J was scathing in his comments on the transfers: 'the Government of India did not choose to disclose the principle on which these 16 High Court Judges were picked out for being transferred. It is indeed strange that the Government of India should have selected for transfer, by and large, those High Court Judges who had decided cases against the Government during the emergency.'

The unfettered discretion vested in the President, in most cases in the Government of India, is hardly checked by consultation with the Chief Justice. There ought to be a widening of the range of the persons who should at least be consulted. The Law Commission, in its 80th Report, recommended that in both cases of the Supreme Court and that of the High Courts, the respective Chief Justices should consult the two next ranking judges and should state in their letter of recommendation both the fact of the consultation as well as the views of their colleagues. It also recommended against transfer without consent. The report, requested during the Janata period, was presented to Parliament only after the return of the Congress to power. Later, and specifically with respect to the High Courts, the National Front government of V.P. Singh, although a minority government, did attempt to extend the consultation group. In 1989 it suggested that a committee comprising the Chief Justice of India, the Chief Minister of the state, the Chief Justice of the state High Court, the leader of the opposition in the state Legislative Assembly and a representative of the governor of the state, recommend names to the central government.[46] This is, effectively, a commission or collegium.

Australians must wonder whether such a political reaction such as we have noted above in India with respect to supersession and transfers is solely the product of an aberrant political period or something more. As noted previously, the High Court in 1992 found Australian legislation restricting political advertising to be unconstitutional. The media judgement was that the court had made a political decision. In the aftermath of this controversy, we are again looking at the need to justify judicial appointments in political terms.

In statements made prior to its election in 1995, the Liberal/National party coalition led by John Howard, indicated a desire to consult widely on the appointment of judges but gave little detail about how it intended to do this. We are left where we have been for sometime, with no immediate signs of change.

Is it likely that the concept of a 'representative' judiciary will be adopted? The answer must surely be 'no'. The Law Council of Australia, in its response to the Labor Government's Discussion Paper, indicated its belief that the concept of a 'representative' judiciary is fundamentally dangerous—insofar as it is inconsistent with judicial independence and appointment on merit—and should be rejected. Criteria for appointment, the Law Council argued, should be drafted—not with the force of law but placed in a protocol. Having the capacity to change over time would make the process more 'transparent'. As to consultation, it suggests a wide group of legal bodies 'to reassure the community that appointments were of the highest standard'. In short, its conclusion is that the present method of selection and appointment of judges should be retained, but the Attorney-General should be encouraged to consult well informed bodies and persons, including present judges, more widely.

NOTES

1. At least subject to a certificate granted under Sec. 74 of the Constitution. Only one such certificate has been granted (*Colonial Sugar Refining Co.* v *Commonwealth* (1912) 15 CLR, p. 182) and the tenor of the statements of

the Court in *Kirmani* v *Captain Cook Cruises Pty Ltd* (No. 2) (1985) 159 CLR, p. 461 are the strongest indications to date that it is unlikely to occur again.

2. *Nelungaloo Pty Ltd* v *Commonwealth* (1952) 58 CLR, p. 573.
3. In 1912 a cable was sent to a leading member of the Sydney Bar, A.B. Piddington, in which he was asked his views on the question of 'Commonwealth versus State rights'. He replied that he favoured Commonwealth power. He was subsequently offered a position on the High Court and accepted on the condition that it was realized he was completely independent on all constitutional questions. The storm against the appointment, particularly from the Bar, was such that he resigned before ever sitting on the Court.
4. In the Australian Law Reform Commission Report No. 69, 1994, *Equality before the Law: Justice for Women*, it was noted in para 9.39 that there was only one of seven on the High Court and that she, Justice Mary Gaudron, was the first. And only 17 out of 230 other Federal, State and Territory judges are women. Of the 52 Family Court judges, only 7 are women. Some states—Victoria, Tasmania and Western Australia—have no women on their Supreme Courts.
5. (1992) 177 CLR, p. 106.
6. *High Court of Australia Act 1979* (Cth), Sec. 6.
7. Blackstone, *Commentaries*, p. 69.
8. Attorney-General's Department, *Judicial Appointment—Procedure and Criteria. Discussion Paper*, Canberra, 1993, para 4.3.5. This places a new colour upon the story set out in Heuston, 1964, *Lives of the Lord Chancellors 1885-1940*, pp. 36-7, that Lord Halsbury, when asked whether, *ceteris paribus*, the best man would be appointed to a judicial position, was said to have replied. '*Ceteris paribus* be damned, I'm going to appoint my nephew.'
9. Attorney-General's Department, *Judicial Appointment—Procedure and Criteria. Discussion Paper*, para 4.3.4.
10. The doctrine of separation of powers implied in the Australian Constitution has been strictly interpreted, particularly since *R* v *Kiby; Ex parte Boilermakers' Society of Australia* (1956) 94 CLR, p. 254, notwithstanding some periods during wartime when members of the High Court have accepted extra-curial positions. One such appointee was Sir Owen Dixon who took leave of absence from the Bench between May 1942 and November 1944 to become Commonwealth Minister Plenipotentiary to the United States. This was specifically provided for by the *Judiciary (Diplomatic Representation) Act 1942* (Cth) and followed a similiar appointment to Japan of Sir John Latham, Chief Justice, from November 1940 until December 1941. Later Sir Owen was to publicly doubt the correctness of accepting the appointment. See 1955, *The Australian Law Journal* 253, vol. 29, p. 272. This must now be accepted as the current view of the Court. While members of the Federal

Court have accepted both ambassadorial and Royal Commission appointments, the High Court recently examined the position of all federal judges who hold a variety of executive positions, not as members of the Federal Court, but in persona designata. In *Wilson* v *Minister for Aboriginal and Torres Strait Island Affairs* (Unreported, High Court judgement of 6 September 1996) it was held that a Federal Court judge, appointed under Chapter III of the Australian Constitution, could not provide a report to the Minister under the *Aboriginal and Torres Strait Islander Protection Act 1984* (Cth). This function was incompatible with the Commonwealth judicial power exercised by such a Judge.

11. The states, which are not under the same constitutional strictures as the Commonwealth with respect to the doctrine of separation of powers, vary in attitude to such appointments. The Victorian Chief Justice, Sir William Irvine, wrote to the Attorney-General when a request was made to supply a judge to examine an allegation of bribery involving a public contract. In the letter Chief Justice Irvine refused the request and set out the reasons. This has become known as 'Irvine Memorandum' and has been the basic attitude of the Victorian Supreme Court ever since. There was a gloss in 1952 when after another request for a judge was made, the Court met and indicated that in future no judge should be obliged to undertake any such duties; that where the matter was of national importance arising in times of national emergencies, the communication should be relayed to a meeting of the judges who should consider the matter. New South Wales has no such historic reluctance to provide judges although in 1984 the appointment of Justice Donald Stewart to head the National Crime Authority brought the question into national prominence when the Chief Justice of NSW, Sir Laurence Street, opposed the appointment. After six months of public debate, Justice Stewart resigned from the NSW Supreme Court. Commonwealth legislation has given him the status of a Supreme Court Judge of the Australian Capital Territory and appointed him to the office of full-time Deputy President of the Administrative Appeals Tribunal. The background to the origins of the Irvine Memorandum and its subsequent history, as well as Justice Stewart's problems with the NSW Supreme Court are well set out in *Judges as Royal Commissioners and Chairmen of Non-Judicial Tribunals: Two Views Presented at the Fourth Annual Seminar of the Australian Institute of Judicial Administration, 31 August 1985, Adelaide,* AIJA, Canberra, 1986. The case against such appointments was written by Sir Murray McInerney, QC and Garrie Moloney, the case for such appointments was written by D.G. McGregor, QC.
12. For the attitude of the other Australian States, see the AIJA publication noted above, at pp. 31-2. In the case against, there is considerable comparative material from Great Britain, New Zealand, Canada and the United States as well.

13. Attorney-General's Department, *Judicial Appointment—Procedure and Criteria. Discussion Paper*, Canberra, 1993, para 2.2.1. The following list come from a variety of sources. They can also be expressed in many, and varied ways. Thus Lord Hailsham, the Lord Chancellor, said in a public address: 'My first and fundamental policy is to appoint solely on merit the best potential candidate ready and willing to accept the post. No consideration of party politics, sex, religion, or race must enter into my calculations and they do not. Personality, integrity, professional ability, experience, standing and capacity are the only criteria, coupled with, of course, the requirement that the candidate must be physically capable of carrying out the duties of the post, and not disqualified by personal unsuitability. My overriding consideration is always the public interest in maintaining the quality of the Bench and confidence in its competence and independence.' *Law Society Gazette*, 28 August 1985, p. 2335, quoted in Sir Harry Gibbs, 'The Appointment of Judges', *The Australian Law Journal* 7, 1987, p. 61.
14. Attorney-General's Department, *Judicial Appointment—Procedure and Criteria. Discussion Paper*, Canberra, 1993, para 2.5.2.
15. George Winterton, 'Appointment of Federal Judges in Australia', *Melbourne University Law Review*, 16(185), 1987, pp. 186-7, referring to work undertaken by Duncan Chappell and Peter Cashman for the Australian Law Reform Commission in all Australian jurisdictions except Western Australia and the Northern Territory in 1981. See also Duncan Chappell, 'Judicial Responsibility: A Review of the selection process for Australian Judges', *Australian National Report for the Eleventh International Congress of Comparative Law* (1982), pp. 6-12.
16. *Report from the Select Committee of the NSW Legislative Assembly upon the Appointment to the High Court of Australia*, NSW Parliamentary Papers, 5, 1974-5, pp. 321-405.
17. See the Judicature Sub-Committee, 'Second Report to the Standing Committee', in *Proceedings of the Australian Constitutional Convention*, 1985, II.
18. *Final Report of the Constitutional Commission*, 1, para 6, 1988, pp. 162-78.
19. *Australian Judicial System, Report of the Advisory Committee to the Constitutional Commission* (chaired by Justice D.F. Jackson), 1987, paras 5.11-5.33.
20. In its Chap. 4, 'Options for Reform', there is acknowledgment of the work undertaken by George Winterton, and contained in 'Appointment of Federal Judges in Australia', *Melbourne University Law Review*, 16, 1987, pp. 85-211. In a more recent paper by Michael Lavarch, Commonwealth Attorney-General, another option was added—a register of expression of interest. This could well be used by most of the options set out here. See his paper 'The Appointment of Judges' delivered at the *Australian Institute of Judicial Administration Conference Courts in a Representative Democracy, 13 November 1994.*

21. See the references in Winterton, n. 42, but particularly Sir Robert Megarry, 'The Anatomy of Judicial Appointment: Change but not Decay', *University of British Columbia Law Review*, 19(113), 1985, pp. 115-16.
22. Alabama, Arkanasas, Illinios, Mississippi, North Carolina, Pennsylvania, Texas and West Virginia.
23. The Illinois Supreme and Appellate Court judges must stand for an initial ten-year term. Circuit court judges stand for an initial 6-year term, with retention elections every six years. For the various terms for the various judges in all of these States, see Patrick McFadden, *Electing Justice, the Law and Ethics of Judicial Election Campaigns* (1990). See also Ruth Gavison, 'The Implications of Jurisprudential Theories for Judicial Election, Selection and Accountability', *Southern California Law Review,* 61, 1988, p. 1618.
24. See particularly Anthony Champagne, 'Judicial Reform in Texas', *Judicature*, 72, 1988, p. 146. Much of the information, not only from Texas but other States, is gathered and summarized in Peter Webster, 'Selection and Retention of Judges: Is there one "Best" Method', *Florida State University Law Review*, 23, 1995, p. 1.
25. Georgia, Idaho, Kentucky, Louisiana, Michigan, Minnesota, Montana, Nevada, North Dakota, Oregon, Washington and Wisconsin.
26. For one perceptive study, see Thomas Brennan, 'Nonpartisan Election of Judges: The Michigan Case', *Southwestern Law Journal,* 40, 1986, p. 23.
27. 'Good judges tend to be unopposed'. See John Korzen, 'Changing North Carolina's Method of Judicial Selection', *Wake Forest Law Review*, 25(253), 1990, p. 270.
28. See George Winterton, 'Appointment of Federal Judges in Australia', *Melbourne University Law Review*, 16(185), 1987, pp. 194-6.
29. Canadian Bar Association Special Committee on the Method of Appointment of Judges, *The Appointment of Judges in Canada* (1985), p. 49. An explanation for this must be the nature of the Canadian Senate and the fact that its reform was probably part of the 'package'. It was not reformed so the other parts lost their appeal. This is noted in Winterton, 'Appointment of a Federal Judge', p. 196. That report is also examined in *Australian Judicial System, Report of the Advisory Committee to the Constitutional Commission*, 1987, paras 5 and 16-21.
30. Winterton, 'Appointment of Federal Judges', p. 196.
31. *Final Report*, etc., para 6.163.
32. P. Nygh, in Annexure D of the *Report from the Select Committee of the NSW Legislative Assembly upon the Appointment to the High Court of Australia*, NSW Parliamentary Papers, 5, 1974-5, p. 55.
33. See the pros and cons set out in some detail in Attorney-General's Department, *Judicial Appointment—Procedure and Criteria. Discussion Paper*, Canberra, 1993, paras 4.3.1-4.4.10. Indeed, compared to the space devoted in the *Discussion Paper* to the alternate options, by far the greater space was

devoted to questions arising under this heading. It was supported by the Canadian Committee, for various types of advisory committees for various types of judicial appointments. It is dealt with at length by Professor Winterton in his 1987 article and a judicial nominating committee is his preference. Ramakrishna Hegde, Chief Minister of Karnataka, recommended a collegium in a speech to the Bar Association of India Conference in 1986. See *The Judiciary Today: A Plea for a Collegium*, published by the Government of Karnataka, 1986. There was a similiar plea by Bhagwati J, *S.P. Gupta* v *Union of India*, Supp SCC 87, 1981, p. 233.

34. See the various groups operating or suggested, in Ontario, Israel, New Zealand, and recommended by the British Section of the International Commission of Jurists (JUSTICE), and the Law Society of Great Britain, set out in the Attorney-General's Department's *Discussion Paper*, para 4.4.5. Even Sir Garfield Barwick, former conservative Attorney-General and Chief Justice, has supported the idea of a nominating commission. See his 'The State of the Australian Judicature', *Australian Law Journal*, 51(480), 1977, p. 494.
35. The historic reluctance to select from the universities in Australia is gradually breaking down. Starting with the Family Court Bench and the appointment of senior academics who have a specialist reputation in the field, for example Justices Peter Nygh and Richard Chisholm, it has now extended to general jurisdictions, for example Justice Paul Finn to the ACT Supreme Court, and more recently the acting appointment on the NSW District Court of Professors Colin Phegan and John Goldring.
36. See Harold Laski, 'The Technique of Judicial Appointment', *Michigan Law Review*, 24, 1926, p. 529.
37. See Glen Winters, 'The Merit Plan for Judicial Selection and Tenure: Its Historical Development', in Glenn Winters and Stanley Lowe (eds.), *Selected Readings on the Administration of Justice and its Improvements*, 1971; Peter Webster, 'Selection and Retention of Judges: Is there one "Best" Method', *Florida State University Law Review*, 23, 1995, fn. 18 notes that under the Missouri Plan and the California Plan, judges participate in the selection process.
38. Neal Roberts, 'The Supreme Court in a Developing Society: Progressive or Reactionary Force? A study of the Privy Purse Case in India', *American Journal of Comparative Law*, 20, 1972, p. 79.
39. AIR 1967 SC, p. 1643. In this case the Court denied to Parliament the power to amend the Constitution in a way which would take away or abridge fundamental rights. To many people this was judicial activism—in much the same way as the Supreme Court prior to 1937 obstructed President Roosevelt's New Deal legislation. See particularly Upendra Baxi, *The Indian Supreme Court and Politics* (Lucknow, 1980), pp. 16-26.
40. Professor P. Nygh, in Annexure D of the *Report from the Select Committee of*

the NSW Legislative Assembly upon the Appointment to the High Court of Australia, NSW Parliamentary Papers, 5, 1974-5, p. 50.

41. *XIV Rep*, I, pp. 39-40.
42. It was probably no accident that on 24 April 1973 the Supreme Court handed down its historic ruling in *Keshavananda Bharati* v *State of Kerala* (1973) 4 SCC, p. 225; AIR 1973 SC, p. 1461. The three judges passed over were in the majority. Mr. Justice Ray was in the minority. The appointment of Chief Justice occurred on the following day.
43. *A.D.M. Jabalpur* v *Shiv Kant Shukla* (1976) 2 SCC, p. 521: AIR 1976 SC, p. 1207. This decision is extensively discussed in Baxi, *The Indian Supreme Court and Politics* (1980), pp. 79-117.
44. *Union of India* v *Sankalchand Himatlal Seth* (1977) 4 SCC, p, 193; AIR 1977 SC, p. 2328.
45. Chandrachud J at AIR 1977 SC, p. 2347.
46. T.K. Tope, *Constitutional Law of India*, 2nd edn. (Lucknow, 1992), p. 626.

5

Bureaucracies as Instruments of Federalism: Administrative Experience from India

BERYL A. RADIN

Despite the increasing prevalence of federal systems across the globe, few governments have attempted to fashion their national bureaucracies as direct instruments of federalism. While concern about mechanisms that link levels of government in federal systems is not unusual, these mechanisms are most frequently devised as political structures (e.g. upper houses that represent states or provinces) or more informal modes of representation (e.g. premiers' conferences or chief ministers' meetings). India, by contrast, has used senior bureaucrats, assigned to states and rotated between the states and the central government to link levels of government.

Most systems have been premised on the doctrine of administrative dualism with each level of government equipped with its own set of administrative instrumentalities and mechanisms.[1] Countries such as Australia and the United States have separate and distinct levels of public administration that reflect the interests and concerns of the specific levels of government. The separate administrative structures have tended to emphasize the differences between the levels of government rather than accentuate areas of interdependence.

Increasingly, however, students of governance have come to recognize the importance of developing mechanisms that can cope with the emerging political realities. Pure unitary systems and pure federal systems are becoming less effective and may not be able to deal with the problems of the twenty-first century. Concepts such as collaborative decision-making, networks and other mechanisms that link levels of government have been associated with the field of inter-governmental management in recent years.[2]

Nearly fifty years ago, however, India grappled with these issues at Independence. Concern about mechanisms that would preserve unity and, at the same time, acknowledge the diversity and specific interests of the provinces (now called the states) were balanced through the transformation of the civil service system of the Raj into the All-India Services. This essay reviews the historical development of the Indian form of administrative federalism and examines its relevance in light of the dramatic changes that have occurred in the nation's political, economic and social fabric. The tradition will be contrasted with data on the current composition and attitudes of one batch in the Indian Administrative Service. This data was collected in July 1995 from the 1993 batch of recruits into the system.[3]

The Historical Backdrop

The framers of India's Constitution opted for continuity, building on the structures and experience of the Indian Civil Service (ICS) and the Indian Police (IP) of the British period.[4] Built upon the selection of highly competent individuals who would exert appropriate discretion, that colonial system was devised to respond to the size and diversity of the Indian subcontinent.

The decision to build on a unified administrative system was advanced by Vallabhbhai Patel and argued on the basis of maintaining efficiency, giving the civil service experience at the centre as well as the districts, and serving a liaison function between the then-provinces and the centre.[5] This came to be known as the 'steel frame' argument. The bureaucracy would provide a mechanism for national integration through members of the services allocated to the various states on the basis of ability. They would provide the nation with an all-India outlook. The constitutional debate reflected a distinction between recruitment and control, supporting recruitment of personnel on an all-India basis but provincial control over such personnel. It has been noted, however, that even at the time of independence, the provinces 'evinced little enthusiasm for the All-India Services; the latter were pushed down their reluctant throats by Vallabhbhai Patel'.[6]

According to Maheshwari, three grounds were given for the creation of All-India Services. 'Firstly, an all-India service is considered to be a bulwark of national integration as its members possess an all-India outlook. Secondly, being based on all-India recruitment, it attracts the best talent in the country, a vital necessity for the accomplishment of national tasks. Thirdly, it reinforces the sense of independence and impartiality of its members by affording protection against local pressures and influences.'[7]

Although nine All-India Services existed in 1924 under the British, upon Independence only two were retained. The ICS became the Indian Administrative Service (IAS) and the IP became the Indian Police Service (IPS). Maheshwari notes that little attention was given to the services until 1955 when the States Reorganization Commission focused on the reorganization of states on linguistic lines and, as well, the necessity for preserving the 'unity of India'.[8] The Administrative Reforms Commission, reporting in 1969, called for the establishment of new All-India Services. However, it warned that these services would be effective only when the relations between the centre and the states were cordial.[9] During this period, the Centre-State Relations Inquiry Committee, set up by the government of Tamil Nadu (one of the few states that was not controlled by the Congress party) argued against the addition of new services. This Committee noted: 'It cannot be denied that there may be a feeling among the non-Congress state governments that the All-India Service officers are the agents of the centre, and may not carry out the policies of those states.'[10]

The system that was established (and continues today) recruits and examines applicants through a single examination held at a number of locations across the country. The examination is used for the All-India Services as well as a number of specialized services. Top performers on the written examination appear for an oral exam. According to one observer, historically this 'examination is rightly regarded as representing an "equal opportunity" for obtaining public employment and access to highest bureaucratic levels at the Central as well as the States' levels, by all sections of society and all regions of the country, and it arouses country-wide interest on a sustained basis.'[11] The IAS and IPS individuals who are selected begin an intensive training course at the Academy in Mussoorie and are immediately allocated to a state within the union. Individuals who score highest on the exam may be given their preferences for assignment to particular states (usually the state of their origin). Candidates who are assigned to a state (called the state cadre) are given instruction in, and must demonstrate competency in, the regional language. The specific allocation of individuals to states is based on a complex formula after consultation between the centre and the individual states. The initial training period (called the foundational course) emphasizes the constitutional, economic and social framework within which the officers function and also covers such matters as the rights and obligations of the civil services and the ethics of the profession. After completing this course, IAS trainees are sent for a year of district training in the state to which they have been assigned; they then return to the training academy for the second phase of training. When they complete this training, they are full-fledged officers of the service.

Although the pattern of specific postings and assignments of the members of the IAS varies by time period as well as by state, there is a general model of career development that structures the process. New officers are expected to spend approximately seven years in the district, often assuming different roles in that most decentralized level. Following that experience, they are assigned to jobs in the state secretariat for a number of years. At that point, individuals are likely to be assigned to a job in the central government. Supposedly states are obligated to fulfil a 'quota' for secondment to the centre. Individuals may work for a limited period in Delhi (or another location in which there is a central government function) and return to their states for a higher level state job. A small number of individuals will return to the central government for further assignments.

This process has had many supporters over the years. A typical argument for the system follows:

> The system of secondment and recirculation is of great value in bringing about an exchange of experience between the Centre and the States, and in giving to the Centre access to the most recent experience of policy-making at the State level and the ground level situation in different areas. This informal, personal insight into regional conditions becomes available to the Central Ministries and serves as a valuable supplement to the information obtained through formal communications, reports and reviews, as well as assessments made in the course of discussions in inter-governmental conferences. For States, the access to a broader perspective and experience of Central policy imperatives and the development situation in the other States is a parallel gain. Of course, this mutual reinforcement of experience is of direct value mostly in respect of

the work done by these officers in fields of common or joint endeavour of the Centre and the States.[12]

Those who have been sceptical about the system have not accepted this argument, however. For example, the Communist Party of India (Marxist) observed in its manifesto of 1971 that the All-India Services have 'meant that the bureaucracy is responsible only to the centre, acts as its spies against the elected ministry, subverts the policies of the legislature and conspires with the centre to bring down an unwanted ministry'.[13] Others have argued that the states ought to enjoy the right to recruit and control the civil service for the performance of tasks allotted to them in the Constitution; their autonomy and patronage are thought to be restricted by the system. In addition, some noted that the presence of the services has a demoralizing effect on state civil servants.[14]

An essential part of the system focuses on confidence in the abilities of the individuals selected for the two services. At least one student of the system noted that concern about levels of representativeness is less important in a developing country because efficiency values are the most important. 'Let us be grateful if such selection produces a fairly representative bureaucracy, but let us not go madly after it by diluting or manipulating the selection.'[15] Although the system sought to assign most individuals to states other than their own, historically the composition of the services does not reflect the geographical, caste or class dimensions of the Indian nation. Geography, for example, was based on the declaration of regional affiliation by the recruit; one observer noted that 'it does not disentangle the different components that constitute regional affiliation, nor does it help one to study inter-state movements and involvements meaningfully'.[16] In addition, the majority of recruits were drawn from middle class urban salaried and professional families.

In his study of the IAS composition, Subramanian found that for the 1947-56 period, Kerala, Mysore, Madras and Punjab were over-represented; in addition, displaced persons from Pakistan and those born in Delhi were 'strikingly' over-represented. Andhra Pradesh, Assam, Bihar, Gujarat, Jammu & Kashmir, Madhya Pradesh, Orissa and even Maharashtra and West Bengal were considerably under-represented while Uttar Pradesh (the largest State) just 'holds its own'. During the period from 1957 to 1963, Kerala, Madras, Mysore and Punjab were still over-represented but to a lesser extent. Displaced persons and those from Delhi were also still strongly over-represented. Assam and Orissa changed from under- to over-representation. Rajasthan increased its representation by almost three-fold and Maharashtra had 'come into its own'. Uttar Pradesh lost somewhat while Andhra Pradesh, Bihar and Madhya Pradesh were still under-represented.[17] Subramanian gives different reasons for these patterns, noting that in West Bengal students were going into other avenues (engineering and medical studies), Gujarat students were attracted to commerce, while Madhya Pradesh and Andhra Pradesh had poorer facilities for higher education and lacked a tradition of taking the examination.

Although there was concern about geographical representation, Indian policy-makers were much more focused on problems of representation of those in castes and groups that had been excluded from the benefits of citizenship in the society. The Constitution itself dealt with public employment by calling for 'reservation of appointments or posts in a favour of any backward class of citizens which, in the opinion of the State, is not adequately represented in the services under the state'.[18] The first amendment to the Constitution further allowed special provision 'for the advancement of any socially and educationally backward classes of citizens or for the Scheduled Castes and the Scheduled Tribes'.[19] The preferential treatment that followed these constitutional provisions was also justified in the quest for unity of the nation.[20] During the twenty years from 1971 to 1991, the representation of the Scheduled Castes in the higher levels of the federal government public service moved from 2.6 per cent to 9.1 per cent while the Scheduled Tribes increased from 0.4 per cent to 2.5 per cent.[21] In 1963, the Supreme Court ruled that total reservations (including three categories: Scheduled Castes, Scheduled Tribes and Other Backward Castes) should be less than 50 per cent of positions. To that point, however, the reservations did not include the category called Other Backward Castes. Some state governments had already established reservation quotas above the 50 per cent limit set by the Supreme Court. Andhra Pradesh announced a policy in 1986 to raise the quotas in government positions and all professional colleges to 71 per cent. Tamil Nadu had already raised its total to 69 per cent.

In 1990, the National Front government dusted of a ten-year-old report from the Mandal Commission and included the Other Backward Castes (OBCs) category in its reservation policy. This policy provoked extensive division within Indian society. The Mandal Report acknowledged that forty years from Independence, society still remained caste-based but, paradoxically, it recommended a policy that every member of a lower caste, regardless of economic or educational standing, would be eligible for benefits of reservation.[22]

A series of recent developments within Indian society and in the services themselves have set the framework for an understanding of the contemporary Indian administrative scene.

During the past decade, there is clear evidence of the demise of the one-party state dominated by the North. As the 1996 election makes clear, the Congress party no longer can be viewed as the controlling political force within the society. Regional parties, formerly found only in the southern states, now are present throughout the nation. They are based on religious, caste and ideological perspectives. Political differences between state and central government leaders are now common.

These shifts have raised a number of issues for members of the administrative services, particularly those within the Indian Administrative Service. State cadre members are dependent on decisions of state political leaders for postings. At least two aspects of postings are affected by political shifts. First, state political leaders may not be willing to move individuals who are valuable to them to central government posts controlled by political rivals. Cadre members who had invested in relationships with political figures as a method of assuring good postings in Delhi may now find themselves without political patronage.[23] Similarly, when new political leaders come into power within a state, cadre members sometimes find themselves subject to unexpected job transfers.[24] Some have noted that state-level politicians from different political parties can always blame the central government for their problems; the officers of the All-India Services are convenient whipping boys for that blame.

Even before the recent shifts, however, all higher civil servants did not experience posting to the centre. Two groups appear to have developed: one that seeks central postings and finds ways to stay out of its 'home' state; another that avoids these postings and does not want to come to the centre at all.[25]

This behaviour compounds what some already found to be a problem. In his 1974 book, *A Tale Told by an Idiot*, R.P. Noronha, who retired as Chief Secretary of Madhya Pradesh, wrote:

Today the politician distrusts the IAS man. . . . He distrusts him because he belongs to an All-India Service, whose loyalty must be more to the centre than to the state. This is utter nonsense, but the politician believes it, and it is what he believes that is the important thing, not the truth. . . . At state level, therefore, the IAS is a foundling. So far as the centre is concerned, he has been put out for adoption and they wash their hands off him. The state can kick him around as much as they [*sic*] please and the centre will not interfere, even unofficially.[26]

At the same time, it is not clear whether the political shifts will create new pressures for elimination of the All-India Services. Maheshwari has noted that 'Only when in opposition, political parties in India articulate a concern for civil service reform including the need for impartiality and objectivity in public administration. Once in power, all parties appear to forge [a] relationship of a dubious kind with the members of the civil service.'[27]

The recent establishment of a third tier of government, the panchayats, has the potential of creating a new set of political expectations that may affect the All-India Services. While the constitutional amendments establishing this decentralized form has established a new level of elected officials, at the time of writing the relationship between the officers and this tier is not clear. At the present time, the youngest (and least experienced) officers are usually assigned to district level posts; some observers of the process believe that the creation of the panchayats will require skill and experience from administrators and thus require the posting of more senior officials.

Despite the rhetoric, it has been noted that deregulation of the economy has not moved very far at the state level. Top level bureaucrats within states have been socialized to act in a manner that accentuates command and control methods, rather than processes that create opportunities for citizens. The changes in the economic structure raise new demands related to control and accountability of the services as well as new definitions of professional obligations. In a 1995 paper on 'Reforms for the Indian Administrative Service', the Lal Bahadur Shastri National Academy of Administration, Mussoorie, contrasted the work culture of young IAS officers with those coming out of the Indian Institutes of Management:

Both come from the same social and educational background, and both enter their respective organisations at senior positions at a young age, while their other colleagues and subordinates are much older to [*sic*] them. The young manager has to establish himself by proving his effectiveness and utility to the organisation by generating more sales or showing greater savings etc. With no prospects of a time bound promotion, he must strive hard to earn a name for himself in the market and keep growing. The young administrator, on the other hand, relies more on acquiring traditional and ascriptive traits which distinguish him from others; aloofness, greater use of English, calling on seniors and trying to achieve social integration with them, and at the same time enforcing symbols of subordination on others.[28]

The individuals who have joined the services in recent years exhibit a somewhat different profile than those in the past. Creation of new opportunities in the private sector have combined with the fruits of the reservation policy to explain this. A trend analysis of IAS recruits from the 1987 to the 1991 batches indicated that increasingly they were from a lower socio-economic status, from families of government servants, from engineering backgrounds and decreasingly from liberal arts backgrounds. During this period, Uttar Pradesh produced the largest number of recruits, followed by Bihar and Andhra Pradesh. Goa did not send a single person to the IAS during the period of the study.[29]

The concept of the All-India Services was to foster national integration by recruitment of personnel through a nation-wide competition that puts those selected under state control. However, selection of state service members for promotion into the IAS was expected to balance a national perspective with more local views. Despite policy shifts that increased the percentage of insiders (including new IAS candidates selected via national competition but from the state who were allowed to choose their cadres as well as the promotees), in a number of states the outsiders exceed the local component. This has been true in both Gujarat and Maharashtra.[30] In addition, several commentators have noted that in practice new candidates opt for assignment to a neighbouring state and are not really 'outsiders' in the manner that the concept of the All-India Services imagined. Maheshwari called the response to the provision for outsiders in the services 'technical and not substantive'.[31]

Some of this has contributed to increasing conflict between the IAS and the state administrative services over quality of assignments, pay and status.

The changes that have occurred in Indian society since Independence have made some commentators doubtful of the continued utility of the administrative system. With the installation of the United Front government today, these concerns may move from academic queries to real policy debate. For example, on 5 June 1996, *India Abroad* reported that 'during its term of office, the United Front government will advance the principles of political, administrative and economic federalism. In each of these spheres, powers will be devolved and authority will be decentralised'.

Does the current system allow enough flexibility for the All-India Services to adapt to these developments? Do the states have adequate powers in terms of discipline and control of members of the services? With increasing devolution from a unitary government, do the existing services actually restrict State autonomy? Is it possible to maintain high standards of performance (particularly in those areas requiring skill as modernizing agents) and, at the same time, create an administrative apparatus that plays an appropriate role as integrating forces in a new set of governing relationships?

While we can expect these questions to structure future debate, the individuals who have recently entered the services have had to grapple with these issues as they begin their careers. As part of the ongoing study of these issues, data were gathered from a recent batch of trainees of the Indian Administrative Service. Two research questions informed the questionnaire that was completed at the LBS National Academy of Administration in Mussoorie in July 1995 by 57 of 80 individuals who were a part of the 1993 batch of IAS officers:

1. How has India reconciled a nation-wide and nationally recruited bureaucracy with a federal system which has regionally diverse, strong state governments? How does this interaction work in practice in Delhi and the states?
2. How do different accountability theories and practices explain the perceptions and behaviour of administrators who are required to function at different levels of government?

The questionnaire elicited a range of responses among the trainees. In terms of geographical origins, the respondents were divided into groups from the northern Hindi belt (Rajasthan, Uttar Pradesh, Bihar, Haryana, Madhya Pradesh), the north-east and north-west (Jammu & Kashmir, Punjab, West Bengal, Orissa, Assam, Manipur and Meghalaya) and others (Maharashtra, Tamil Nadu, Andhra Pradesh, Karnataka, Kerala Andaman and Nicobar Islands). They were divided on the basis of their having a rural, urban or mixed background. The measure of family background divided the respondents on the basis of whether or not their parents were in government service. The educational background of the respondents was defined as those trained in engineering, medicine, liberal arts or other fields (such as commerce, physics, etc.).

The trainees were asked to react to specific statements that elicited their opinions on a number of matters. Questions were put to the respondents that tried to gauge their perceptions of the changing situation of Indian politics and government and changing centre-state relations. Ten statements regarding these perceptions were given to the respondents and they were asked whether they agreed or disagreed with the statements. These statements were:

- As my career develops, I expect to experience conflict between expectations of state officials and those of the centre.
- I expect to have pressures on me that come from political figures.
- I assume that my postings will be based on my competence not on my personal relationships.
- I expect to be able to develop a policy specialization (e.g. health) that will define my career pattern.
- I believe that my batch of officers is more interested in personal career enhancement than batches who entered the service ten years ago.
- I believe that my career development will be enhanced by my family background.
- Officers who become whistle-blowers are not effective in changing the policies they oppose.
- Developments in centre/state relationships in India over the past five years make an All-India Service an inappropriate institutional form.
- My career progression is dependent on my performance in the state.
- My career progression is dependent on my performance in Delhi.

The questionnaire then asked the respondents to answer two questions that dealt with their views about accountability relationships:

- To whom (or what) do you think that a public servant is accountable?
- What are the mechanisms that ensure that the public servant is accountable?

The first question presented the respondents with fourteen factors which they were expected to rank in order of importance. These factors were the minister, the secretary, the political party in power, the people, the parliament, the prime minister, the law, citizens who are recipients of the services provided, the public servant's own morals and values, the public servant's own community of origin, the Constitution, the public service, and citizens who are politically, socially or economically disadvantaged. Respondents could also add factors to this list.

The second question presented the respondents with nineteen factors which they were also expected to rank in order of importance. These factors were Indian law, fiscal accounts and financial reports, personal values of the public servant, natural law, political parties in opposition, publication of information, elections, the hierarchy, politicians, the public servant's family, the central government, the state (of origin or cadre), professional norms, fear of legal action, the press, the service batch, and NGO activity. Respondents could also add other factors to this list.

Of the 57 respondents, 36 came from the Hindi belt, 8 from the north-east and north-west, and 12 from other states (largely from the south). In terms of the urban/rural background, 34 came from an urban setting, 15 from a rural setting and 7 were from a mixed setting. Of the 57 respondents, 29 came from a family where either one or both the parents were in government service (including three in the Armed Services of India). In terms of the education received by the respondents prior to joining the service, 37 were trained as engineers, 22 as doctors, 10 in the liberal arts and 8 in other fields (ranging from veterinary science, physics, agricultural science, biotechnology, commerce and law). See Tables 1-4 for details.

For the most part, responses by the various groups were more similar than dissimilar. However, several of the questions evoked different levels of intensity in their answers (see Appendix 1 for the percentages reported). For example, in response to the statement, 'As my career develops, I expect to experience conflict between expectations of state officials and those of the centre', respondents from the north-east, urban respondents and those whose parents were in government service were most likely to agree. The statement, 'I expect to have pressures on me that come from political figures', was most likely to evoke agreement from individuals from southern states, urban residents, doctors and liberal arts majors.

TABLE 1A: OPINIONS ABOUT CAREER, I

Respondents	Conflict Centre and State	Pressure from Politicians	Postings Based on Competence	All India Services Appropriate	Career Progression Based on State	Career Progression Based on Centre
Northern India	Yes	Yes	Yes	Yes	Yes	Yes
North-west/ North-east India	Yes	Yes	Yes	Yes	Yes	Yes
Other/Southern India	Yes	Yes	Yes	Yes	Yes	No
Urban Residents	Yes	Yes	No	Yes	Yes	Yes
Rural Residents	Yes	Yes	Yes	Yes	Yes	No
Semi rural Residents	Yes	Yes	Yes	Yes	Yes	Yes
Parents in Govt Service	Yes	Yes	Yes	Yes	Yes	Yes
Medical Education	No	Yes	Yes	Yes	Yes	No
Engineering Education	Yes	Yes	Yes	Yes	Yes	Yes
Liberal Arts Education	Yes	Yes	Yes	Yes	Yes	No
Other Education	Yes	Yes	Yes	Yes	Yes	Yes

TABLE 1B: OPINIONS ABOUT CAREER, II

Respondents	Develop Policy Specialization	Batch More Interested in Career	Family Background Enhance Career	Whistle-Blowers Effective
Northern India	Yes	No	No	Yes
North-west/ North-east India	Yes	Yes and No	No	Yes
Other/Southern India	Yes	Yes and No	No	Yes
Urban Residents	Yes	No	No	Yes
Rural Residents	Yes	No	No	Yes
Semi rural Residents	Yes	No	No	Yes
Parents in Govt. Service	Yes	No	No	Yes
Medical Education	Yes	Yes	Yes and No	Yes
Engineering Education	Yes	No	No	Yes
Liberal Arts Education	Yes	No	No	Yes
Other Education	Yes	Yes	No	Yes

TABLE 2. REASONS FOR JOINING THE IAS

Respondents	Job Diversity	Status/ Best Govt. Service	Job Satis- faction	Helping to Serve People	Challenging Job/Career Opportunities	Back- ground
Northern India	Yes	Yes	Yes	Yes	—	—
North-west/ North-east India	Yes	Yes	—	Yes	—	—
Other/Southern India	Yes	—	—	Yes	—	—
Urban Residents	Yes	Yes	—	—	—	—
Rural Residents	Yes	Yes	—	Yes	Yes	—
Semi rural Residents	—	Yes	—	Yes	Yes	Yes
Parents in Govt. Service	Yes	Yes	—	—	—	—
Medical Education	Yes	—	—	—	Yes	—
Engineering Education	Yes	—	—	—	Yes	—
Liberal Arts Education	Yes	Yes	Yes	Yes	—	—
Other Education	Yes	Yes	Yes	—	Yes	—

TABLE 3: ACCOUNTABLE TO WHOM

Respondents	The People	The Constitution	Their Own Morals	The Law	The Disadvantaged	The Clients	The Public Service
Northern India	xx	xx	xx	xx	—	—	—
North-west/ North-east India	xx	xx	—	xx	xx	—	—
Other/Southern India	xx	xx	xx	—	xx	—	—
Urban Residents	xx	xx	xx	—	xx	—	—
Rural Residents	xx	xx	—	xx	xx	—	—
Semi rural Residents	xx	xx	xx	—	—	—	—
Parents in Govt. Service	xx	xx	—	xx	xx	—	—
Medical Education	xx	xx	xx	xx	—	xx	xx
Engineering Education	xx	xx	xx	xx	xx	—	—
Liberal Arts Education	xx	xx	xx	xx	—	—	—
Other Education	xx	xx	xx	xx	xx	—	—

TABLE 4: ACCOUNTABILITY MECHANISMS

Respondents	Own Values	The Press	Indian Law	Natural Law	Professional Norms	Legal Action	Official Reports	NGOs	The State
Northern India	xx	xx	xx	xx	xx	xx	xx	—	—
North-west/ North-east India	xx	xx	xx	—	—	—	xx	—	—
Other/Southern India	xx	—	xx	—	—	xx	—	—	—
Urban Residents	xx	xx	xx	xx		xx	xx	—	—
Rural Residents	xx	—	xx	xx	xx	—	—	—	—
Semi rural Residents	xx	—	xx	xx	—	xx	—	—	—
Parents in Govt. Service	xx	—	xx	—	xx	xx	xx	—	—
Medical Education	xx	xx	xx	—	xx	xx	—	xx	xx
Engineering Education	xx	xx	xx	xx	xx	xx	—	—	—
Liberal Arts Education	xx	—	xx	—	xx	xx	—	—	—
Other Education	xx	—	xx	xx	xx	—	—	—	—

While a majority of individuals in the study did not agree with the statement, 'Developments in centre/state relationships in India over the past five years make an All-India Service an inappropriate institutional form', rural residents, liberal arts graduates and respondents from the south were more likely to agree with it than others.

When asked whether they agreed with the statement, 'My career progression is dependent on my performance in the state', respondents from the north-east and north-west, rural residents and respondents from a mixed setting, and individuals whose educational background was from 'other fields' were most likely to agree. Liberal arts graduates and respondents from the south had a somewhat lower agreement rate (although all groups agreed with this statement).

The converse statement, 'My career progression is dependent on my performance in Delhi', evoked a lower agreement rate. Hindi belt respondents, respondents from the north-east and north-west, and urban respondents were most likely to agree. By contrast, individuals from the south had a very low agreement rate. All respondents except those that come from an urban background agree that their postings will be based on their competence rather than their personal contacts.

All respondents in groups largely disagree that their careers will be enhanced by their family background except those with a medical educational background who agree and disagree to the same extent. All respondents, except the doctors who again agree as much as they disagree, also disagree that whistle-blowers are ineffective in changing policies they oppose.

The accountability questions indicate that there was not any systematic variation between responses and the groups. Overall, the respondents ranked the people as the factor they consider themselves most accountable to, followed by the Constitution, the law, their own morals and values and the citizens who are politically, socially or economically disadvantaged.

Respondents were also consistent in referring to certain factors over and over again as being the most salient mechanisms that ensure accountability. As in the first case, there were no systematic variations observable in the responses and the groups. The mechanism ranked most important and relevant across all the groups was Indian law, followed by personal values, the press, professional norms, fear of legal action, and natural law.

These preliminary data are interesting on several grounds. They acknowledge the ascendancy of the state perspective in terms of centre/state relationships. They indicate that new recruits into the IAS are well aware of the pressures and conflicts they are likely to experience between the centre and state perspectives. At the same time, these recruits do not appear to be overwhelmed by this 'reality'. Their views about accountability also suggest that there is an increasing responsiveness towards citizens in general and the disadvantaged in particular.

The data provide a sense of the changing demographic and educational composition of the IAS. The number of individuals in the service from the Hindi belt is significant as is the background of these individuals as urban residents with family members in government service.[32] Perhaps most striking is the educational background of these individuals, with more than 60 per cent trained as engineers.

These new members of the IAS are not likely to be the individuals who, in the near future, will determine the fate of the All-India Services. Indeed, these decisions are likely to be political calculations that will be made on grounds other than those of concern to the government officers. Yet the responses in this preliminary study suggest that the structure may be flexible enough to respond to changes in Indian society, yet continue some semblance of the current system. Tension between levels of government is inherent in most federal systems today. Despite the dramatic changes that have occurred in India, it would appear that, unless Indian government becomes much more decentralized, the All-India Services will continue to provide a mechanism to deal with that tension and serve as a conflict management instrument for the future. Time will, of course, tell.

APPENDIX 1

RESEARCH QUESTION ONE

Given below are the responses to the agree/disagree opinion questions:

In response to the first statement, '*As my career develops, I expect to experience conflict between expectations of state officials and those of the Centre*', 75 per cent of the Hindi belt respondents agreed,[33] 87.5 per cent of the respondents from the north-east and north-west agreed (12.5) and 58.3 per cent of the respondents from the other states agreed (41.7). 77.1 per cent of the urban respondents (20), 66.7 per cent of the rural respondents (33.3) and 71.4 per cent of the respondents from a mixed setting (28.6), agreed. 83 per cent of those whose parents were in government service agreed (14). 73 per cent of the engineers (24.3), 0 per cent of the doctors (100), 70 per cent of those who studied the liberal arts (30) and 100 per cent of the category that studied other fields agreed.

In response to the second statement, '*I expect to have pressures on me that come from political figures*', 83.3 per cent of the respondents from the Hindi belt agreed that they expected the pressure (16.7), 87.5 per cent from the north-east and north-west agreed (12.5) and 100 per cent of the respondents from the other states agreed. 91.4 per cent of the urban (8.6) , 86.7 per cent of the rural (13.3) and 71.4 per cent of the mixed background respondents agreed (28.6) to this statement. 86 per cent of those whose parents were in government service agreed (14). In the educational background category, 89.2 per cent of the engineers (10.8), 100 per cent of the doctors, 90 per cent of the liberal arts majors (10) and 75 per cent of the respondents from other fields agreed (25) to the statement.

In response to the third statement, '*I assume that my postings will be based on my competence not on my personal relationships*', 47 per cent of the Hindi belt respondents agreed (39), 75 per cent of the respondents from the north-east and north-west agreed (25) and 58.3 per cent of the respondents from the other states agreed (33.3). 40 per cent of the urban respondents (48.6), 86.6 per cent of the rural respondents (6.7) and 57.1 per cent of the respondents from a mixed setting (28.6), agreed. 55 per cent of those whose parents were in government service agreed (35). 48.7 per cent of the engineers (37.8), 100 per cent of the doctors,

60 per cent of those who studied the liberal arts (30) and 62.5 per cent of the category that studied other fields agreed (37.5).

In response to the fourth statement, '*I expect to be able to develop a policy specialization (e.g. health) that will define my career pattern*', 75 per cent of the Hindi belt respondents agreed (22.2), 62.5 per cent of the respondents from the north-east and north-west agreed (37.5) and 91.7 per cent of the respondents from the other states agreed (8.3). 77.1 per cent of the urban respondents (22.9), 80 per cent of the rural respondents (20) and 71.4 per cent of the respondents from a mixed setting (14.3), agreed. 83 per cent of those whose parents were in government service agreed (17). 75.7 per cent of the engineers (21.6), 100 per cent of the doctors, 80 per cent of those who studied the liberal arts (20) and 75 per cent of the category that studied other fields agreed (25).

In response to the fifth statement, '*I believe that my batch of officers is more interested in personal career enhancement than batches who entered the service 10 years ago*', 30.6 per cent of the Hindi belt respondents agreed (50), 50 per cent of the respondents from the north-east and north-west agreed (50) and 50 per cent of the respondents from the other states agreed (41.7). 37.1 per cent of the urban respondents (42.9), 40 per cent of the rural respondents (53.3) and 26.6 per cent of the respondents from a mixed setting (71.4), agreed. 28 per cent of those whose parents were in government service agreed (55). 32.4 per cent of the engineers (54.1), 100 per cent of the doctors, 20 per cent of those who studied the liberal arts (50) and 62.5 per cent of the category that studied other fields agreed (37.5).

In response to the sixth statement, '*I believe that my career development will be enhanced by my family background*', 16.7 per cent of the Hindi belt repondents agreed (80.5), 12.5 per cent of the respondents from the north-east and north-west agreed (87.5) and 16.7 per cent of the respondents from the other states agreed (83.3). 11.5 per cent of the urban respondents (85.7), 13.3 per cent of the rural respondents (86.7) and 42.9 per cent of the respondents from a mixed setting (57.1), agreed. 7 per cent of those whose parents were in government service agreed (93). 13.5 per cent of the engineers (83.8), 50 per cent of the doctors (50), 10 per cent of those who studied the liberal arts (90) and 25 per cent of the category that studied other fields agreed (75).

In response to the seventh statement, '*Officers who become whistle-*

blowers are not effective in changing the policies they oppose', 36.1 per cent of the Hindi belt respondents agreed (58.3), 25 per cent of the respondents from the north-east and north-west agreed (75) and 25 per cent of the respondents from the other states agreed (50). 28.6 per cent of the urban respondents (62.9), 33.3 per cent of the rural respondents (53.4) and 42.9 per cent of the respondents from a mixed setting (57.1), agreed. 42 per cent of those whose parents were in government service agreed (55). 32.4 per cent of the engineers (59.5), 50 per cent of the doctors (50), 40 per cent of those who studied the liberal arts (50) and 12.5 per cent of the category that studied other fields agreed (87.5).

In response to the eighth statement, '*Developments in centre/state relationships in India over the past 5 years make an All India Service an inappropriate institutional form*', 13.9 per cent of the Hindi belt respondents agreed (83.3), 12.5 per cent of the respondents from the north-east and north-west agreed (87.5) and 16.7 per cent of the respondents from the other states agreed (66.6). 14.3 per cent of the urban respondents (85.7), 36.8 per cent of the rural respondents (52.6) and 0 per cent of the respondents from a mixed setting (85.7), agreed. 10 per cent of those whose parents were in government service agreed (90). 13.5 per cent of the engineers (78.4), 0 per cent of the doctors (100), 20 per cent of those who studied the liberal arts (80) and 12.5 per cent of the category that studied other fields agreed (87.5).

In response to the ninth statement, '*My career progression is dependent on my performance in the state*', 80.6 per cent of the Hindi belt respondents agreed (16.7), 100 per cent of the respondents from the north-east and north-west agreed and 75 per cent of the respondents from the other states agreed (25). 77.1 per cent of the urban respondents (20), 93.3 per cent of the rural respondents (6.7) and 85.7 per cent of the respondents from a mixed setting (14.3), agreed. 79 per cent of those whose parents were in government service agreed (21). 83.8 per cent of the engineers (13.5), 100 per cent of the doctors, 70 per cent of those who studied the liberal arts (30) and 87.5 per cent of the category that studied other fields agreed (12.5).

In response to the tenth statement, '*My career progression is dependent on my performance in Delhi*', 63.9 per cent of the Hindi belt respondents agreed (33.3), 62.5 per cent of the respondents from the north-east and north-west agreed (25) and 15.7 per cent of the respondents from the other states agreed (83.3). 68.6 per cent of the urban respondents (28.6), 26.7 per cent of the rural respondents (73.3) and 57.1 per cent of the respondents from a mixed setting (42.9), agreed. 66 per cent of those whose parents were in government service agreed (31). 56.8 per cent of the engineers (40.5), 50 per cent of the doctors (50), 40 per cent of those who studied the liberal arts (50) and 62.5 per cent of the category that studied other fields agreed (37.5).

RESEARCH QUESTION TWO

Given below are the responses to the first part of the accountability questions. The first part of this research question was, '*To whom (or what) do you think that a public servant is accountable?*'

Rank 1

44 per cent of the Hindi belt respondents ranked people, 25 per cent ranked Constitution and 13.9 per cent ranked morals.[34] 37.5 per cent of the respondents from the north-western and north-eastern states ranked Constitution, 25 per cent ranked disadvantaged, 25 per cent ranked people and 12.5 per cent ranked morals. 25 per cent of the respondents from other states ranked Constitution, 25 per cent ranked morals, 16.7 per cent ranked disadvantaged and 16.7 per cent ranked people. 34.3 per cent of the respondents from an urban background ranked people, 31.4 per cent ranked Constitution, 14.3 per cent ranked morals and 11.2 per cent ranked disadvantaged. 46.7 per cent of the respondents from a rural background ranked people, 26 per cent ranked Constitution and 13.3 per cent ranked morals. 28.6 per cent of the respondents from a mixed background ranked morals, 14.3 per cent ranked Constitution, people, spouse, minister and disadvantaged. 42.1 per cent of the respondents whose parents were in government service ranked people, 31.6 per cent ranked Constitution and 10.5 ranked disadvantaged. 50 per cent of the doctors ranked Constitution and 50 per cent ranked morals. 60 per cent of the respondents with a liberal arts degree ranked people, 30 per cent ranked Constitution and 10 per cent ranked clients. 29.7 per cent of the respondents with an engineering degree ranked people, 24.3 per cent

ranked Constitution, 18.9 per cent ranked morals and 16.2 per cent ranked disadvantaged. 37.5 per cent of the respondents with other degrees ranked Constitution and people while 12.5 per cent ranked morals and minister.

Rank 2

22.2 per cent of the Hindi belt respondents ranked law, 19.4 per cent ranked people, 16.6 per cent ranked morals and 13.9 per cent ranked Constitution. 37.5 per cent of the respondents from the north-western and north-eastern states ranked Constitution, 25 per cent ranked law, 25 per cent ranked people and 12.5 per cent ranked clients. 25 per cent of the respondents from other states ranked Constitution and 16.7 per cent ranked clients and people. 22.9 per cent of the respondents from an urban background ranked people and law, 17.1 per cent ranked Constitution, 14.3 per cent ranked morals and 11.22 per cent ranked clients. 33.3 per cent of the respondents from a rural background ranked Constitution, 20 per cent ranked law and 13.3 per cent ranked disadvantaged and people. 28.6 per cent of the respondents from a mixed background ranked public service and 14.3 per cent ranked secretary, people, morals, chief minister and law. 42.1 per cent of the respondents whose parents were in government service ranked law, 21.1 per cent ranked morals, 15.8 per cent ranked people and 10.5 per cent ranked Constitution. 50 per cent of the doctors ranked people and 50 per cent ranked clients. 50 per cent of the respondents with a liberal arts degree ranked law and 10 per cent ranked Constitution, people, morals, public service and disadvantaged. 25 per cent of the respondents with an engineering degree ranked Constitution, 22.2 per cent ranked people, 16.7 per cent ranked law and 13.9 per cent ranked morals. 12.5 per cent of the respondents with other degrees ranked Constitution, disadvantaged, law, morals, people, secretary and parliament.

Rank 3

30.5 per cent of the Hindi belt respondents ranked Constitution, 19.4 per cent ranked disadvantaged, 13.9 per cent ranked law and 11.1 per cent ranked people. 37.5 per cent of the respondents from the north-western and north-eastern states ranked law, 25 per cent ranked public service and 12.5 per cent ranked Constitution, minister and people. 33.3 per cent of the respondents from other states ranked law and 25 per cent ranked Constitution. 25.7 per cent of the respondents from an urban background ranked law, 20 per cent ranked Constitution and 11.2 per cent ranked public service and people. 33.3 per cent of the respondents from a rural background ranked Constitution, 20 per cent ranked law and 13.3 per cent ranked disadvantaged and public service. 42.8 per cent of the respondents from a mixed background ranked Constitution, 28.6 per cent ranked disadvantaged and 14.3 per cent ranked people. 31.6 per cent of the respondents whose parents were in government service ranked Constitution, 15.8 per cent ranked law and people and 10.5 per cent ranked morals. 50 per cent of the doctors ranked law. 30 per cent of the respondents with a liberal arts degree ranked Constitution, 20 per cent ranked law and 10 per cent ranked people, morals, public service, clients and disadvantaged. 32.4 per cent of the respondents with an engineering degree ranked Constitution, 20.6 per cent ranked law and 17.6 per cent ranked disadvantaged. 25 per cent of the respondents with other degrees ranked law and people and 12.5 per cent ranked minister, public service and Constitution.

Given below are the responses to the second part of the accountability questions. The second part of this research question was, '*What are the mechanisms that assure that the public servant is accountable*?'

Rank 1

41.7 per cent of the Hindi belt respondents ranked values, 27.8 per cent ranked Indian law and 16.7 per cent ranked legal action.[35] 50 per cent of the respondents from the north-western and north-eastern States ranked Indian law and 25 per cent ranked values. 41.7 per cent of the respondents from other States ranked values and 16.7 per cent ranked Indian law. 34.3 per cent of the respondents from an urban background ranked values, 28.6 per cent ranked Indian law and 14.3 per cent ranked legal action. 46.7 per cent of the respondents from a rural background ranked Indian law, 40 per cent ranked values and 13.3 per cent ranked professional norms. 57.1 per cent of the respondents from a mixed background ranked values, 28.6 per cent ranked legal action and 14.3 per cent ranked opposition party. 36.8 per cent of the respondents whose parents were in government service ranked Indian law, 21.1 per cent ranked values and 15.8 per cent ranked legal action. 50 per cent of the doctors ranked values and press. 40.5 per cent of the respondents with an engineering degree ranked values, 32.4 per cent ranked Indian law and 16.2 per cent ranked legal action. 40 per cent of the respondents with a liberal arts degree ranked Indian law, 30 per cent ranked values and 10 per cent ranked legal action and press. 37.5 per cent of the respondents with other degrees ranked values and 12.5 per cent ranked Indian law, natural law, opposition party and professional norms.

Rank 2

17.5 per cent of the Hindi belt respondents ranked natural law and 12.5 per cent ranked Indian law, professional norms and reports. 25 per cent of the respondents from the north-western and north-eastern States ranked reports and 12.5 per cent ranked legal action, professional norms and natural law. 16.7 per cent of the respondents from other States ranked Indian law, information, legal action and professional norms. 15.9 per cent of the respondents from an urban background ranked Indian law and reports and 10.5 per cent ranked natural law and values. 20 per cent of the respondents from a rural background ranked natural law and legal action and 13.3 per cent ranked professional norms, values and press. 42.9 per cent of the respondents from a mixed background ranked professional norms, 28.6 per cent ranked natural law and 14.3 per cent ranked information and politician. 15.8 per cent of the respondents whose parents were in government service ranked Indian law, professional norms, reports and values. 50 per cent of the doctors ranked professional norms and information. 21.1 per cent of the respondents with an engineering degree ranked natural law, 15.8 per cent ranked Indian law and 13.2 per cent ranked legal action, reports and values. 18.1 per cent of the respondents with a liberal arts degree ranked professional norms and press. 25 per cent of the respondents with other degrees ranked professional norms and 12.5 per cent ranked reports, politicians, natural law, family and values.

Rank 3

18.9 per cent of the Hindi belt respondents ranked Indian law and 13.5 per cent ranked legal action and press and 10.8 per cent ranked natural law. 25 per cent of the respondents from the north-western and north-eastern states ranked press and 12.5 per cent ranked legal action, information and values. 33.3 per cent of the respondents from other states ranked hierarchy and 16.7 per cent ranked information, legal action and professional norms. 17.1 per cent of the respondents from an urban background ranked legal action and 11.4 per cent ranked press and Indian law. 20 per cent of the respondents from a rural background ranked Indian law and hierarchy and 13.3 per cent ranked professional norms, legal action and press. 25 per cent of the respondents from a mixed background ranked Indian law and 12.5 per cent ranked politician, legal action, natural law, press, state and values. 15.8 per cent of the respondents whose parents were in government service ranked professional norms and 10.5 per cent ranked Indian law, information, natural law, press, reports, values and legal action. 50 per cent of the doctors ranked state and Indian law. 14.7 per cent of the respondents with an engineering degree ranked Indian law and press and 11.8 per cent ranked natural law, information and professional norms. 20 per cent of the respondents with a liberal arts degree ranked legal action and 10 per cent ranked Indian law, hierarchy, professional norms, politicians, press and values. 37.5 per cent of the respondents with other degrees ranked legal action, 25 per cent ranked Indian law and 12.5 per cent ranked press and values.

NOTES

★ Support for this research was provided by Center for the Advanced Study of India at the University of Pennsylvania, the Centre for Policy Research in New Delhi, and the U.S. National Science Foundation. A version of this paper was published in *Seminar* in September 1997.

1. Shriram Maheshwari, *Problems and Issues in Administrative Federalism* (Bombay, 1992), p. 2.
2. See, for example, Beryl A. Radin, Robert Agranoff, Ann Bowman, C. Gregory Buntz, Steven Ott, Barbara S. Romzek, and Robert Wilson, *New Governance for Rural America: Creating Intergovernmental Partnerships* (Kansas City, 1996).

3. This paper grew out of a collaborative study of the All-India Services in which I have been engaged along with Balveer Arora at the Jawaharlal Nehru University in New Delhi and Douglas Verney at the University of Pennsylvania, sponsored by the Centre for Policy Research in New Delhi and the Center for the Advanced Study of India at the University of Pennsylvania. I wish to thank Douglas Verney for comments on an earlier draft of this paper. Research assistance on the questionnaire results reported in this paper was provided by Radhika Nath, a Ph.D. student in the Department of Public Administration and Policy at the State University of New York at Albany.
4. The British actually built the district level system on the structures devised by the Mughals for tax collection. The British used that decentralized system to perform tasks of social control (e.g. law and order) as well as for tax collection.
5. See Shriram Maheshwari, *Indian Administration,* (New Delhi, 4th revd. edn., 1990), p. 237.
6. Ibid.
7. Ibid., p. 239.
8. Maheshwari, *Problems*, p. 63.
9. Ibid., p. 64.
10. Ibid., p. 67.
11. R.K. Dar, *The All India Services in India, with Special Reference to Their Role in Promoting Intergovernment Co-operation,* Centre for Research on Federal Financial Relations, The Australian National University, Reprint Series: Number 28, 1979, p. 7.
12. Dar, pp. 9-10.
13. Quoted in Maheshwari, *Problems*, p. 69.
14. In part this argument was met by a procedure that allowed State civil servants to come into the IAS as promotees. However, they enter the IAS at an older age and are rarely accorded the secondment opportunities to the Central Government.
15. V. Subramanian, *Social Background of India's Administrators* (New Delhi, 1971) p. 6.
16. Ibid., p. 10.
17. Ibid., p. 26.
18. Sec. 4, Article 16.
19. Sec. 4, Article 15.
20. See Krishna K. Tummala, 'Politics of Preference in Public Service: Mandal and Since in India' (paper presented at the annual meeting of the American Political Science Association, Chicago, August 1995).
21. Data from the Planning Commission, Government of India, quoted in ibid.
22. Ibid.
23. Maheshwari has noted (p. 110) that 'without political patronage, a civil servant

is unlikely to get a senior posting at the centre, at least in a prestigious ministry'.

24. When Mulayam Singh Yadav came into power as Chief Minister in Uttar Pradesh, transfers of some IAS officers were frequent. Indeed, some service members decided not to move their families to the posting because they could not assume that the assignment would go through a full school year.
25. Described in ibid., p.111.
26. Quoted in ibid., p. 139.
27. Ibid., p. 186.
28. 'Reforms for the Indian Administrative Service', LBS National Academy of Administration, Mussoorie, 1995, p. 13.
29. *IAS Probationers: A Trend Analysis (1987-91 Batches)*, Training, Research and Development Cell, Lal Bahadur Shastri National Academy of Administration, 1992.
30. Maheshwari, *Problems*, p. 143.
31. Ibid., p. 144.
32. Government service includes both State services as well as All-India Services.
33. All figures in brackets correspond to the percentage who responded 'disagree' as per the opinion questions. Residuals reflect no responses to the questions.
34. Percentages shown are those where, at least, above 10 per cent of the respondents have ranked a particular factor.
35. Ibid.

6

Federalism as a Response to Ethnic Regionalism

SURI RATNAPALA

The man of system . . . seems to imagine that he can arrange the different members of a great society with as much ease as the hand arranges the different pieces upon a chessboard. He does not consider that the pieces upon the chessboard have no other principle of motion besides that which the hand impresses upon them; but that, in the great chessboard of human society, every single piece has a principle of motion of its own, altogether different from that which the legislature might choose to impress upon it. If those two principles coincide and act in the same direction, the game of human society will go on easily and harmoniously, and is very likely to be happy and successful. If they are opposite or different, the game will go on miserably and human society must be at all times in the highest degree of disorder.

ADAM SMITH[1]

History reveals that in some conditions, federations disintegrate owing to ethnic regionalism while in other conditions, they provide a means of accommodating regional ethnic diversity. The aim of this paper is to support the hypothesis that the capacity of federations to withstand regionalism and promote inter-ethnic harmony is enhanced by three conditions, territorial devolution (which allows ethnically distinct regions a high degree of political autonomy), the guarantee of personal security and individual liberty to all residents within each region, and freedom of individuals to engage in economic and cultural intercourse across the territorial borders of such regions.

Though this proposition may seem simple enough, history shows that it is often disregarded at great human cost. Conflicts directly or indirectly fuelled by ethnic sentiment continue in the territories of the former Yugoslavia, in parts of Russia, in many African countries and in West Asia and South Asia. Sri Lanka which is gripped by a thirteen year old civil war between the government and Tamil separatists is a case with which I am familiar. The unitarist ideal which dominates Sinhala politics has frustrated the attempts of successive governments to reach a political-economic solution on federal lines. Yet, it is increasingly evident that Sri Lanka's unitarism is only a military reality. In contrast, Sri Lanka's much larger and potentially more fractious neighbour India has preserved its nationhood by following a federalist strategy. India, at present, has simmering regional problems concerning Jammu & Kashmir and the Punjab which it has so far contained. Though military muscle has played a part in this containment, the decisive factors have been regional autonomy and the Indian common market which has produced a 200 million strong and rapidly growing pan-Indian middle class.[2] In 1946, the Indian government decided to terminate direct rule in Jammu & Kashmir, to hold state elections and to move towards autonomy of that state as a means of ending the violence between separatists and the central government's security forces. The then Indian Home Minister was quoted as saying that 'autonomy is necessary if we want to keep Kashmir'.[3] In my view, India provides a highly instructive case study of a federation that has been successful in containing ethnic regionalism and of promoting inter-ethnic cooperation.

The Indian Home Minister's view that India cannot hope to retain Kashmir without granting it greater autonomy than it currently enjoys, reveals the simple truth that enduring national unity is achieved not by military force, but through free association. What kind of free association would bring about unity among nations or regions? Clearly, the freedom of rulers to associate with one another is not enough. In the community of nations, the freedom of governments to deal with one another has hardly promoted the unity of states. On the contrary it has often produced disunity and war. It is the freedom of individuals to associate with each other across borders that promotes national and international cooperation. The history of the Indian republic offers support for this hypothesis. India's constitution fortuitously promotes the three conditions that I have stipulated. I am not, for a moment suggesting that other historical and cultural factors have not contributed to the relative success of the Indian federation. But I believe that substantial political devolution to ethnic or linguistic regions, and personal liberty including the freedom of individual intercourse across state borders have been the most important sources of strength of the Indian federation. While effecting political devolution on ethnic lines, India has maintained through its constitutionalism and it is protection of fundamental rights, the capillary processes that promote inter-communal harmony.

To understand why the freedom of individuals to associate is conducive to optimal federation we must understand the nature of knowledge and how complex systems such as human societies utilize knowledge. But first, we should make certain conceptual clarifications about the federalist idea.[4] Conceptual clarity tends to unearth systems and ideas which remain buried in un-analysed materials. The views canvassed in this paper derive from insights which are gained precisely through such conceptual differentiation.

In recent years, an important distinction has been drawn between 'federalism' and 'federation'. The distinction was drawn first by Preston King who used the term 'federalism' to refer to the philosophical advocacy of the federal principle in political organization and the term 'federation' as descriptive of actual political systems which are structured according to the federal principle. Thus, Madison's celebrated Federalist Paper No. 10 is an example of federalism, while the German state is illustrative of federation. Ronald Watts notices that this dichotomy is understood differently by others who use both terms in descriptive senses. These writers mean by 'federalism' the whole genus of federalist political models including federations, confederations and supra-national organizations, and by 'federation', a particular species of federalist organization.[5] Watts, therefore, proposes the conceptual trichotomy: (1) 'federalism' meaning philosophical advocacy of the federal principle; (2) 'federal political systems' meaning the genus of federalist systems; and (3) 'federation' meaning a particular species of federalist organization.[6]

Watts' analysis is an improvement on King's. Yet, the purposes of this paper demand a further refinement. The Watts trichotomy does not bring out a crucial distinction that has profound consequences for federalism as a philosophical project, namely, the distinction between the process of spontaneous or natural federation in and among human communities and the process of political federation which is brought about by deliberate political action. It is a distinction that reflects the difference between the 'top down' imposition of political order and the 'bottom up' principle of self-organization in complex systems.

Federation as Construction and as Principle of Self-organization

Modern constitutions, whether unitary or federal, are generally regarded as the products of deliberate design. This is certainly true of constitutions in the formal sense, the British Constitution being an apparent exception. True, constitutions are never entirely enacted. Conventions, traditions and doctrines, play critical parts in their working. They are always amalgams of formal and informal law.

Many writers on federalism, including Watts, have argued that federations are dynamic systems in a much more fundamental sense. Watts notes that the understanding of federal systems requires analysis of the interaction of societies, structures and processes. This observation echoes the thoughts of many others.[7] Friedrich regards federalism 'as an evolving pattern of changing relationships'.[8] He explains that federalism is 'perhaps primarily the process of federalising a political community, that is to say, the process by which a number of separate political communities enter into arrangements for working out solutions, adopting joint policies, and making joint decisions on joint problems, and, conversely, also the process by which a unitary political community becomes differentiated into a federally organized whole'.[9] Other evolutionary conceptions of federalism are identified by W.H. Stewart in his lexicographic work, *Concepts of Federalism*.[10] While endorsing this approach, I wish to develop it further with the aid of tools provided by evolutionary theory.

It is easily forgotten that constitutions exist even without formal enactment. The written constitution, though known to antiquity, is mainly a modern phenomenon. In the past, constitutions, like most laws, were customary. Much constitutional theorizing proceeds upon the inarticulate positivist premise that political authority precedes law and is the source of all law. This premise has credence only if we regard law as a property of a certain kind of society only or if we define law semi-tautologously as the projection of authority. This premise is contradicted by anthropology and evolutionary theory. From the evolutionary-theoretical viewpoint, it is possible to argue that it is the emergence of law in the form of social rules which establishes authority. In the evolutionary paradigm, federalism is seen as a naturally occurring phenomenon. This proposition may be explained by an hypothetical narrative of the emergence of political societies. The account is not proffered as the true story of our political evolution, but as an illustration of the kinds of processes that may have produced political-social order.

It is conceivable according to the natural selection paradigm that sometime in the past, the biological ancestors of hominids lived as solitary species. Some of them became social species through natural selection. Behavioural regularity produced rules which produced social order. The social rules aided the survival of the ordered groups, which thus survived selection pressures. The very importance of rules for survival produced mechanisms for the retention and enforcement of beneficial rules. One of the first mechanisms was the process of arbitration or adjudication. Quarrels were settled by respected elders or arbiters. Another mechanism was that of headship, the institution granted power to deal with internal and external threats to the social order. Thus there were laws, judges and administrators who together constituted the rudimentary constitutions. The original human communities were small and tribal. Over time these communities began to deal with each other for mutual gain. Where rules of conduct differed between communities, or were inadequate to resolve transcommunal questions, meta-rules evolved. Overarching institutions emerged to adjudicate disputes concerning these rules and to enforce them. Some of these communities merged, some remained semi-autonomous. Forms of federalism evolved with the increasing interaction and interdependence of communities. Towns, estates, baronies and kingdoms were formed, with their own spheres of authority. Although this narrative is given only as an explanatory device, studies of estate federalism and feudal federalism show that it is not far removed from what might have occurred.[11]

It is not suggested that this federalizing process is totally spontaneous. On the contrary, the process is ever subject to deliberate political interference. As political authority becomes formalized, constitutional designing becomes more common, as does deliberate law making. Federations are legislatively made and unmade. Events such as settlement, conquest, and colonization interfere profoundly with the course of political evolution. However, though these interventions may produce undesirable outcomes, they do not alter the overall character of the process, which remains evolutionary. These interventions, like all other cultural and physical conditions, provide the ingredients of the environment which selects the institutional forms that emerge.

It should not be assumed that deliberate human interventions always produce the outcomes willed by the intervenors. In fact, it is arguable that intervenors hardly ever secure the exact results that they seek. When they do, their success may have as much to do with chance as with design. The complexity of social order makes successful designing virtually impossible. This complexity decrees the law of unintended consequences. The operation of this law on the 'federal' plane is frequently demonstrated. Conquering nations are often themselves transformed in unintended ways by the communities that they conquer and by the cost of conquest. History is also replete with downfalls of nations which over-extended their dominance.

Thus in nature there are two forms of federation at work which are in a state of dynamic equilibrium. Firstly, there is the federal phenomenon that occurs 'naturally' or independent of human design and secondly there is the deliberate creation of federations through political action, which, for want of a better term I will call political federation. Political federation is greatly influenced by the forces of natural federation. The emergence of communalities of interest among politically independent communities may generate incentives for the construction of a federation to that end. Likewise, the emergence or persistence of distinct regional interests within a unitary state may motivate political action to decentralize authority and to create a federation of semi-autonomous regional entities. The converse is also true in that politically-constructed federations may generate forces of natural federation. Where a country which is culturally homogeneous is artificially fragmented into federated states with their own elected legislatures and governments, distinct political communities may be generated with interests in preserving regional autonomy. Such political federation creates several centres of power with capacity to create new regional interests where none exist. Owing to its regulatory power and reach, modern government unavoidably creates special interests and attracts rent seekers to itself. State governments may also confer special benefits on residents which create new incentives for residents to maintain their semi-autonomy. (These incentives may be counter-balanced by incentives provided by central governments.) It seems, therefore, that the two forms of federation interact in a process of negative feedback to produce the stable states which we observe at given times.

Towards Optimally Stable States

It is evident that at a given time a society is in a stable state at some point in the spectrum between absolute unity and absolute separation. It does not follow that the society is at the optimally stable state, which is rare. However, it is my submission that where the three conditions specified at the outset are present, societies will gravitate towards optimal federation. The reason is that these conditions maximize the exchange of information among individuals who compose the society and enhance the responsiveness of the legal-constitutional order to such information.

Why is exchange among individuals important? It is because much of the information upon which the process of natural federation occurs is dispersed among the countless individuals in society. In human affairs, several types of knowledge come into play. One is theoretical knowledge, the knowledge of principles and processes. A second type of knowledge concerns facts relevant to concrete situations. This knowledge is dispersed among the millions of individuals who compose the society. The circumstances which affect individuals are ever changing and are known generally only by the individual and by those who are close to her. A society deprives itself of the benefit of the latter kind of knowledge to the extent that the society impedes its free flow. Natural federation is a process of self-organization which occurs through the synthesizing of this knowledge.

There are two forces at work in the emergence of social order. There is the exogenous or top-down way by which authorities determine what is most beneficial to the members of society. Political federation is one manifestation of this process. There is also the endogenous or bottom-up process by which order emerges spontaneously as the outcome of interactions among countless individuals pursuing disparate aims. Natural federation is part of this process. These two processes operate simultaneously and interact in varying degrees, but it is critically important to understand that the overall process is one of self-organization. No social order can be controlled wholly exogenously not even by the most powerful and ruthless of dictatorships. Those regimes that have gone close to achieving such an object have not, themselves, lasted long. (History seems to indicate that absolute rulerships tend to last when they do not seek to control every detail of society but are content to enjoy a monopoly of power while allowing the established order of society to continue.) As F.A. Hayek demonstrated in his classic work, *Law, Legislation and Liberty,* the overall order of the Great Society is always spontaneous in nature.[12]

Hayek's theoretical insight into the nature of spontaneous orders is being spectacularly and independently substantiated by the multi-skilled researchers developing the new science concerned with the laws of self-organization and complexity.[13] The significance of these developments lies in the fact that they demonstrate the inevitability of the bottom-up process of self-organization, and hence the cognitive significance of the type of dispersed knowledge which is unavailable to social designers. If we deprive ourselves of this type of knowledge, we are unlikely to move in the direction of optimal federation.

The Limits of Federal Optimality

The argument developed thus far is that optimal federation requires the kind of information exchange which can occur only with individual liberty and cross-border freedom of interaction. If this proposition is valid it may seem to imply that the federal ideal is served best by allowing federations to remain in a state of unimpeded flux so that the process of spontaneous or natural federation will determine optimal territorial distributions of power at any given moment. However, on reflection it seems that such a state of affairs is not achievable. To appreciate this point, we need to understand the hierarchical nature of human institutions, by which we mean the rules of human interaction and social order.

It is observed that stable societies display classes of institutions or rules which are distinguished by hierarchy, relative stability and level of abstraction. Towards the bottom of this hierarchy, we find various types of subordinate legislation and decree. Generally, these are made and unmade executively. They are liable to frequent change and, ideally, should deal only with matters of detail. (The decline of constitutionalism in modern democracies increasingly allows this type of executive decrees to determine matters of legislative principle.) Above them are the more general laws of the land which consist of customary law or common law and statutes made by legislatures at the state and federal levels of government. Many of these statutes authorize the making of subordinate law. The courts that recognize and enforce customary law and the state and federal legislatures which make statute laws are themselves authorized by higher order constitutional rules. In federations, the rules which determine the territorial limits of states and their respective powers are often determined by constitutional provisions.

There are two aspects to the constitutional allocation of power in federations. One is the territorial delimitation of the federating states. The other is the distribution of the subjects of power between the central federal authorities and the regional entities. A high degree of instability in one or both of these aspects of allocation will lead to a high degree of instability of lower-order rules within states as the constituency which produces law fluctuates. It need hardly be stressed that the meta-rules of a political system represented by the constitution should have a very high degree of stability. The constitution embodies the fundamental political values of the community, provides for the making or recognition of lower-order rules, and lays down the ground-rules for the exercise of public coercive power. Naturally, if the foundation is unstable, the lower-order rules will be even more unstable. Where lower-order rules are unstable, there is less scope for settled expectations, hence less freedom. Such conditions militate against the natural federative process. Yet, the specific federal distribution of power cannot have the permanence of the cardinal rules of constitutional government for that too defeats optimal federation. It seems, therefore, that optimal federation requires a judicious balance between stability of federal arrangements and capacity for modification when lasting changes in the constituency occur.

For this reason, it would seem that rules of federation should ideally occupy an intermediate position in the institutional hierarchy between the rules of customary and statute law on the one hand and the most fundamental rules of the constitution on the other. Under such a scheme the principle of federation itself can be accorded the status of a constitutional fundamental while the rules concerning the territorial delimitation and subject allocation are assigned the intermediate position.

We could expect to find in an idealized scheme, an institutional hierarchy on the following lines:

- Fundamental principles of the constitution:
  Tripartite separation of powers federalism;
  Freedom of interstate commerce and interaction;
  Representative government;
  Classical (negative) human rights.
- Rules governing the territorial delimitation of federal units and the distribution of powers between centre and regional units.
- Primary legal rules represented by customary or common law and statute law.
- Subordinate legal rules made by executive authorities.

It is not coincidental that some of the great federations of the world reflect this hierarchy. The Constitution of the United States cannot be changed except by an extraordinarily difficult procedure.[14] Yet the Constitution itself provides for a much easier mode of adjusting the territorial limits of states.[15] The position is very similar in the Australian Constitution.[16]

However, one of the most sophisticated attempts to achieve the kind of balance that would harmonize political federation and natural federation is to be found in the Constitution of the Federal Republic of Germany, Article 29 para (1) states:

> Boundaries may be modified to ensure that the Länder, by virtue of their size and capacity, can effectively perform their functions. Due regard shall be given to regional, historical and cultural ties, economic expediency and the requirements of regional policy and planning.

According to para (2), modifications have to be made by federal law with the approval of the affected Länder expressed at a referendum. Section (1), in my view, seeks to balance, on the one hand, the need to recognize existing or emerging cultural and economic commonalities, and on the other to provide the kind of stability and viability of federal units without which cultural and economic emergence can be aborted. Article 29 para (4) reinforces and fine tunes this balance by providing:

> Where in a clearly defined, homogeneous community and economic area whose parts lie in several Länder and which has a population of at least one million, one tenth of those entitled to vote in Bundestag elections submit a

petition to the effect that the area in question belong to one Land, a federal law shall be enacted within two years which shall determine whether boundaries of the affected Länder are to be modified pursuant to paragraph (2) of this Article or that a referendum is to be held in the affected Länder.

There is in truth a second aspect to federation which is the distribution of subjects between the centre and the regions. Ideally, subject distribution should be more dynamic than the permanent principles of the constitution and less dynamic than specific laws. Depending on the provisions of the relevant constitution, a number of options are available in this regard.

- The regions can enact uniform or mirror legislation on a particular subject, making it federal in effect.
- The regions can enact legislation authorizing the federal legislature to make law on a subject.[17]
- The so-called states' houses, namely chambers of the federal legislature where states have either equal or near equal representation, can serve as a means of encouraging federal laws to be responsive to the process of natural federation.
- Federal legislatures may, in the absence of constitutional impediments, delegate or devolve powers to the regions.

In this respect too, the German Constitution is noteworthy. It divides legislative powers into two categories: (1) exclusive powers of the federation and (2) concurrent powers. In the field of concurrent power, the Federation can legislate for the establishment of equivalent living conditions (*glichwertige lebenscerhälnisse*) in the federal territory or the maintenance of legal and economic unity in the interest of the entire state (*gesamstaatlich*). Where the need ceases, the Federation can withdraw from the field, restoring the power of the Länder.[18]

The Problem of Minorities within Federating States

The model herein proposed can be expected to work best where ethnically distinct groups occupy distinct regions. However, in many cases, this condition will fail to some degree. There are two kinds of situations that threaten the success of this model. One concerns disputed border areas where no ethnic community predominates. The other is where a region contains within it one or more significant ethnic minorities, either concentrated in enclaves or dispersed among the majority. These conditions impede the search for federal solutions in countries like Bosnia-Herzegovina and Sri Lanka.

The nationalistic response to these conditions sometimes takes the form of the brutal policy of 'ethnic cleansing'. This response is rejected not only because of its abhorrence, but also because it is likely to foreclose peaceful federation in the short and perhaps medium terms. The theory underlying this model suggests that the option of regional autonomy should be pursued as far as possible. This could mean considering arrangements such as cantonization (as in Switzerland) and asymmetrical devolution whereby special arrangements could be negotiated to devolve degrees of self-government on ethnic enclaves (as in Spain and the Russian Federation). Where a canton is created in an area where no ethnic group predominates, each group may not have full capacity for cultural self-determination, but would at least have some means of avoiding cultural subordination. In such a canton, the democratic process can be expected to promote fair treatment of all the communities.

This still leaves the question of minorities. One of the frequent causes of cross-border strife is the real or perceived mistreatment of ethnic minorities. While the potential for mistreatment of minorities can never be wholly eliminated, the constitutional guarantees of basic individual rights including, most importantly, the right to equal protection of the law and the right of individual exit (emigration), can go a long way in protecting minorities. As seen in the case of India discussed below, this ingredient is critical to the success of multi-ethnic federations. The right of exit is a guarantee of last resort which is of great importance. I have many Tamil friends in Sri Lanka who live in the predominantly Sinhala part of the island. Some of them support the campaign for the establishment of a Tamil state in the traditional Tamil homelands of northern and eastem Sri Lanka, but have no intention of living in such a state if it is established. They have told me that they not only see such a state as a means of Tamil cultural survival, but also as a home of last resort if their lives or liberties are imperilled.

It is legitimate to ask why the federal model is preferred to complete independence of regions as a solution to ethnic problems. In seeking to answer this question we must bear in mind that 'independence' is a relative notion and that nations are never totally independent in the sense of not being associated with other nations in legal and economic terms. If independence is taken to mean conventional state sovereignty, it has to be conceded that there may be situations where, at least in the short term, independence may be preferred to federation, despite the economic advantages which federation confers. However, the federal option has clear advantages in situations where the regions are ethnically differentiated but nevertheless have strong economic and demographic links.

The economies of the relevant regions may be already integrated to the point where total independence could lead to severe dislocation. For example, regions may share vital resources such as harbours and rivers or may depend on each other owing to specialization. Such conditions make it desirable to maintain a common market, which in turn may require overarching institutions. Again, where the ethnic groups have significant minority presence in each other's territories, the federal option offers tangible advantages. Regional representation on federal courts, legislatures and executives (consider the Bosnian settlements[19]) as well as the potential for reciprocity in the treatment of minorities, can serve as powerful safeguards.

Will Federation Lead to Unitarism?

If the thesis of this paper that regional autonomy together with domestic and cross-border freedom is accepted, the question must be asked whether the process generated by these conditions will lead to the obsolescence of federal arrangements as a consequence of economic and cultural integration. Is it possible that the growth of common interests will promote a highly centralized legal and administrative system? Historical experience suggests otherwise. Local government not only survived but thrived through the process of economic integration of communities. Even where countries have become culturally homogenized, federal arrangements have not disintegrated. There is hardly a country more homogeneous than Australia. Until recently, the Australian Labor Party was formally committed to the dismantling of the Australian federation. The party finally abandoned its anti-federalism when it realized that the policy was keeping it out of office.

The process of natural federation is unlikely to lead to unitary forms of government except, perhaps, in very small territories. The reason has to do with the fact that people tend to belong to several communities at the same time. Some of these communities are territorially defined and some are determined by cultural and economic interests. I live in a village outside Brisbane in Queensland, Australia. I belong to a local community with whom I share local concerns such as the cleanliness of my neighbourhood. Residents of other shires have little, if any interest in the condition of my neighbourhood's streets, playgrounds or public toilets. But with some of them, I form a wider community which is concerned with the region's schools, hospitals, trains, bus services and the like. Residents in far away places, such as Sydney, Melbourne, and Adelaide are not too worried about these things insofar as they affect the residents of southern Queensland. But with people all over Australia, I share concerns about the defence of our territory and political system, our communications, the freedom of interstate trade, our relations with other nations, and so on. And, with people all over the world, I share concerns about the freedom of the high seas and of the skies, protection from piracy and terrorism, the territorial integrity of nations and so on. This kind of differentiation is unavoidable in all but the smallest territorial nations. What is required is that constitutions aspire to assign power to the constituency most concerned with the subject of power.

The likely outcome of free cross-border interaction is that the law, insofar as it gives expression to general rules of conduct, will tend towards uniformity as individuals and firms look for a stable and predictable framework of rules for interaction. In this regard it is useful to recall the important distinction which Hayek drew between the abstract and end independent rules of conduct (*nomoi*), and the rules which serve particular purposes of organizations, including the rules of government (*thesei*). The rules of just conduct generally take the form of the private law and, insofar as the state directly intervenes to enforce these rules, the criminal law.[20] As residents of the diferent federating regions interact, they generate the impulses for the endogenous formation of this kind of common rules. In some common law federations such as Australia, there is one superior court which serves as the ultimate court of appeal for all states and territories. This pyramid jurisdiction promotes the uniformity of the private law subject, of course, to local legislative variations. Even in countries such as the United States, where there is no single common law superior court, the state superior courts are guided by each others' precedents and hence promote uniformity. Where legislation has displaced common law rules, cross-border interaction will generate pressure for standardizing relevant statute law. The phenomenon of the universalization of the law through commerce has been evident for centuries on the international plane. The Lex Mercatoria is the classic example of the emergence of a supra national system of rules. In the present age the pressure for the standardizing of national laws affecting international trade is immense and has produced a host of multilateral instruments such as the Vienna Convention on the Sale of Goods, the UNCITRAL Model Law on International Commercial Arbitration and most importantly the GATT and WTO treaty provisions.

While the rules of just conduct will tend to be universalized through the process of cross-border intercourse, a parallel phenomenon is less likely with respect to the rules concerning the provision of public goods. The reason is that in such matters, the local conditions will remain decisive and hence the need will continue for these rules to be determined by the representatives of the constituency most affected. However, even in this respect, the competition among the states may ensure that these rules would not diverge drastically. As Buchanan explains:

> We should predict, of course, that the separate states of a federal system would be compelled by the forces of competition to offer tolerably 'efficient' mixes of publicly provided goods and services, and, to the extent that in the different states exhibit roughly similar preferences, the actual budgetary mixes would not be predicted to diverge significantly one from the other. However, the point to be emphasized here (and which seems to be missed in so much of the discussion about the potential European federalism) is that any such standardization or regularization as might occur, would itself be an emergent property of competitive federalism rather than a property that might be imposed either by constitutional mandate or by central government authority.[21]

Will Federation Lead to Separation?

The hypothesis discussed herein is based on the assumption that individuals generally will act in their own self-interest. It is assumed that this tendency to engage in wealth maximization will prevail over ethno-regional sentiments which promote separatist and isolationist causes. If the assumption is false the model can be expected to catalyse the process of separation. Although there is no proof of this assumption, historical evidence in its support is encouraging. Apart from the Indian case-study which follows, one may point to the fact that similar schemes in places such as Spain and Belgium have not shown signs of leading to the breakup of those countries although each country has witnessed a degree of ethno-regional polarization.[22] Even if we assume that ethno-regionalism will remain strong under such a model, it does not mean that the regions will necessarily pursue isolation or separation. Regional interests may in fact fuel competitive federalism with regions vying for interstate markets and capital infusions, thus consolidating rather than undermining the federation.

The Fate of Soviet Federalism

If the theoretical framework developed in the preceding section is accepted, it would indicate that authoritarian political organization is not conducive to optimal federation. Dictatorships tend to suppress the exchange of the kind of information that is dispersed among individuals upon which the process of natural federation rests. A society under an absolute dictatorship is organized to a large extent on the information possessed by a single authority. The predicament of such a society is best captured in Hayek's memorable passage in *Law, Legislation and Liberty*.

> In none but the most simple kind of organization is it conceivable that all the details of all the activities are governed by a single mind. Certainly nobody has yet succeeded in deliberately arranging all the activities that go on in a complex society. If anyone ever did succeed in fully organizing such a society, it would no longer make use of many minds but would be altogether dependent on one mind; it would certainly not be very complex but extremely primitive—and so would soon be the mind whose knowledge and will determined everything. The facts which could enter into the design of such an order could be only those which were known and digested by this mind; and as only he could decide on action and thus gain experience, there would be none of that interplay of many minds in which alone mind can grow.[23]

Certainly there are no absolute dictatorships capable of controlling every detail of society. Dictators, of necessity, leave many decisions to individuals themselves. Nevertheless, they tend to drastically curtail the exchange of information and keep in their own hands decisions concerning the constitution, the laws and the character of the social order.

It would be misleading to equate the Soviet political system with petty dictatorships which serve personal or oligarchical ends, and it is not my intention to do so. But, it remains the case that the Soviet system was inimical to federalism in two ways.

Geographic federalism sat uncomfortably with Marxist-Leninist doctrine which informed the organization of the Soviet State. Marxist-Leninism tends to divide the world into economic classes as opposed to territorial, racial, religious or other cultural groupings. The struggle is between the capitalists and workers. Hence the slogan: 'workers of the world unite'. The unity of the workers, and their dictatorship, therefore, were the essential transitional conditions on the road to the ideal classless society. There was no place for geographic federalism in Marxist-Leninist theory. However, upon the establishment of the Soviet Union, Lenin was compelled to accept a form of cosmetic federalism to address the 'national problem'. The existence of distinct nations within the socialist compass necessitated the formulation of a theory of socialist federation which sought to reconcile the goal of the unity of the people with the diversity of the nations. As Viktor Knapp puts it, 'in the theoretical foundations of the origin of the Soviet and other socialist federations, the unity of the people and the diversity of nations meet and merge dialectically'.[24]

The synthesis which this federalism represented was, even in theory, a recipe for strong central control. The balance between the unity of the people and the diversity of the nations was undermined by the leading role of the Communist Party which embodied the unity of the people and spoke for the people. Although the Soviet Constitution separated government and Party, the central and regional governments were clearly subject to the policies and programmes determined by the Party in both foreign and domestic affairs.[25] This situation would not have mattered much, had the Communist Party also been organized on the federal principle. But this was not the case. The Central Committee and Presidium of the Party made decisions binding on all republics.[26]

Marxist-Leninism's central tenet of monopolizing the means of production, distribution and exchange as the way to usher in the utopian communist society, provided the greater obstacle for optimal federalism. The programme led to the collectivization or direct state control of vast sectors of the economy, the imposition of central planning and the severe curtailment of private enterprise. The suppression of private economic activity drastically reduced the exchange of knowledge dispersed among individuals upon which the process of natural federation depends.

The tremendous irony of the Soviet brand of federalism was that it achieved enforced unity while it lasted but stifled the spontaneous emergence of intercommunal commonalities of interest which alone foster enduring unity. The result was that when the enforcement ended with the collapse of communism, the federation broke asunder on regional lines. This apparent paradox is easily explained. The state monopolization and the regulation of economic activity within the Soviet Union, minimized the opportunities for individuals to engage in interregional exchange and to seek the satisfaction of their private ends through cross-border transactions. The omnipresent state mediated in most transactions, screening nationalities from each other. The barriers against individual economic intercourse were complemented by restrictions on political communication, association and travel. We know that private enterprise was not eliminated in the Soviet Union. The legendary Soviet black market in goods and services attests to the contrary. Nevertheless, Soviet law managed to localize private economic activity and discourage the growth of grassroots links among regions.

Compounding this problem was the Russian domination of the federation. In any system of unified policy-making, the more powerful regions are likely to predominate. Federalism counters this problem by decentralizing political power. The centralization of policy-making and economic planning in the Soviet Union allowed Russia to dominate the political process, further alienating the other republics. As Knapp points out, the absence of a Russian Communist Party as distinguished from the Soviet Party was symptomatic of this dominance. The Russian Party *was* the Soviet Party.[27]

There is every prospect of a revival of federalism among the republics of the former Soviet Union. Such federalism is likely to be based on emerging common markets engendered by economic liberalization within the republics. This liberalization is likely to regenerate the capillary connections among communities through which the information necessary for the process of natural federation flows.

After the breakup of the old Soviet Union, Russia opted for a multiethnic federation of its own. On 31 March 1992, 19 of the 21 republics

(Tartastan and Chechnya dissenting) adopted a Federal Treaty creating a federation of 21 republics and 11 autonomous territories. The new Russian Federation with its common market and the process of liberalization is likely to provide a new laboratory for testing the hypothesis developed in this paper.

The Union of India: A Fortuitous Federation

In contrast to the fate of the Soviet federation, the Indian republic has endured acid tests to emerge as a highly instructive case of successful federation. Like the Soviet Union, India had, and continues to have, a problem of ethnic regionalism. Yet, in India, the centrifugal forces have been contained with no signs of the nation disintegrating into separate states. While the problem was common to both federations, the constitutional responses could not have been more different. At the birth of each federation, unity was of primary concern. The Soviet Union emphasized the unity of the people while India extolled the unity of the nation. Both countries were ruled by powerful political parties, but the similarity appeared to end there. In the Soviet Union, the unity was sought, unsuccessfully it turned out, through enforcement. In India, unity is maintained, successfully it seems, through the democratic accommodation of ethnic-regional diversity.

Whereas the Soviet Constitution vested sovereignty in the Communist Party, the Indian Constitution transformed the idea of sovereignty by establishing majoritarian parliamentary democracy, constitutional (though defeasible) state autonomy, fundamental rights of individual citizens, protection for vulnerable cultural communities and an independent judiciary with power to oversee and uphold the constitutional order. The complement of rights guaranteed by the Constitution fuelled two apparently contrary forces within the Indian polity. First, the political participation rights combined with the existence of regional governments and legislatures, facilitated centrifugal regional politics. Second, the political and economic freedoms guaranteed under the constitution consolidated the grassroots integration of India in economic and political terms. Although in tension with each other, these two forces interacted to facilitate the process of natural federation.

The Indian world in the past consisted of kingdoms and principalities.

Even the empires which ruled the subcontinent from time to time were highly decentralized.[28] However, the political entities of India were not entirely co-extensive with ethnic homelands. The pre-Independence subdivisions of India had much to do with conquests, dynastic machinations and later, British administrative expedience.[29] The democratization of India after Independence unleashed regional pressures for the readjustment of its subdivisions to reflect better the ethnic distributions.[30] Several such readjustments occurred constitutionally.

The territorial readjustment of India to reflect better the ethnic and linguistic geography of the nation was facilitated by a provision which, in theory, is inimical to federalism. Article 3 of the Indian Constitution empowers the Union Parliament to unilaterally (without the consent of the affected states) alter state boundaries, to transfer territory from one state to another and rename any state. In theory this power could be used to mutilate the federation. Yet, in practice, it has proved fortuitous to the process of natural federation. As the leading Indian jurist H.M. Seervai observed, 'it is not the Union which has re-drawn the map of India; on the contrary, the hands of a reluctant Union have been forced by extra-constitutional agitation in the States, since most of them wanted to be regrouped on a linguistic basis'.[31] What Seervai terms 'extraconstitutional agitation', was, for the most part, perfectly legal and constitutional. The crystallization of regional sentiment, its articulation and political execution were facilitated by the very freedoms secured by the Constitution.

While the Indian political map was re-drawn on ethnic lines, in other respects, the unity of the nation continued to be consolidated under the Constitution. The British administered India as a common market. After Independence, the Congress Party which enjoyed a long period of political dominance at the Union and state levels implemented a policy of maintaining a mixed and regulated economy. To the extent that the policy reduced the scope for private economic activity, it constrained the forces of natural federation. But, unlike the Soviet Constitution, the Indian Constitution contains a panoply of constitutional safeguards which maintain the capillary process of national integration.

For a start, the Constitution devotes Part XII (Articles 301-7) to maintaining the freedom of trade, commerce and intercourse among the states and prohibits preferential or discriminatory treatment of interstate trade. This Part is in addition to the wide-ranging 'Bill of Rights' contained in Part III (Articles 12 to 35). Article 14 of the Constitution guarantees equality before the law to all citizens. This guarantee is supplemented by the provisions of Articles 15, 16, 17 and 18 which prohibit discrimination in all its forms. These provisions have the cumulative effect of placing an important fetter on the capacity of the Union and the states to impede economic and cultural dealings among individuals through discriminatory laws and executive actions. Article 16 has added significance. It prevents the Union and states from discriminating in their hiring practices against any person on the ground, *inter alia*, of residence. The effect of this provision is to make the residents of each State eligible for employment in other states and in the Union public service. In a country served by an immense public sector, this eligibility is a powerful force for integration.

The Indian Bill of Rights goes on to guarantee; in Article 19, the freedom of speech and expression, the right to peaceable assembly, the freedom to form associations, the freedom to move throughout the territory of India and to reside in any part of that territory and the freedom to carry on any occupation, trade or business. Article 20 guarantees the classic personal liberties and due process rights. Article 32 confers enforcement rights by recourse to the jurisdiction of the Supreme Court whose independence the Constitution guarantees. Underpinning the constitutional order are the provisions of Part XV (Articles 324-9) aimed at ensuring free and fair elections at Union and state levels.

It is true that the rights and freedoms conferred by the Constitution are far from complete. The Constitution allows the abridgement of these safeguards on broadly defined grounds. [The most significant restriction, from the theoretical standpoint taken in this essay, is found in the 1951 Amendment to Article 19(6) which permits the Union and the states to establish trading monopolies.] I am also not suggesting that the Indian Bill of Rights is always respected by the Union and state governments and legislatures or that they are amenable to easy judicial enforcement. Mrs Gandhi demonstrated how vulnerable these rights are to the will of a government which commands large legislative majorities. But I do submit that in normal times, the constitutional framework of rights and liberties provides formidable fetters on government, and consequently ensures the degree of individual autonomy which is critical to harmonizing the processes of constructive and natural federation. In recent times, India has embarked upon a programme of extensive economic liberalization. In my view, the new policy is likely to strengthen the Indian federation by intensifying grass-roots interaction among individuals.

The history of Indian federation contains important lessons. There is a tendency to overlook these lessons because of simplistic inferences concerning India's serious problems with poverty, ethnic strife, political and corporate corruption and technological shortcomings. I suspect that there is a widespread inarticulate assumption that a nation which manifests these kinds of problems cannot be instructive on questions of good governance. Those who judge the Indian Constitution by reference to conditions prevailing in contemporary Western society are making a serious mistake. The efficacy of the Indian Constitution must be judged in terms of the challenges posed by the Indian situation. In my view, no constitution of a Western democracy has been subjected to harsher tests. The Indian experience suggests that the success of federations depends on the extent to which the federal arrangement gives expression to the natural or self-organized pattern of human communities. It follows that federations which deny substantial autonomy to ethnically self-conscious regions are inherently unstable.

NOTES

1. A. Smith, *The Theory of Moral Sentiments* (London, 1759), Part 6, Chap. 2.
2. S. Corbridge, 'Federalism, Hindu Nationalism and Mythologies of Governance in Modern India', in G. Sunith (ed.), *Federalism: Multiethnic Challenge* (London, 1995), p. 123.
3. 'Kashmir autonomy after poll: India', *The Australian,* 2 July 1996, p. 9.
4. On the need for conceptual clarity, see R.L. Watts, 'Contemporary Views on Federalism', in B. de Villers (ed.), *Evaluating Federal Systems* (Cape Town, 1994), p. 7.
5. Ibid.
6. Ibid.
7. Ibid.
8. C.J. Frederick, *Trends of Federalism in Theory and Practice* (London, 1968), p. 173.
9. Ibid.

10. W.H. Stewart, *Concepts of Federalism* (Lanham, MD, 1984), p. 72.
11. See studies cited by Stewart, *Federalism*, p. 72 (estate federalism) and p. 70 (feudal federalism).
12. F.A. Hayek, *Law, Legislation and Liberty*, vol. 1 (London, 1982), pp. 46-7.
13. For a summation of the state of this discipline, see S. Kauffman, *At Home in the Universe: The Search for the Laws of Self-Organization and Complexity* (New York, 1995), particularly Chap. 4.
14. Article 5. The procedure requires two-thirds of both Houses of Congress or two-thirds of State legislatures to *propose* an amendment and three-fourths of state legislatures or state conventions (as Congress determines) to *approve* it.
15. Article 4, Sec. 3. The procedure requires the consent of the legislatures of the concerned states of Congress?
16. Section 123 of the Australian Constitution requires the Parliament and the majority of electors of a State to approve the lateration of the limits of such State. Contrast this procedure with the referendum procedure prescribed by Sec.128 for the amendment of the Constitution.
17. See for example, Sec. 51 (xxxii) of the Australian Constitution.
18. Article 72.
19. The terms of the Dayton Peace Agreement signed on 14 December 1995 provides for a Constitution of Bosnia and Herzegovina under which Bosnians, Croats and Serbs are guaranteed representation on the Parliamentary Assembly, the Presidency and the Constitutional Court. Source: United States, Defence Intelligence Agency, *Handbook on the Dayton Peace Agreement*, Defence Intelligence Reference Document PC-1510-100-96 (Washington, DC, 1996), pp. 10-11.
20. The Crown's intervention in criminal cases was initially driven by the profit motive. Since convicted felons forfeited their lands and goods to the Crown, it made revenue sense to convert customary law wrongs into felonies. See historical sources cited in B. Benson, *The Enterprise of Law: Justice Without State* (San Francisco, 1990), pp. 50-1.
21. J.M. Buchanan, 'Federalism as an Ideal Political Order and an Objective for Constitutional Reform', *Publis*, Spring 1995, pp. 22-3.
22. For Belgium, see A. Murphy, 'Belgium's Regional Divergence: Along the Road to Federation', in Smith, *Federalism: The Multiethnic Challenge*, pp. 93-6; for Spain see M. Guibernau, 'Spain: A Federation in the Making?', ibid., pp. 246-52.
23. Hayek, *Law, Legislation and Liberty*, p. 49.
24. V. Knapp, 'Central and Eastern European Federations: Communist Theory and Practice', in K. Knop, S. Ostry, R. Simeon and K. Swinton (eds.), *Rethinking Federalism: Citizens, Markets and Governments in a Changing World* (Vancouver, 1995), p. 321.
25. Ibid., pp. 322-3.

26. Ibid., p. 323.
27. Ibid.
28. D.J. Elazer, *Federal Systems of the World* (2nd edn., Harlow, 1994), p. 104. The most centralized, perhaps, was the last one, that of the British Raj.
29. Freidrich, *Trends of Federalism,* note 6, p. 136.
30. Ibid., pp. 135-6.
31. H.M. Seervai, *Constitutional Law of India: A Critical Commentary*, vol. 1 (3rd edn., Bombay, 1983), p. 154.

7

Regionalism, Hindu Nationalism, and Party Politics in India's Federal System

PAUL R. BRASS

Fifteen years ago I attempted to assess the long-term tendencies in Indian politics in the light of Mrs Gandhi's unprecedented extensions of central government power during the Emergency, the subsequent defeat of the Congress and the installation of India's first non-Congress government at the centre, and the increasing abuse by central governments, Congress or non-Congress, of the powers of President's Rule to dismiss state governments and administer them directly from the centre. I argued then that the long-term tendencies were towards regionalism, pluralism, and decentralization, but that some features and aspects of Indian government and politics persisted in favour of centralization. In the past five years, momentous changes have taken place in India that I believe are working towards the further evolution of regionalizing tendencies and the weakening of centralism. These include the increased competitiveness of politics at the central level, the end of the Nehru dynasty consequent upon the assassination of Rajiv Gandhi in 1991, the results of state legislative and parliamentary elections held between 1993 and 1996, and the installation of India's third coalition government at the centre in the aftermath of the 1996 Lok Sabha elections. However, a major force in favour of centralization also persists, reflected in the increased strength and militancy of Hindu nationalism and its manifestation in a multiplicity of organizations in the Rashtriya Swayamsevak Sangh (RSS) 'family', including especially the Bharatiya Janata Party (BJP) and the Vishwa Hindu Parishad (VHP). Here I re-assess the arguments made fifteen years ago and consider the likely future direction of the opposed tendencies and their consequences for the Indian federal system.

The Implications and Sustainability of Coalition Politics in India's Federal System

The centering force in India from the inception of the federal system was the Indian National Congress, occupying its place as the dominant party at the centre and in nearly all the states under the leadership of a succession of scions of the Nehru family. In its heyday, the Congress ruled alone, offering to opposition parties and dissident factions only two prospects: join or remain in the Congress and hope to exercise power, or go into the political wilderness where defeat and loss of power were most likely. Congress dominance prevailed until the Fourth General elections of 1967.

Since 1967, increased competitiveness has marked Indian politics, though the decline of the Congress has been slow and the rise of alternative parties and coalitions has been gradual, uncertain, and often ephemeral. Nevertheless, it is now evident that increased competitiveness and coalition politics have brought to an end the Congress-dominant system at the centre and in all the Indian states. It is important, therefore, to begin by assessing past experience with coalition politics and comparing it with the coalition that came to power at the centre in the aftermath of the 1996 parliamentary elections.

The first large-scale experiment with coalition politics occurred between 1967 and 1971 when the Congress lost power in half the states and was replaced for the most part by fragile, unstable, and short-lived governments. Although this period was marked by apparent chaos, instability, and increased personal opportunism and corruption, it proved to be a prelude to fundamental changes in the nature of Indian politics, of which two seem to me to have been especially important. The first is that chaos and instability were followed by the establishment in several states of either stable regimes dominated by regional parties, or parties whose strengths were confined to one or two states, or by the emergence of stable patterns of competitive politics and alternations in power. These included most notably the entrenchment of the Dravida Munnetra Kazhagam (DMK) and later the All-India Anna Dravida Munnetra Kazhagam (AIADMK) as the dominant party in Tamil Nadu, the

Communist Party of India (Marxist) (CPM) in West Bengal, and alternating coalitions in Kerala. In most other states, however, the Congress ultimately recaptured power as Mrs Gandhi consolidated her leadership of the party and the country and seemed to restore in large measure the old Congress-dominant system. In still other cases, most notably Punjab, no stable pattern emerged and the results were ultimately disastrous. Overall, however, the return of Congress dominance proved temporary while the entrenchment of regional parties and unique party systems in particular states proved to be more long-lasting.

The second important development in this period was the rise of parties based on the middle peasantry and backward castes and the beginnings of the entry of backward caste politicians into positions of political power in several states, particularly in the north. The changes that began then are still working themselves out and have become increasingly important not only in the various states but at the centre as well. In fact, the introduction of the caste divide at the centre, deliberately avoided for the first four decades after Independence, has been a direct consequence of struggles in north India by backward caste leaders, groups, and parties against the dominance of elite castes in politics, administration, and the rural economy. Those struggles also came to the fore initially in the days of coalition politics in Uttar Pradesh (UP) between 1967 and 1971.

In addition to the experience with coalition politics in the states, there were two periods of coalition politics at the centre, which preceded the United Front government established in 1996. The first was the post-Emergency Janata regime, which lasted from 1975 to 1977. The Janata government achieved its main purpose of reestablishing the basic structures of the parliamentary regime that Mrs Gandhi had begun to dismantle. However, it disintegrated as a consequence of both leadership and inter-party conflicts involving struggles for control over the states. The leaders of the non-Congress parties knew and practised precisely what Mrs Gandhi knew and practised, if not so well: that no leader, party, or coalition could remain in power in Delhi without maintaining effective control over most state governments.

A further development in central politics in this period was the increasing importance of conflicting personal interests, which had for long been critical in state politics and which have since this period been critical as well for the stability of governments at the centre.

Conflicting personal interests not only split the Janata Party and brought down the government, they also brought down the government that succeeded it, that of Charan Singh at the head of a breakaway faction. Originally brought to power with the support of Mrs Gandhi and the Congress, it fell within a few weeks when Mrs Gandhi insisted as a condition for her continuing support upon the withdrawal of all cases against her and her son, Sanjay, concerning their abuses of power during the Emergency regime. Thus, struggles for power, not ideology, brought down the Janata government. Those struggles then, before, and since have revolved around two axes: relations between the centre and the states, and relations between individual leaders.

The second experiment with coalition politics at the centre, the Janata Dal National Front government of V.P. Singh, which was in power between 1989 and 1991, bore some similarities with the previous one, but inaugurated profound new developments as well. The element of personal confrontation was central to the rise of the Janata Dal, which arose as a consequence of issues concerning personal political corruption. V.P. Singh, who had been Finance Minister in the central government, uncovered evidence suggesting that the highest level leaders of the Congress, including Rajiv Gandhi, had been siphoning off millions of dollars from defence contracts for their personal use. The Congress organization in north India, particularly in UP, was actually definitively destroyed as a consequence of Rajiv Gandhi's efforts to prevent the revelation of the alleged proofs of his malfeasance and corruption. The Congress allied with non-Congress parties and leaders to stave off V.P. Singh, who was expelled from the party. Subsequently, Singh formed a new opposition alliance against the Congress. These forces with which the Congress then allied, especially what is now known as the Samajwadi Party (SP) led by Mulayam Singh Yadav and the RSS, whose cadres man the local BJP organizations, ultimately displaced the Congress from power in UP.

The second Janata experiment ended in some ways quite similarly to the first, but in other ways profoundly differently. The end of the first experiment was marked by rancorous divisions between the former Socialist and Congress components of the Janata party and the remnants of the former Jan Sangh. The BJP, the reincarnation of the former Jan Sangh, chose not to repeat the mistakes its leaders thought they had made in 1977-9, and refused to join the National Front government in 1989, choosing instead to support it from outside. The government ultimately fell when it withdrew its support.

On this occasion, however, fundamental issues of national and social policy were involved: reservations for backward castes in public sector jobs and Hindu-Muslim relations. The government was, in effect, brought down as a consequence of competing manoeuvres by the Janata Dal and the BJP to establish firm bases of political support in the electorate, both eyeing in particular the north Indian electorate. The Janata Dal sought to consolidate its base among the backward castes while the BJP sought to gain support among upper caste Hindus by inciting anti-Muslim feelings. It was during this process of competition between these two non-Congress forces, concentrated mostly in north India, that the Congress was reduced to third place and decisively eliminated as a serious contender for power in the two most important states, Uttar Pradesh and Bihar. Therefore, divisions at the centre and in the states interlocked with substantial mutual consequences, making it clear once again that stable governance at the centre requires effective political control in most states.

It must now be considered how the post-1996 election coalition at the centre compares with its predecessors. In important respects, it continued social and political trends initiated by them, principally the increasing importance in its leadership and support bases of backward castes and the increasing prominence of non-Westernized politicians with rural roots, who initially held the most important Cabinet positions in the central government, including the prime ministership and such important portfolios as defence. The most important difference between this coalition and its forerunners was the predominance within it of regional or regionally-confined political parties.

The fragility of the United Front coalition formed after the 1996 elections was evident from the beginning. Within a year of its formation, in 1997, it faced several crises that threatened its continuance, of which the most serious was caused by the withdrawal of Congress support in the Lok Sabha in April, leading to the replacement of Prime Minister Deve Gowda by Inder Kumar Gujral in April and the temporary withdrawal from the coalition of one of its regional components, the Tamil Manila Congress. It had also to face internal divisions concerning the formation of a new government in Uttar Pradesh and concerning corruption charges against Laloo Yadav, the leader of the Janata Dal and the chief minister of Bihar.

There are several reasons for the fragility of the United Front coalition. First, the governing components consisted of a multiplicity of small parties. Second, its continuance depended on the support of the Congress, which was larger by far than any single element in the coalition. Furthermore, Congress support for the coalition depended primarily on the government continuing to refrain from prosecuting powerful Congress people, including the former prime minister, Narasimha Rao, other prominent Congress leaders, and persons associated with the Gandhi family, on corruption charges. Overall, therefore, the fragility of the coalition arose from its heterogeneity and the fragmentation of its components, on the one hand, and the importance of personal interests and corruption as powerful forces determining the fate of alliances, on the other. I consider below what might come next, after presenting a brief overview of the history of centre-state relations after 1947.

Centre-state Relations in the Absence of a Dominant Centre

Broadly speaking, there have been three distinct periods in the evolution of centre-state relations. Under Nehru's leadership, the centre provided unchallenged national leadership and policy guidance to the states, but left a large measure of political autonomy to them in practice. During the period of Mrs Gandhi's dominance of Indian politics, the federal system was transformed. The boundaries between central and state politics were eroded and state party bosses were destroyed. The predominant pattern was one of central intervention in state politics, that is to say, penetration by the central government through party politics, including constant efforts to divide state political organizations, including even the Congress itself, in order to maintain the supreme authority of Indira Gandhi and her control over the entire country. It also involved increasing use of central government funds for patronage purposes in the states and to establish an independent base for her in the countryside through such measures as the anti-poverty programmes.

India in 1996 entered a new, third period, marked by three important features. First, there was no strong single party in the governing coalition at the centre. Second, the central government was now penetrated by regional elites, reversing the predominant pattern under Indira Gandhi. Third, the main defender of a strong centre was now the party of militant Hindu nationalism, the BJP, which was the only opposition party waiting for this government to collapse, hoping for a new election from which it would emerge as the majority party in the country.

The question now is which of these conflicting tendencies, apparent for decades, will ultimately prevail and with what consequences. Several of the regional parties have, in the past and since the 1996 election as well, made demands for more autonomy for the states.[2] These demands will be more difficult to ignore than formerly since some combination of regional parties is likely to be indispensable for any future government as for the present one. The BJP, as I will show below, is not in a position now, and is not likely soon, to be in a position to rule alone. It too, therefore, will ultimately have to compromise on issues of regional autonomy. That issue however is very much tied up with Kashmir, which makes such a compromise on the part of the BJP quite difficult. It is necessary now to consider these alternative tendencies in the light of the election results of the early 1990s—those for the state legislative assemblies held between 1993 and 1996[3] and the parliamentary elections of 1996, and to see how they compare with previous elections.

Centralizing and Regionalizing Tendencies in Indian Politics in Light of Recent Election Results

The vote for the Congress

The Congress organization clearly has been the leading political institution in post-Independence India. Since Independence, there has always been one predominant Congress organization in the country, which has always been either in power or has been the largest opposition party in Parliament and which has also always had broader support in most states of the Indian Union than any other party, even though it has never won a clear majority of the popular votes in the country (Table 1). Fifteen years ago I had argued that the most important support for maintaining if not strengthening central government powers was the continuing universal presence of the Congress as the only national party. What is the situation today? Despite the disastrous results of the 1996 election for the Congress, the party has retained in form if not

TABLE 1: VOTE AND SEAT SHARES FOR CONGRESS AND SECOND PLACE PARTY IN ELEVEN PARLIAMENTARY ELECTIONS, 1952-96

Election	Vote (%)			Seats (N)		Seats (%)		
	Congress	2nd Party	Interval	Congress	2nd Party	Congress	2nd Party	Interval
1952	45	11	34	364	16	74	3	71
1957	48	10	38	371	27	75	5	70
1962	45	10	35	361	29	73	6	67
1967	41	9	32	283	44	54	8	46
1971	44	10	34	352	25	68	5	63
1977	35	41	-6	154	295	28	54	-26
1980	43	19	24	353	41	67	8	59
1984	48	7	41	415	30	77	6	71
1989	40	18	22	197	143	37	27	10
1991	37	20	17	227	119	45	23	22
1996	29	20	9	140	161	26	30	-4

NOTE: The TDP (Telugu Desam Party), a regional Andhra party, actually won the second largest number of seats in this Lok Sabha.

in substance its traditional place in three respects: it retained support in all major states of the Indian Union; although its vote share in the country was by far the lowest in its history, it polled a larger percentage of the total vote than any other party; and although the post-1996 election parliament has been divided for purposes of defining government and opposition into sets of coalitions rather than into single parties, the Congress remained in 1996 the second largest party in parliament, after the BJP.

A more detailed study at the 1996 election results in comparison with previous elections, however, reveals how far the Congress has fallen and suggests quite unfavourable prospects for its future role in the Indian political order. Consider first the overall picture of Congress strength in the country and the dramatic change from its former position of dominance, as revealed in Table 1 and Figure 1, which show the vote shares for the Congress and the second place party in the eleven parliamentary elections held between 1952 and 1996. Note first the enormous gap between the Congress and the second place party in the heyday of Congress dominance 1952-71 and what has happened since. In 1977, in the aftermath of the Emergency, the Congress was displaced

FIGURE 1: VOTE SHARES FOR CONGRESS AND SECOND PLACE PARTY IN ELEVEN PARLIAMENTARY ELECTIONS, 1952-96

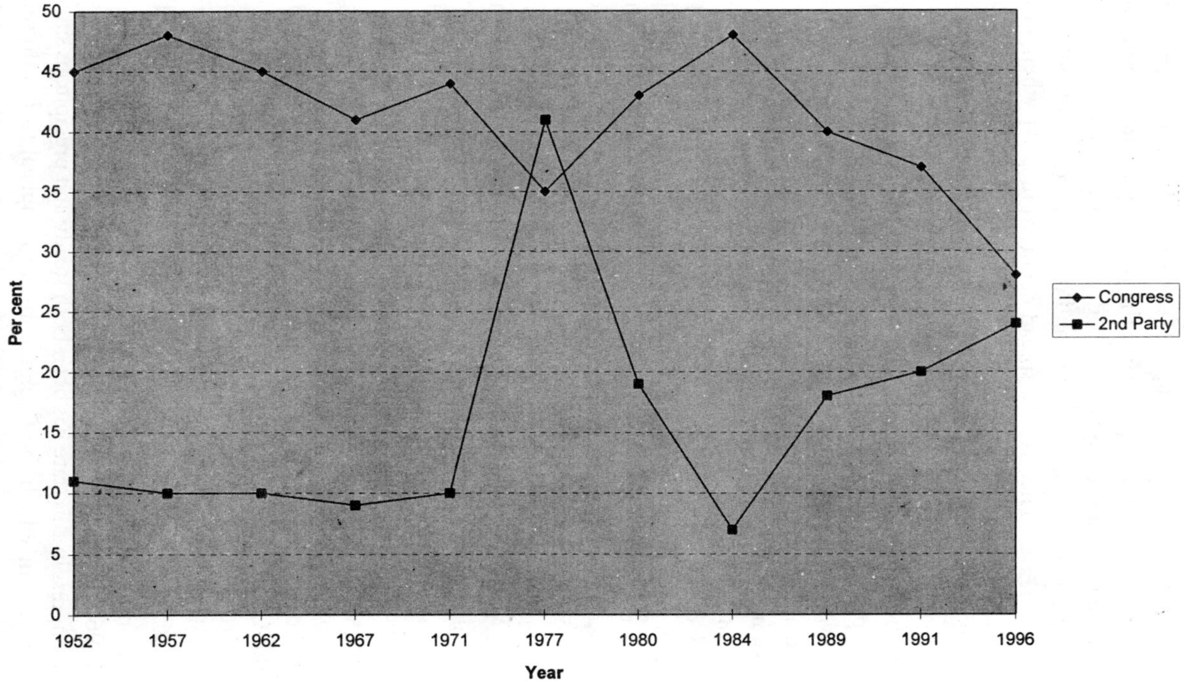

from power at the centre for the first time and polled a smaller percentage of votes than its principal rival, the Janata Party. However, after the disintegration of the latter party, the return of Indira Gandhi to power and then the succession to her son after her assassination in 1984, the old gap between the Congress and its nearest rival not only returned, but increased. The greatest spread occurred in 1984 when an interval of 41 percentage points of vote share separated the dominant Congress from the second place party, the BJP, which won a mere 7 per cent of the vote. This resurgence of the Congress and the precipitous decline in the national strength of its nearest competitor, however, proved temporary. Subsequent elections have shown a new pattern of convergence, a gradually descending line of support for the Congress and an ascending line of support for its nearest competitor the Janata Dal in 1989, and the BJP in 1991 and 1996. Less than nine percentage points of vote share separated the Congress and the BJP in 1996.

Consider next Table 2, which compares the Congress vote share with that of the second largest party in the 1991 Lok Sabha elections and the subsequent legislative assembly elections held in ten states between 1993 and 1995. In 8 of the 10 states, the Congress vote declined, the exceptions being Himachal Pradesh and Gujarat. Further, in half these states in 1993-5—in Bihar, Uttar Pradesh, Gujarat, Karnataka, and Andhra Pradesh—the vote for the largest non-Congress party was higher than that for the Congress. Finally, in the two most populous states, UP and Bihar, the Congress vote in 1993-5 declined below 20 per cent and in UP, the Congress vote was below 20 per cent in both 1991 and 1993, the year in which the most recent UP Legislative Assembly elections were held.[4]

For a retrospective view, consider Figure 2, showing vote shares for the Congress in six states at the parliamentary elections from 1952 to 1996.[5] Note first that in all previous elections, in only one of these, Tamil Nadu, and only in 1971, did the Congress vote go below 20 per cent. In 1996, there were three such states: Uttar Pradesh and Bihar in the north and Tamil Nadu in the south. Further, in UP the vote in 1996 fell below 10 per cent. Consider further that the decline of the Congress in this state has been both steady and precipitous since 1984, the year in which the Congress began its appeal to Hindu sentiment and began to lose decisively the Muslim vote. In Bihar, where similar changes have taken place with respect to both the loss of the Muslim vote and the rise of backward and lower caste groups, the Congress

FIGURE 2: LOK SABHA VOTE SHARES FOR CONGRESS IN SIX STATES, 1952–96

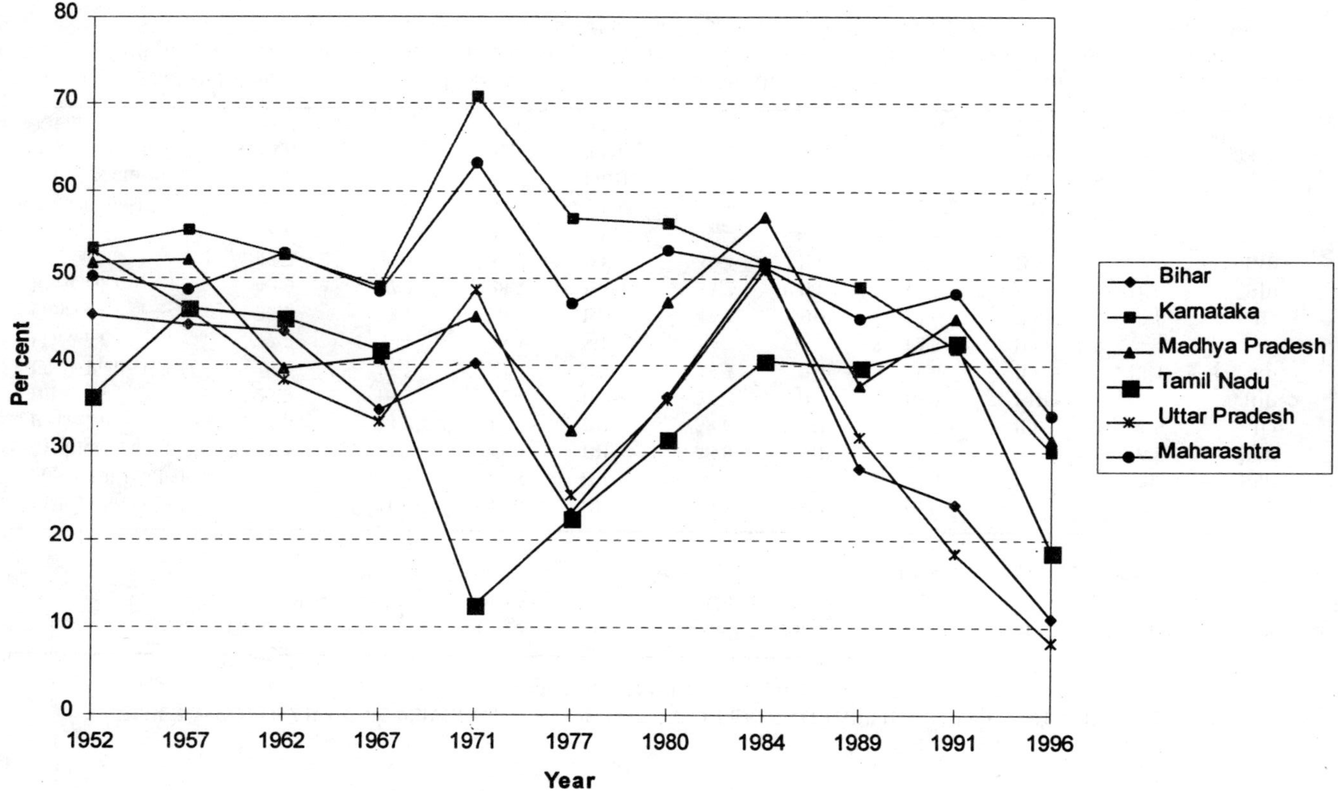

TABLE 2: POPULAR VOTE PERCENTAGES OF THE TWO LEADING PARTIES IN THE 1991 LOK SABHA 1993-95 LEGISLATIVE ASSEMBLY ELECTIONS, BY STATE

State	Congress Vote 1991	Congress Vote 1993-5	Largest Non-Cong. Vote 1991	Party	Largest Non-Cong. Vote 1993-5	Party	Second Largest Non-Cong. Vote 1991	Party	Second Largest Non-cong. Vote 1993-5	Party
Maharashtra	48.3	31.0	20.6	BJP	16.1	SHS	10.9	JD	12.8	BJP
Himachal Pradesh	46.2	49.4	42.8	BJP	36.1	BJP	7.0	JD	2.2	BSP
Madhya Pradesh	45.3	40.7	41.9	BJP	38.8	BJP	4.2	JD	6.8	BSP
Rajasthan	44.0	38.7	40.9	BJP	38.6	BJP	6.2	JD	6.9	JD
Bihar	23.9	16.5	32.4	JD	27.6	JD	16.9	BJP	13.1	BJP
Uttar Pradesh	18.3	15.1	32.9	BJP	33.3	BJP	21.6	JD	18.1	SP
Haryana	37.2	—	25.4	SJP	—	—	12.5	JD	—	—
Gujarat	28.2	32.7	50.6	BJP	42.5	BJP	12.6	JD(G)	2.8	JD
Karnataka	42.0	27.3	28.7	BJP	33.2	JD	18.5	JD	16.7	BJP
Orissa	43.7	39.4	34.2	JD	35.4	JD	9.9	BJP	7.9	BJP
Kerala	38.8	—	20.7	CPM	—	—	5	ML	—	—
West Bengal	36.2	—	35.1	CPM	—	—	11.7	BJP	—	—
Tamil Nadu	42.6	—	22.7	DMK	—	—	18.1	AIADMK	—	—
Andhra Pradesh	44.6	32.3	32.6	TDP	42.2	TDP	9.5	BJP	3.88	TDP
Assam	28.5	—	17.6	AGP	—	—	9.6	BJP	—	—

SOURCES: The 1991 figures come from All India Radio, Lok Sabha Poll: An AIR Analysis (New Delhi: Government of India, All India Radio, News Services Division, 1991), pp. 17-42; the 1993 figures come from Yogendra Yadav, 'Reconfiguration in Indian Politics: State Assembly Elections, 1993-95', *Economic and Political Weekly,* XXXI, Nos. 2 and 3 (13-20 January 1996), p. 100.

decline has also been steady and precipitous, its vote share being barely above 10 per cent in 1996 and just above the Congress' vote share in UP in that election.

In substance, therefore, the results of this past election though not in the least surprising in view of the declining performance of the Congress over the last several national and state assembly elections represent a far more serious blow to the position of this formerly dominant party than would appear at our first glance at the 1996 election results, which appeared to sustain the idea of its continuing universal presence. Though it retained support in all states of the Indian Union, it was no longer a serious competitor for power in three of the largest states, UP, Bihar, and Tamil Nadu. If its vote share remained the largest of any party in the country, it was not far ahead of that for the BJP. More seriously, its share had fallen below the critical level of one-third which had allowed it in the past because of the working of the single member plurality district system (first-past-the-post)to win a disproportionate share of seats in relation to its votes as long as the opposition was divided. Finally, though it has retained more even support among most segments of the electorate than any other party, this support is more of a residual vote than a reflection of its continuing broad appeal. That is, a segment of nearly every category of the population continues to vote for the Congress, but there are fewer categories of voters who support the Congress strongly, as for example Muslims and Scheduled Castes formerly did in large parts of the country and upper castes in north India. It is a more serious matter for the Congress that it has lost the disproportionate and intense support of major categories of numerically strong and economically powerful voting groups and critical blocs. Its even support among many categories of voters does not compensate for these heavy losses. Consequently, it appears that the Congress, now a minor party in the most populous states, has definitively and irretrievably lost its position as the centre and centering force in the Indian political order.

The vote for the non-Congress parties

With the exception of the 1977 elections, no other party ever polled even as much as half the Congress vote in the country as a whole, before 1991. However, in recent elections, the BJP has done so. Less than nine percentage points of vote share separated the BJP from the Congress in the 1996 elections.

The Election Commission has always made a distinction in publishing the figures for parliamentary elections between 'national' parties and other parties. For a time, there appeared to be a trend toward 'nationalization' of the party system, with the vote for the 'national' non-Congress parties having gone up from the 20-30 per cent range in the 1950s to the 30-40 per cent range between 1962 and 1971 to the 40-50 per cent range in 1977 and 1980, with a corresponding decline in the relative vote shares of the category of 'other parties and independents' (Table 3). The trend, however, was partly illusory and appeared especially chimerical in the face of the 1984 election results, when the collective vote share of the 'national' opposition parties was reduced to 29.7 per cent, a figure lower than any in the previous five elections. In the last three elections, in 1989, 1991, and 1996, the balance between the combined vote for all national parties (Congress and opposition), on the one hand, and other parties and independents, on the other hand, has reverted to the pre-1977 range. A significant difference, however, is that the relationship between the Congress and other 'national' parties has been reversed: the Congress no longer completely dominates the national arena. The combined strength of other 'national' parties outweighs that of the Congress while, at the

TABLE 3: VOTE SHARES FOR THE CONGRESS, 'NATIONAL' OPPOSITION PARTIES, AND OTHERS IN PARLIAMENTARY ELECTIONS, 1952-96

(per cent)

Year	Congress	'National' Opposition	All National Parties	Other Parties & Independents	Total
1952	45.0	22.8	67.8	32.3	100.0
1957	47.8	25.2	73.0	27.0	100.0
1962	44.7	33.7	78.4	21.5	100.0
1967	40.8	35.5	76.3	23.8	100.0
1971	43.7	34.1	77.8	22.2	100.0
1977	34.5	50.1	84.6	15.3	100.0
1980	42.7	42.4	85.1	14.9	100.0
1984	48.1	29.7	77.8	22.2	100.0
1989	39.5	39.8	79.3	20.7	100.0
1991	36.4	40.7	77.1	22.8	100.0
1996	28.8	40.3	69.1	30.9	100.0

TABLE 4: CONGRESS AND ITS CLOSEST COMPETITOR, BY STATE,* PARLIAMENTARY ELECTIONS 1991

(per cent)

State	Congress (I)	Closest Competitor
Andhra Pradesh	44.6	32.6 (Telugu Desam)
Assam	28.5	17.6 (AGP)
Bihar	23.9	32.4 (DMKP/Lok Dal(B))
Gujarat	28.2	50.6 (BJP)
Haryana	37.2	25.4 (SJP)
Himachal Pradesh	46.2	42.8 (BJP)
Karnataka	42.0	28.7 (BJP)
Kerala	38.8	20.7 (CPM)
Madhya Pradesh	45.3	41.9 (BJP)
Maharashtra	48.3	20.6 (BJP)
Orissa	43.7	20.6 (Janata)
Rajasthan	44.0	40.9 (BJP)
Tamil Nadu	42.6	22.7 (DMK)
Uttar Pradesh	18.3	32.9 (BJP)
West Bengal	36.2	35.1 (CPM)

NOTE: * Only the larger states of the Indian Union have been included. Excluded are Goa, Manipur, Meghalaya, Nagaland, Sikkim, and Tripura, which elect only one or two seats each to the Lok Sabha. Elections were not held in Jammu & Kashmir because of disturbed conditions prevailing there at the time of the 1991 General Elections. Elections in Punjab were postponed for the same reasons until March 1992, but per cent vote shares were not available at the time of writing.

SOURCE: *Lok Sabha Poll,* pp. 17-42.

same time, the total vote share for other parties and independents, 30.9 per cent, is higher than for any previous general election except the first. Thus the Congress faces simultaneously stronger competition from national parties as well as from regionally specific parties and other parties lacking a national or even a cross-regional reach.

Except for the Congress, the Bharatiya Janata Party (BJP), and the Communist parties, none of the other 'national' parties has endured. Moreover, the second-place party changed in every election between 1952, when the Socialist Party (SP) came in second with 10.6 per cent of the vote, and 1991 when the BJP polled 20.8 per cent. The BJP is the only political party in the post-Independence period to come second in vote shares in two successive elections, 1991 and 1996. It is also important to note that in any single parliamentary election the second-place party is likely to be different in different states, as for example in

1991 (Table 4). Finally, many of the so-called national parties did not have a genuine national spread at all. In general, therefore, despite the considerable evidence of Congress institutional and electoral decline, it remained the case after the 1996 elections that the Congress was 'the only party with a base all over the country' and that no national alternative to the Congress existed.[6] At the same time, it is evident that the Indian political order is at a turning point in which the decline of the Congress seems irreversible and that the BJP is intent upon establishing itself as the only viable alternative to a formerly dominant, but now sinking, Congress, on the one hand, and a fragmented third force of disparate parties, on the other.

The BJP seeks to replace the Congress in every respect as the national party of India and is assiduously striving to attain a universal presence in every state of the Indian Union. Let us look first at the regional spread of the BJP in the legislative assembly elections between 1993 and 1995, as revealed in Figure 3. This shows the deviation of the BJP vote share from its combined total vote share in all the states in which elections were held in those years, and gives a very striking result, especially when compared with Figure 4, which does the same thing for the distribution of the Congress vote. Figure 3 shows a very clear and abrupt demarcation between those states—all in north India plus Gujarat—where the BJP polled significantly above its combined total vote, on the one hand, and all the other states—all of them except Bihar in non-Hindi-speaking states—in which the BJP vote share deviated negatively from its overall vote share, on the other hand. Let us compare this figure with that for the Congress which, as I have noted earlier, despite its decline, retains a universal presence in the states. Figure 4 shows a gradually descending deviation by state in which many of the states do not deviate very far from the Congress' total vote share. In fact, the score for the standard deviation of the Congress vote in these elections is 10.6, significantly lower than that for the BJP, which stood at 16.4.

Unfortunately, comparable figures by state for the 1996 Lok Sabha elections were not available at the time of writing. Results were available for parliamentary vote shares for the 1996 elections for five states only, but even so they are revealing, as indicated by Figure 5 showing the vote share for the BJP for the Lok Sabha from 1952 to 1996 in those five states. First, there is no national trend for the BJP in these states:

FIGURE 3: DEVIATION OF BJP VOTE SHARE FROM ITS TOTAL VOTE SHARE IN LEGISLATIVE ASSEMBLY ELECTIONS BY STATE, 1993–5

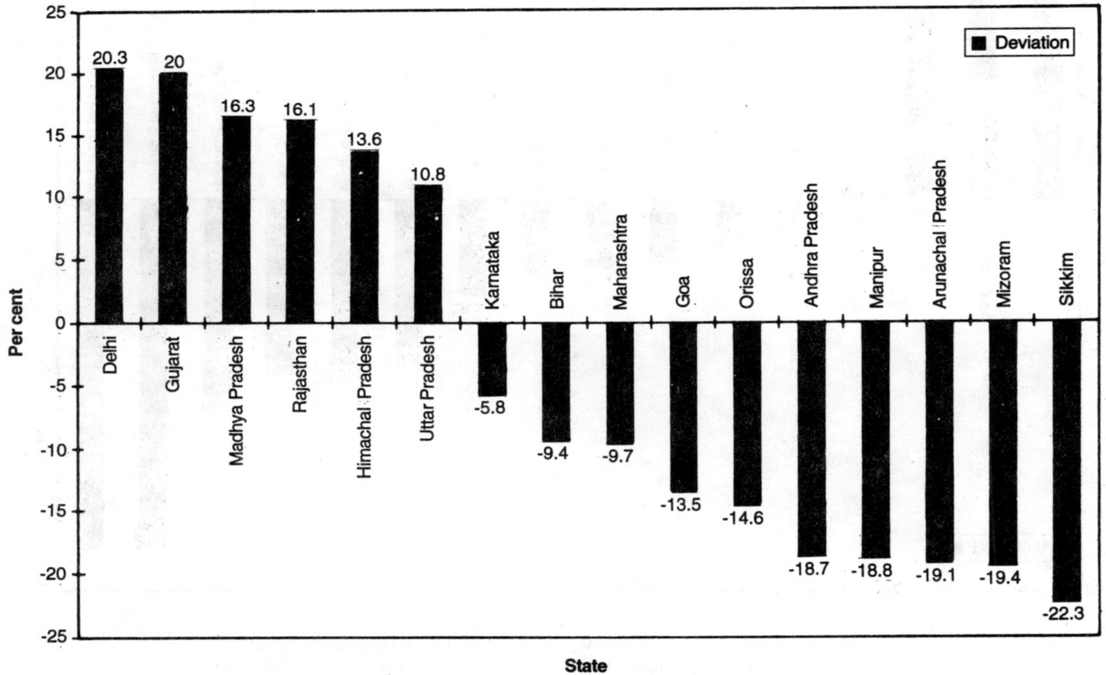

FIGURE 4: DEVIATION OF CONGRESS VOTE SHARE BY STATE FROM ITS TOTAL VOTE SHARE IN LEGISLATIVE ASSEMBLY ELECTIONS, 1993–5

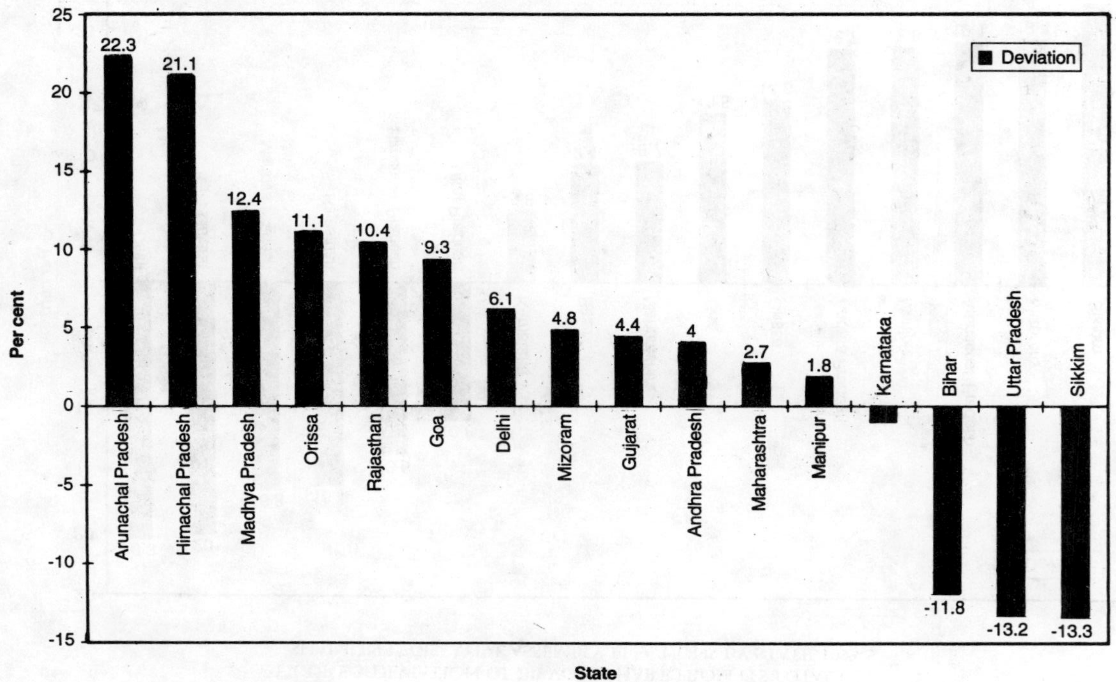

FIGURE 5: VOTE SHARE FOR BJP FOR PARLIAMENT, 1952-96

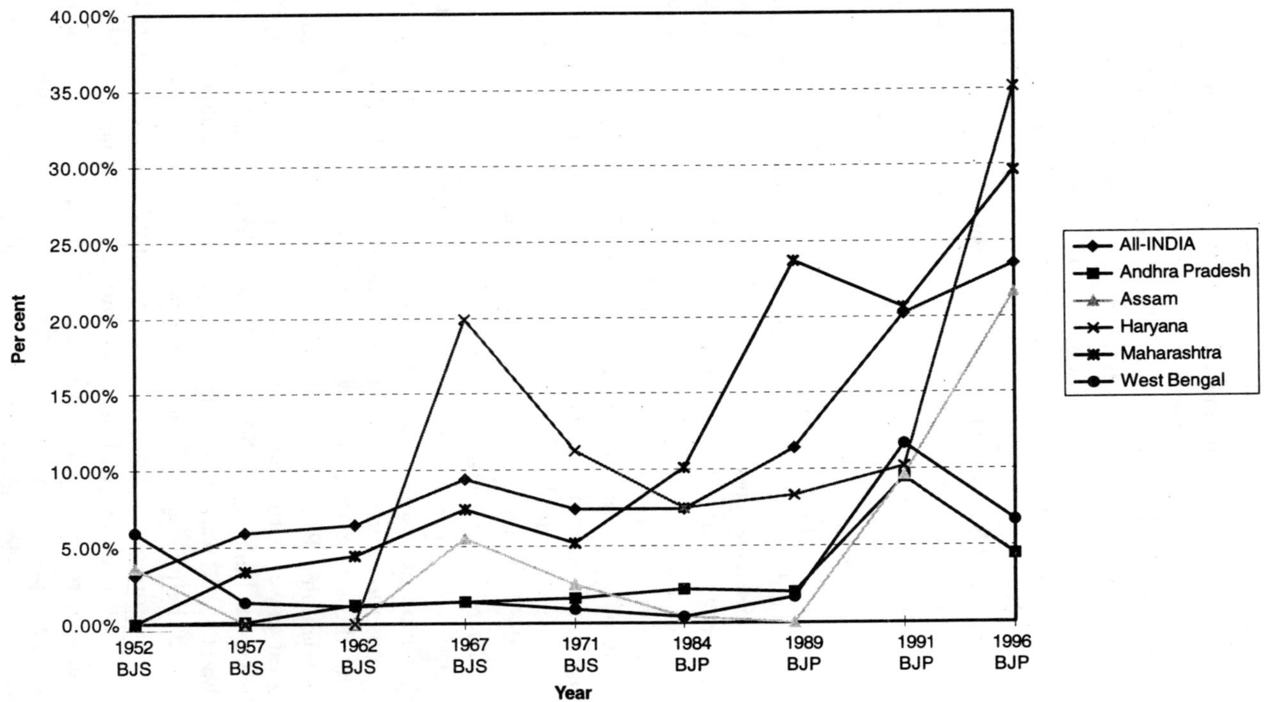

its vote went up in Haryana, Maharashtra, and Assam and down in West Bengal and Andhra Pradesh. The BJP vote in the latter two states is, in effect, inconsequential, below 7 per cent in both cases. The highest BJP vote was in Haryana, in the Hindi-speaking belt. Its second best performance was in Maharashtra, where it maintains an alliance with a hooligan-fascist party, the Shiv Sena. This alliance is critical for the BJP in this state where the Congress remains a strong force. The BJP's third relatively strong performance among these states was in Assam, where it appeals to anti-Muslim-migrant sentiment, but where the AGP, a regional party, emerged stronger and still maintains a much stronger base among the Assamese Hindus than does the BJP.

In short, partial analysis of the limited election results available so far suggests that the Congress in 1996 barely held on to its place as a national party, that the BJP was very far still from replacing it in that regard, and that all other parties were (and are) so fragmented that there appears no possibility of a third alternative. However, this analysis ignores a vital aspect of Indian political and cultural life, namely, that there is a strong sense of national identity among important, elite segments of society everywhere in India and a desire to maintain the unity of the Indian state and to strengthen it in order to maintain its place in the current world order, sentiments which are most effectively articulated by the BJP. We cannot, therefore, rule out the possibility that the BJP may yet achieve its goal, but how?

There is a general feeling that the BJP intends now to downplay anti-Muslim actions and mass mobilizations in order to present itself as a moderate party, which no reasonable persons should fear. It will in this mode stress the more conventional themes of Indian politics and those that have an easy popular appeal: opposing corruption, condemning Pakistan, squashing Kashmir separatism, and achieving great power status and respect in the world for India through such means as building nuclear weapons and delivery capabilities. In this way, the BJP wants to present itself as the only viable alternative when and if the present coalition disintegrates.

It is conceivable that such tactics might work well enough to bring the BJP to power, with its allies, with a slight majority in the next election,[7] but much more than that will be required to establish it as a universal presence and the new centre party in the Indian political order. Achieving the latter would require at the minimum three further developments: (1) undermining and capturing the social bases of the left parties among the backward castes, who comprise the majority of the country; (2) making deals with regional parties that would amount to reducing the powers of the centre in relation to the states, which goes against its fundamental goals; (3) establishing itself as a genuine national, rather than merely a Hindu, anti-Muslim party, which would require giving up some of its goals, such as the elimination of Article 370, the establishment of a uniform civil code, and the building of the temple at Ayodhya, if not the destruction of some more mosques. If, however, the BJP gives up on the latter goals, it risks losing the energy of its cadres and its ability to mobilize large masses of voters around emotional appeals to Hindu sentiment, faith, and solidarity.

The future of Indian politics, therefore, still constitutes a struggle between centralizing and decentralizing tendencies, on the one hand, and militantly nationalist and secular, pluralist forces on the other. My own prediction is that regional forces will ultimately prevail and that there is now a genuine possibility that effective regional autonomy will come to all the states, not just to Kashmir. However, either the strength of Hindu nationalist sentiment in the north and among the upper caste elites nor the single-mindedness of the BJP-RSS leadership should be underestimated.

Insofar as the next election is concerned, the disintegration of the present coalition will leave only the BJP and the Congress as viable potential alternatives. The Congress has the greater spread, the BJP the organization. The most that can be expected is that one of these parties will win enough seats to form a more stable coalition government.

The evidence for continuing fragmentation and regionalization

The strongest evidence against either a return of Congress dominance or the replacement of the Congress by the BJP as the dominant centering party are the electoral figures themselves, which suggest a future of continuing fragmentation and regionalization. The fragmentation in the 1996 elections, for which the vote share figures were not yet available at the time of writing, was preceded and anticipated by the results of the legislative assembly elections held in 15 states between 1993 and 1995. Comparisons are available for ten of those states for the Lok Sabha elections in 1991, as shown in Tables 2 and 5. Note in Table 5 that, in all ten states for which comparative figures are available, the combined three-party vote share was significantly lower in the 1993-5 legislative assembly series than in the 1991 Lok Sabha elections in the same states.

This fragmentation has also affected the party configurations within each state. In the aftermath of the 1991 Lok Sabha elections, I noted the continuing regionalization of state party systems, which I then classified into five types: one-party dominant, competitive two-party, competitive multi-party, competitive dualist, and competitive regionally specific.[8] With regard to the first category, the hallmark of the Indian political order in earlier years, there is now not a single state in the Indian Union that can be characterized as having a one-party dominant system; its last bastion was Maharashtra where the Congress vote declined from 48.3 per cent in the 1991 Lok Sabha elections to a mere 31 per cent in the most recent Legislative Assembly elections. The Congress vote share in the 1996 Lok Sabha elections in Maharashtra was only slightly above its share in the previous legislative assembly election.

The second category of states which, after the 1991 elections, appeared to be emerging two-party systems, comprised Himachal Pradesh, Madhya Pradesh, and Rajasthan. In these there were two principal parties, Congress and the BJP. The BJP had come to power in all three in the March 1990 Legislative Assembly elections. In the 1991 Lok Sabha elections, the vote shares of Congress and the BJP were quite close in each state and the combined vote shares of the two parties were between 84.9 and 89.0 per cent. There are now four states in which something approaching two-party competitiveness exists, in which the Congress and the BJP are the two main competitors and together capture between 75 and 86 per cent of the vote. These are Himachal Pradesh, Madhya Pradesh, Gujarat, and Rajasthan; in other words, Gujarat has been added to the previous list of three. However, as in all other states, the combined two-party vote share declined between 1991 and 1993-5.

In 1991, there were six states which could be characterized as competitive multi-party systems in which there was three-way competition for vote shares and seats between the Congress, the BJP, and the Janata Dal. The six were Bihar, UP, and Haryana plus Gujarat, Karnataka, and Orissa. Gujarat, as just noted, may perhaps better be described as approaching two-party competitiveness. Bihar and UP,

TABLE 5: POPULAR VOTE PERCENTAGES OF THE THREE LEADING PARTIES IN THE 1991 LOK SABHA AND 1993-5 LEGISLATIVE ASSEMBLY ELECTIONS

State	Combined 2-party Vote 1991	Combined 2-party Vote 1993-5	Combined 3-party Vote 1991	Combined 3-party Vote 1993-5
Maharashtra	68.9	51.7	79.8	64.5
Himachal Pradesh	89.0	85.5	96.0	87.7
Madhya Pradesh	87.2	79.5	91.4	86.3
Rajasthan	84.9	77.3	91.1	84.2
Bihar	56.3	44.1	73.2	57.2
Uttar Pradesh	51.2	48.4	72.8	66.5
Haryana	62.6	—	75.1	—
Gujarat	78.8	75.2	91.4	78.0
Karnataka	70.7	60.5	89.2	77.2
Orissa	77.9	74.8	87.8	82.7
Kerala	59.5	—	64.5	—
West Bengal	71.3	—	83.0	—
Tamil Nadu	65.3	—	83.4	—
Andhra Pradesh	77.2	74.5	86.7	78.3
Assam	46.1	—	55.7	—

however, further fragmented in the last Legislative Assembly elections so that the combined two-party vote was less than 50 per cent and the combined three-party vote less than two-thirds in both states. Only in Karnataka and Orissa could it still be said after the 1993-5 Legislative Assembly election series that a predominantly three-way pattern of party competition persisted in which the Congress, the BJP, and the Janata Dal captured more than three quarters of the total vote.

I characterized two states in 1991 as having competitive dualist systems between Congress- and CPM-dominated alliances, West Bengal and Kerala; this pattern persists. I characterized five states as competitive regionally specific: Tamil Nadu, Jammu & Kashmir before the insurrection, Punjab, Andhra Pradesh, and Assam. These are states in which the principal non-Congress party has been neither the BJP, the Janata Dal, nor the CPM, but a party specific to the state. There has been no change in any of these. Furthermore, the regional parties have maintained their place or, as in Tamil Nadu, changed place with each other despite the deaths of founding charismatic leaders, loss of power, and bloody insurrections.

The 1996 election results in Tamil Nadu

What about Tamil Nadu, the prototypical example of a regionalized party system? What can we learn about the future of centralizing and regionalizing tendencies from the Congress decline there and the otherwise extraordinary results of the 1996 Lok Sabha and Legislative Assembly election results? In 1991, the Congress won 28 of the 39 Lok Sabha seats from this state while its traditional alliance partner, the AIADMK, won 11. In 1996, the Congress and its alliance partner were completely routed as all 39 seats went to the National Front Left Front DMK alliance (37 of them to the DMK).

The rout of the Congress and the AIADMK was equally devastating in the 1996 Legislative Assembly elections. It is more important for our purposes, however, to look at the Legislative Assembly results retrospectively, comparing the 1996 results with those for all previous elections back to 1952. What is important about Tamil Nadu is that it is a kind of exemplar of the way in which the Congress maintained its dominance at the centre despite its loss of dominance in particular states. In Tamil Nadu, it did so by encouraging and exploiting a split in the then dominant DMK, which occurred after the death of Annadurai in 1969, and then forming an alliance with the splinter party, which became the AIADMK. (As always, an important device used by the Congress was the threat of filing corruption charges, first against the DMK leader Karunanidhi, whose duly elected government was dismissed during the Emergency in 1975, and then against the AIADMK leader, M.G. Ramachandran, to keep him in line.) That alliance lasted through five elections, between 1977 and 1996, in which the arrangement was that the Congress would ally with the AIADMK against its rival in Legislative Assembly elections, leaving most seats to the latter, while the AIADMK would leave a number of parliamentary seats for the Congress and support it in the Lok Sabha. The value of the alliance, however, declined dramatically in 1996 when Narasimha Rao made the decision to dump his own Congress organization in Tamil Nadu altogether for the sake of maintaining the old alliance with the AIADMK, which had, however, become extraordinarily unpopular under its then chief minister, Jayalalitha. The results of that mistake are shown in Figure 6: the Indian National Congress won no seats and the AIADMK 4 out of 234. Thus both popular vote shares in former areas of relative strength and the value of old alliances with regional parties worked decisively against the Congress in this election.

FIGURE 6: VIDHAN SABHA SEATS WON BY SELECTED PARTIES, TAMIL NADU, 1952-96

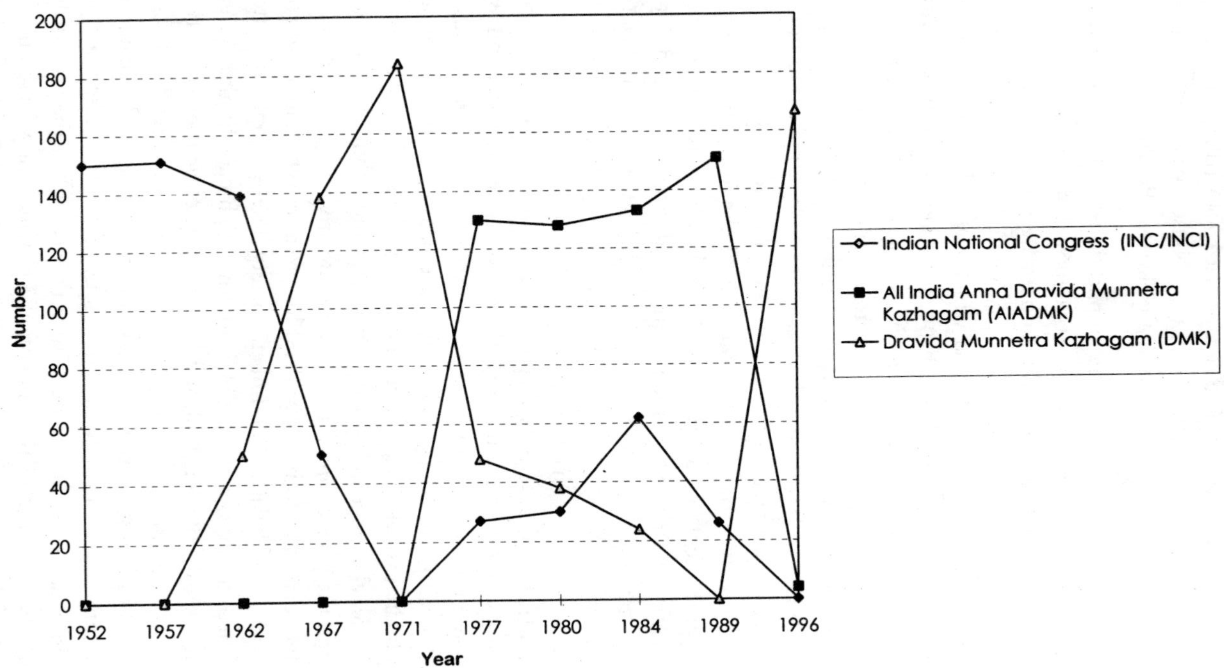

Communal and Caste Conflict and their Implications for the Future of Nationalism and Regionalism in Indian Politics

I conclude by considering the implications for the future of nationalism and regionalism in India of the two most dramatic sets of social changes and conflicts that continue to dominate politics in large parts of the country and at all levels of society. These are the questions of Hindu-Muslim relations and violence, which have ebbed and flowed for more than a century, on the one hand, and intercaste relations, which have shown a long-term tendency in a single direction, on the other hand.

It must first be recognized that Hindu nationalist sentiment has become pervasive among upper castes in north India. I believe this sentiment is based on a dual *ressentiment* on which I do not have the space to elaborate here, but can only state in outline.

First, it is based on *ressentiment* of the West, arising out of disappointment at the failure of the Indian State to achieve most of its major goals of development, equity, and progress. Secondly, it is based on fear and resentment at the rise of the lower classes and castes in the Indian polity, which has so far been its greatest achievement. For, these upper caste elites have reproduced in slightly varied forms for generations under British rule and Independence the same hierarchical social order, an *ancien regime* upon which they have sat with satisfaction while the lower castes have continued to live in poverty and degradation, illiteracy, ill health, and malnutrition, and have had to sell themselves and their children as bonded labourers and child workers. That order is increasingly under challenge in India as government and politics, the rural economy, and the police force in state after state are being manned increasingly by persons from backward and lower castes who intend to rectify the age-old imbalances of Indian society. These people are often rude, uncouth, do not speak English with a high class English accent or do not speak English at all, and have no particular respect for Brahmans. They are also secular, partly because of their very class background, partly because of the compulsions of political coalition-making that require inter-caste and inter-religious alliances to overcome upper caste dominance. Whatever the reasons, they constitute the principal obstacle to the rise of the BJP, which would provide a new lease on life for the old order and the upper caste elites who dominated that order, despite the fact that the BJP too must appeal to the backward and lower castes to achieve power.

The changes that have taken place in north India in the last quarter of the twentieth century and have now reached the centre are momentous in these respects. Upper castes have now been definitively displaced at state and national levels throughout the country as the dominant political elites. They are being displaced also in the police forces in north India. They retain strength in the north Indian countryside, in the landed economy, and in the IAS, the IPS, and other elite all-India services. They also remain politically important in north India. However, their old political dominance is a thing of the past.

Let us make no mistake about militant Hindu nationalism being the product of this dual *ressentiment* and, in classic fashion, finding a scapegoat for all its ills, the Muslim, so-called disloyal, minority. It needs the Muslims as a scapegoat for both psychological and political reasons. Militant Indian or Hindu nationalism (they shade into each other amongst the upper caste elites) can gain no real satisfaction from opposing the West. Indeed, they cannot oppose the West on what really matters for the future of India. They must accept World Bank and IMF conditionalities, while they can only make gestures in other spheres which irritate all the great powers, such as refusing to sign the Comprehensive Test Ban Treaty (CTBT), but which do not bring sanctions down upon them. Nor can they oppose too vigorously the rise of the backward and lower castes, for they constitute the majority of the country. The Muslims, therefore, stand in for the West, for do not the Muslims represent India's greatest enemy, Pakistan, which in turn is a dagger held against the Indian heart by the West? Although this statement appears ridiculous to most of us in the West, it is certainly believed whole-heartedly by many upper caste Indians.

Further feeding upper caste, militant Hindu nationalist hostility against the Muslims is the extent to which they constitute an obstacle to their continuing hold on power and the rise to power of the BJP, for the road to power at the centre can only be through north India, and Muslims hold the political balance there and have thrown their weight heavily against the BJP and with the backward and lower castes and secular parties. That being the case, the prospect of further mass mobilizations designed to consolidate Hindu sentiment and extend it to the backward castes and, along with it, the danger of further violence against Muslims will remain a significant factor in north Indian politics for sometime. It has been deliberately used for political advantage by the BJP and the Congress especially in the past and may be so used again in future. I want to repeat and emphasize this statement that Hindu-Muslim violence is predominantly a creation of political organizations in India. Not only do I have ample positive evidence for this assertion,[9] but there is negative evidence as well. For, it has been shown in West Bengal and in Bihar that there are ways of preventing the expression of Hindu-Muslim antagonism in violent form.

In contrast, the BJP has reached its new heights of proximity to power on the basis of anti-Muslim sentiments. It wants us now to believe that it has no ill designs against Muslims. The problem for it is that it cannot attain power in north India and, through north India, at the centre, without breaking the Muslim-backward caste-scheduled caste alliance. It succeeded in 1995 in Uttar Pradesh in shaving off the BSP from its alliance with the SP and supported a BSP government under the chief ministership of Mayawati only to withdraw its support within a few months. In the ensuing 1996 Legislative Assembly elections in UP, the BSP forged an electoral alliance with the Congress that led to a three-way division of the vote in which no party or coalition was in a position to form a government, as a consequence of which President's Rule was imposed on the state shortly after the election returns. The BJP succeeded later, in March 1997, in forming a coalition government with the BSP, with Mayawati once again installed as chief minister. The BJP has also developed a considerable base of support among the backward castes in this state.

Nevertheless, the potential for mobilization of anti-Muslim sentiment remains a resource that the BJP cannot afford to discard. It cannot afford to do so partly for reasons already elaborated above, namely, in order to isolate or fragment the Muslims in north Indian politics to prevent them from voting *en masse* against it and for the secular parties of the Left. It also cannot afford to do so because its leaders believe that India must become a Hindu nation-state and because its lower-level cadres and affiliated organizations such as the Vishwa Hindu Parishad expect it to make good on its declared aims of getting rid of Article 370 which means utterly destroying for all time Muslim separatism in Kashmir by any means, imposing a uniform civil code on the country, and building the new temple to Ram at Ayodhya, not to speak of destroying a few more mosques. Under the circumstances, therefore, it must be acknowledged that the BJP, in its drive for national power through Hindu consolidation, represents a continuing threat to the unity and peace of India.

NOTES

1. Paul R. Brass, 'Pluralism, Regionalism and Decentralizing Tendencies in Contemporary Indian Politics', in A. Jeyaratnam Wilson and Dennis Dalton (eds.), *The States of South Asia: Problems of National Integration* (London, 1982), pp. 223-64. A slightly revised and updated version appears also under the same title in my *Ethnicity and Nationalism: Theory and Comparison* (New Delhi and Newbury Park, CA, 1991).
2. The demands and the issues of centre-state relations that came up soon after the formation of the new government are summarized in *India Today*, 30 June 1996, pp. 42-5.
3. I have made extensive use in this paper of the figures provided in an excellent article on these elections by Yogendra Yadav, 'Reconfiguration in Indian Politics: State Assembly Elections, 1993-95', *Economic and Political Weekly*, XXXI, Nos. 2 and 3 (13-20 January 1996), pp. 95-104; see esp. Table 6, p. 100.
4. The Congress vote declined further in the Vidhan Sabha elections held in 1996 after this essay was prepared. Although the official figures are not available, the Congress vote share probably fell below 10 per cent.
5. The data in this Figure are unfortunately incomplete and provisional, referring only to the six states for which results were available for 1996 at the time of writing.
6. Pratap Bhanu Mehta, 'India's Disordered Democracy: Review Article', *Pacific Affairs*, LXIV, No. 4 (Winter, 1991-2), 538.
7. This is exactly what occurred in the 1998 general election, held after this paper was written [eds.].
8. Paul R. Brass, *The Politics of India Since Independence* (Cambridge, 2nd edn., 1994), pp. 125-35.
9. See Paul R. Brass, *Language, Religion, and Politics in North India* (New York, 1974), pp. 265-7, where I said in an analysis of the Ranchi riots of August 1967: 'Communal riots in India have been in the past and were in Ranchi a continuation and extension of communal politics by other means. . . . In effect, there is a continuum from political rivalry leading to communal riots to political rivalry feeding on communal riots.' For more recent evidence, see the contributions on India in Paul R. Brass (ed.), *Riots and Pogroms* (New York, 1996) and Paul R. Brass, *Theft of an Idol* (Princeton, N.J., 1997).

8

Region and Nation in India's Political Transition

ZOYA HASAN

Over the last decade Indian politics is marked by a struggle between two rival conceptions of the nation: one wants to establish a unicultural nation that ought to be governed by a strong centre; the other argues that India is a social mosaic that can be sustained by a democratic and federal structure held in place by strong states. Strains between national and regional identity and the unsatisfactory functioning of federalism constitute the underlying base of these differences. At the heart of these differences are varying conceptions of modern India and the struggle to reconstitute the state and society in a more secular and federal direction, on the one hand, and, in a more conservative and unitary direction, on the other.

Scholars and journalists writing about Indian politics have paid most attention to the apex or the centre—who controls the leadership at the top—as if those at the summit of power speak and act for the complex of state organizations and different levels of governance in the polity. Not enough attention has been paid to the political changes at the regional/state level and contestations between the states and the centre and how the state/region rather than the centre is reshaping the polity. This paper examines the emerging relationship between nation and region by exploring the process of regionalization triggered off by social change and upward mobility in the states and shifts in the structure of party politics induced by the institutional and ideological decline of the Congress party, and assesses their impact on the political order in India. Political trends over the last few years have shown that we should not over-emphasize the top level or the centre or major battles among large-scale social classes/forces operating at some grand level. Struggles at multiple planes and especially the regional level provide us the key to understanding the major transitions in Indian politics. The political system is rapidly moving from a centralized system toward a multi-layered distribution of political and economic powers. Many aspects of the unfolding political scenario are indicative of greater democratization and empowerment yet, there are many issues of equity and growth, both regionally and individually, that the emerging polity does not necessarily have answers to.

I

The priority of the political leadership presiding over the transition from colonialism was to weld together a unified nation-state from culturally and linguistically distinct and economically disparate regions; consequently, the Constitution and the policy-makers, especially Jawaharlal Nehru, followed ideologies of social transformation and composite nationalism to integrate all strands of the people. Religion, culture and language, were accommodated as long as these groups did not make demands for recognition as corporate groups in state and society. The linguistic reorganization of states was the single most important policy in this period to facilitate the process of accommodation of both national and regional identities.[1] The combination of composite nationalism and linguistic reorganization in conjunction with a centralized state committed to the goal of planned economic development and social transformation, managed to check any reassertion of centrifugal tendencies for the first two decades. The dominance of the Congress party at the centre and the states also helped in creating political homogeneity between the two arenas.[2] Granville Austin in his assessment of the functioning of the Constitution in the first two decades noted that 'Congress ministries had not aggrandized their authority at the expense of constitutional government either in the states or in New Delhi'.[3] In effect, the powers of the central government were not abused or misused.

But the project of integrating the nation through the centralizing drives of the state ran into rough weather in the post-1967 period. Some of these tensions related to cultural diversities, but more often conflicts were generated by uneven economic and political development. Nevertheless, during the sixties the centre demonstrated elements of flexibility and pragmatism in dealing with the regional opposition. As a result, Tamil nationalism—the first major expression of nationality centred opposition—was accommodated within the parameters of the Indian union, a process no doubt facilitated by the Dravida Munnetra Kazhagam's (DMK) electoral triumph in the 1967 elections. The centre also succeeded in turning the tide of secession in Nagaland and Mizoram through a combination of coercion and the disbursement of development funds that consolidated a regional elite whose aspirations changed from independence to autonomy to centre-sponsored development.[4]

A new dimension was added to centre-state relations in the 1980s, until then dominated by differences over an interpretation of the Constitution and dissatisfaction with the distribution of powers between the centre and states.[5] Regional autonomy from New Delhi in financial, administrative and political matters now became the key issue in confrontations between the centre and states. Regional politics acquired a new force with the rise of militancy in Punjab, Assam and Kashmir.[6] Led by regional elites who mobilized cultural identities, rather than just economic grievances or political discrimination by the centre, these movements demanded greater autonomy from the centre and in some cases even sovereignty. At stake in all three conflicts was the varying conception of the single unified nation pitted against the demands for autonomy and independence. The central government's counter-offensive based primarily on coercion and a majoritarian ideology of national unity, complicated the political terrain in all the border states.

The operation of Indian federal politics over the last five decades has basically given rise to three kinds of regional assertions with very different implications for adaptation in the polity. The first, mentioned earlier, are militant movements in Kashmir, Punjab and Assam, directed against an overpowering centre and claiming varying degrees of autonomy and independence from the Indian state. In at least two of these instances of political conflict, region and nation are on a collision course, representing a break in the accepted conception of a unified nation. The second type of regional assertion grounded in the distinctiveness and underdevelopment of regions—Uttarakhand, Chattisgarh and Jharkhand—demands autonomy within the Indian federal framework.

The third are the regional assertions whose area of operation coincides with the federal territorial division of the union. In this category can be grouped centre-state and inter-state conflicts, that is, tensions in which the state government is the leading agent.[7] These assertions, impelled as they are by an aspiration for change in centre-state relations and devolution of powers to the states are not quite autonomy movements. In the forefront of demands for a greater voice in national policy and decision-making are Tamil Nadu, Andhra Pradesh, Karnataka, West Bengal and Assam.

The emergence of these regional pressures should be seen in the background of the defeat of the Congress in the 1967 elections and the formation of non-Congress governments in several states. To reverse this trend, Indira Gandhi shattered the boundaries between the centre and states and sought to control the Congress and states through central domination.[8] The keystone of her political strategy was an unprecedented centralization of power, within the ruling party, within the prime minister's office, and excluding parliament and cabinet from decision-making.[9] The Emergency accelerated the concentration of power within the offices in New Delhi. The specific measures taken by Indira Gandhi to centralize political authority involved most crucially the delinking of parliamentary and legislative assembly elections, selection of chief ministers by her advisers in New Delhi rather than by the state legislative parties, and frequent impositions of President's rule in various states to influence state politics. The principal effect of these policies was felt by the Congress party itself but its centrality in the political arena ensured that its actions transformed the relationship of the centre to the states by decreasing their relevance and that of districts as critical arenas of political competition and mobilization independent of the centre.[10] This strategy proved to be counter-productive in managing tensions and cleavages: it made the Congress more vulnerable by undermining the regional leadership of the party and thus cutting at the roots of autonomy necessary for a centrist party operating in a heterogeneous society.[11] This marked a departure from past trends: since the 1930s, a combination of strong central command and relatively independent provincial leadership has been the spindle of the Congress machine.

Democratic functioning within the Congress declined all through the 1970s and 1980s just when democracy was assuming a new importance in the polity and civil society.[12] The defeat of the Congress party in the 1977 election brought about further changes in centre-state relations. A new feature of the post-1977 period was greater competition between political parties and also greater social polarization in the states with reduced manoeuvre for the central government since the control of the centre itself was beginning to be contested. During this period, the Congress party continued to wield power over a highly centralized state but its political authority was greatly reduced in the states. This opened up the space for new alignments to reinforce the growing opposition in the states.

Central control reached unprecedented levels in the context of worsening government-opposition relations between 1974-84. Demands of states for greater participation in policy processes were met with stiffening controls and continuation of the centralized set-up. One effect of excessive centralization was manifest in the continually shrinking support base of national parties, and the rise of regional parties to power at the state level,[13] the most dramatic example being the electoral success of Telugu Desam in Andhra Pradesh in the 1982 Assembly elections. The rise of Telugu Desam indicates that regionalism can be kindled simply by the discernment of political discrimination or centralized decision-making by the centre.[14] Against this new development, non-Congress chief ministers of Andhra, Karnataka, West Bengal and Jammu & Kashmir organized several conclaves in 1983-4 with the explicit purpose of creating a united anti-Congress front. The front's chief demand was a fundamental renegotiation in centre-state relations and vesting of greater powers in the states.

But the central government continued to intrude into spheres reserved for the states. Several states felt aggrieved that they were getting a raw deal from the centre. By the early 1990s, there was substantial resentment against excessive centralization of economic and political power. Alienation and disaffection was strengthened by the failure of the state in lessening regional disparities or level out economic inequalities. The basic issue is the balance in the economic equation between the centre and states. Presently it is heavily tilted in favour of the centre. States receive a rather small share of the central pool of taxes.[15] In 1995-6 the states' share of the gross tax revenue of the centre was little over 20 per cent.[16] Apart from taxes, only 40 per cent of the funds given to the states are decided by the Finance Commission, a statutory body, while the larger share is decided by the Planning

Commission, an executive body, which increases the scope for arbitrariness. As for resource transfer to states and central assistance to state plans, only 30 per cent of the Rs. 62 crores in 1996 set aside for this was given to state plans; the rest went to central plans.[17] Not surprisingly, states are discontented. Assam is sore it cannot benefit from its own resources like coal, oil and natural gas; Karnataka's chief minister asked for quick clearance of power projects in view of the power crisis in the state, but the centre would not oblige; Maharashtra complains that it receives too meagre an amount from the central divisible tax pool; Telugu Desam chief ministers believed that poverty in Andhra Pradesh can be tackled by the Rs. 2 per kilogram rice scheme whereas the centre wants them to implement an employment generation programme like the Jawahar Rozgar Yojna.[18]

Critical changes in Indian politics generated by the expansion of democratic forces and the persistence of militant movements in the north-east, Punjab and Kashmir prompted some rethinking on questions of regional autonomy. The centre was compelled to entertain these demands owing to its ramifications for national unity. Attempts were made to resolve them through a series of high level 'accords' such as the Assam and Punjab accords.[19] Greater autonomy in decision-making was promoted with democratic decentralization and revitalization of local-self-government institutions through the devolution of power to elected panchayats in 1991 and the creation of autonomous councils for Jharkhand and Gorkhaland in the early 1990s.[20] On the whole the Indian state can claim considerable success in nation-building—it was able to incorporate regional dissensions using the persuasive and coercive means at its disposal. But these initiatives have not mitigated the desire to create centres of autonomous power.

II

To understand this we need to turn attention to the changes in the polity caused by the decline of Congress hegemony. At the centre of political transformation (1989-97) is the crumbling of the Congress system which for over four decades occupied a position of dominance at the national level and in the states. The Congress party has not been able to win a national majority since 1984, even that mandate was secured in the context of an emotional wave generated by Indira Gandhi's assassination. Realignments caused by the Ayodhya and Mandal issues have shrunk the party's social base and reduced the party's vote share to an all-time low of 28 per cent in 1996.[21] The aspiring Bharatiya Janata Party (BJP) which won seats in 12 states in 1996, is mainly strong in the northern states. Ironically, for a party claiming to replace the Congress at the all-India level, the principal reason for its improved performance is the regional concentration of its support in Uttar Pradesh, Haryana, Rajasthan, Maharashtra, Gujarat and Karnataka. By contrast the Congress' weakness stems from its national spread: it won seats in 26 of 31 states.[22]

The most striking feature of the 1996 elections was the spectacular rise of regional parties and the challenge posed by these alterations to the 'nationalization of politics' which had gained ascendancy in the previous two decades.[23] As the importance of regional and state parties began to emerge and government formation became rather dependent on them, one newspaper report in May 1996 quipped that 'the world's largest democracy now has the distinction of electing the world's largest opposition'. This sally summed up the dramatic political change which has occurred: from a dominant party system to a multi-party system. Congress dominance was replaced by minority and multi-party coalitions at the centre and the states, reflecting the major changes that have occurred in political life over the last two decades. Similarly the 1998 election also reveals how much Indian democracy has changed in the last ten years. It confirms the tendency towards the regionalization that has been apparent since the 1989 election which propelled the National Front coalition government of V.P. Singh to power. About two hundred seats in the twelfth Lok Sabha have gone to parties that have essentially local or regional support. What has emerged, then, is a multi-party system involving the Congress, BJP and regional parties. However, the combination of parties differs from state to state and this has intensified political conflict at the state level and complicated the transition to a post-Congress polity at the national level.[24]

These momentous changes are partly an outcome of specific social and political circumstances in different states propelling the growth of contending regional formations with their own social and political agendas. The process of change is closely linked to the differential dynamics of Congress decline and to the emergence of specific regional and vernacular discourses that have eroded centralized political authority.

This decentering of politics has shifted its locale from New Delhi to the states with their distinct political cultures, political discourse and caste-class and caste-community mobilization and alliances. The single most important source of change is the entry of hitherto peripheral groups into the political system. This is the result of the immense social awakening among the lower castes and dalits, particularly in north India—a region that for decades constituted the citadel of the upper caste dominated Congress system.

The centrepiece of Congress hegemony was the politics of social consensus and a strategy of mobilization which aggregated the interests of different sections of society on the basis of an inclusive ideological package of nationalism, secularism and Nehruvian version of socialism. The Congress operated as a centrist party, representing no single category of interest, and its coalitional character enabled it to attract a wide range of individuals and groups. The party ruled for so long because it deftly persuaded the lower orders to believe that existing political arrangements worked in their interests, whereupon the business of governance could be left to the Congress. From the 1980s, however, its claims to ideological leadership was challenged by the counter-hegemonies that were generated by new social forces. The crucial question for them was not the failure to accommodate the claims and counter-claims of backward and lower castes for power-sharing, but the very structure of representation and centre-state relations which was at odds with the way groupings now wanted to conduct political business and representation. People preferred to invoke the strength of caste and community or regional majorities on the ground; they wanted to be represented by their own community/regional leaders. However, the decline of the Congress has also meant the decline of a particular type of politics organized around a universalist secular-nationalist discourse.

Marking a break from the presuppositions of this discourse are competing attempts to redefine political identity. The Hindu Right made the most infuential attempt to redefine political identity. The Ayodhya movement played a crucial part in the reconstruction. The 'Ayodhya strategy' succeeded in winning new adherents largely because the BJP and affilitated organizations seized the opportunity provided by the communal compromises made by the Congress to arrest its own decline in the 1980s. The escalation of political competition from the late 1970s saw the Congress appealing to community identities. Unable to respond to the groundswell of social discontent and opposition brewing in civil society, the Congress chose the easier option of stoking majoritarian and minoritarian politics. This shift, though prompted by electoral compulsions, was part of the retreat from the central principles of the Nehruvian project and the long-term decline in the secularity of the state. The BJP took advantage of this to rework the balance of power by taking the communal issue beyond the boundaries set by the Congress and thus forcing open the ambivalences in the relationship between secular and communal politics. Its main appeal, however, was to the insecurities of upper castes who were willing to switch after the decline of the Congress. The destruction of the Babari Masjid by Hindu extremists in December 1992 persuaded many lower castes that this was an upper caste backlash against the Mandal move by the Janata Dal government. In the post-demolition period caste assertions signalled an attempt by marginal groups to claim the middle ground vacated by Congress decline. They combined with other subaltern groups to strengthen their own bargaining position *vis-a-vis* national parties and the bigger parties in the states. Consequently, the political map is dotted with regional, state and locally-based parties. Their leaders perceive the politics of regionalization and fragmentation as the best chance to transform their control over vote banks into autonomous power at the state and at the national level.[25]

III

The internal decimation of the Congress weakened its control over regional politics; if anything, regular central interference in regional politics bolstered disgruntlement with the Congress which fuelled regional aspirations of autonomy from Congress domination.[26] The broader impetus for regionalization can be traced to the rapid pace of socio-economic change in the last three decades, giving rise to strains and pressures, and the dissatisfaction of new groups with the Nehruvian paradigm. The early contours of this challenge was epitomized in the 1970s by Charan Singh's critique of the urban-industrial-metropolitan policy of the Congress and the upper caste dominated power structure. Initially, the sub-national and sub-state pressure directed against the Congress and the centre or both came mainly from the agrarian surplus producers, the chief beneficiaries of commercialization of agriculture in the last few decades. The new rural bloc accused the centre and state governments of being biased in favour of urban India and sought a place for its non-farming members in the government and state bureaucracies. Over the years they courted alternative political formations and resorted to mass agitations to enhance their influence, knowing full well that they stand to gain the most from the success of non-class farmers or regional movements in which all groups or classes participated.

There are other regional assertions which combined popular grievances with elements of political manipulation from above. Many of the leaders of regional movements seek to use their political authority to accumulate wealth and power in order to become part of the regional economic elite. Besides the agrarian bourgeoisie whose interests are demarcated regionally,[27] significant sections of the urban middle classes also benefit from greater decentralization of power, greater industrialization or investment of public resources, or the state getting a greater share of central resources. State governments employ millions of people and very often public employment exceeds that offered by large-scale industry. State-based linguistic exclusivity, articulated by the Shiv Sena type of sons-of-the-soil movement in Maharashtra or the Assam type movement against the influx of foreigners favours the urban middle classes seeking government employment.[28] This is true of linguistic politics in most states and is partly a result of the success of the regional language policy which has produced new generations of youth who have no exposure to any other language except the vernacular and who as a result, cannot hope to gain employment in any state except their own. The new middle classes thrown up by the two decades of economic change across the small towns of India are vernacular in culture and many of them have used regionalism for the fulfilment of economic and political aspirations of upward mobility.[29]

The close connection between new regional bourgeoisie and business groups and regional parties demonstrates the social character of many of the regional upsurges. Parties such as the DMK and Telugu Desam have become powerful advocates of regional business interests. Agrarian change and agricultural growth played a critical part in shaping the process of capitalist development in the regions and in creating the new class of regional capitalists, who have in the post-Green Revolution period moved into industry. Typically, such businessmen are born in agrarian merchant/trading, money-lending or professional middle class families and invariably have agrarian and rural roots.[30] They are often first or second generation business families and have moved into areas like cement, sugar, pharmaceuticals and electronics backed by the state governments and public financial institutions. They promote regional political parties to gain support and leverage with foreign investors and national big business.

To be sure, regional pressures have shifted the centre of regional gravity to the more prosperous states of the southern and western India with capital accumulating and gravitating there in new industries, new information technologies, research and development complexes. The relatively higher level of economic development in these states demonstrated the benefits of regional assertion which has clearly helped in building broad-based political affinities that can then make claims on the central government to augment development opportunities and public investment. Both the state and central governments have intervened to support industrial enterprise in states where the regional capitalists were already influential: as in Gujarat, Maharashtra, Karnataka, Tamil Nadu, Andhra Pradesh, Punjab and Haryana. In contrast the four north Indian states of Uttar Pradesh, Bihar, Madhya Pradesh and Rajasthan, though they account for nearly one-third of the members of Parliament, have neither singly nor collectively pulled their weight in favour of economic development.

The most visible outcome of the struggle for economic and political power is an increase in representation in government of the vernacular elite who have established themselves at local and regional levels. It is illustrated in the strategic shift from protests against the symbols of Brahman domination to an appropriation and consolidation of political power through an acquisition of economic clout, control over the educational system and jobs in the government sector. The scale of the transfer of power, as indeed the social constellations giving rise to these shifts, has varied from state to state, but the unmistakable aftermath of regionalization has been the displacement of upper castes from positions of power and the rise to power of intermediate classes and castes. This had already happened in Tamil Nadu, Karnataka, Andhra Pradesh, Kerala, Gujarat and Maharashtra and is now under way in Bihar, Madhya Pradesh and Uttar Pradesh.

One feature of political transformation is the diffusion of power downwards and greater autonomy and power for the states.[31] The emergence of states as pathways to power marks a decisive change from Indira Gandhi's regime under which the centre was deliberately given priority over the states. Then the centre was the most important avenue for a quick rise to power, whereas now states are strong and new groups find they can quickly establish their dominance through control of the state arena. This tendency has been fortified by nearly a decade of liberalization.

Three principal changes are underway: the centre is not pre-eminent in the way it was during Indira Gandhi's rule; there has been a growth in the power of state governments after the collapse of the centralized Congress party; and politically and ideologically a perception has taken root that the state is an important arena for both political power and economic development. Meanwhile, liberalization and economic reforms are accelerating the shift of power from the centre to the states as states compete with each other to attract foreign direct investment, establish tax structures and institutional mechanisms for clearance of such projects. After industrial deregulation the number of industries under central government control declared by Parliament to be in national interest has shrunk to eight.[32] Indeed, some state governments such as Tamil Nadu, Andhra Pradesh, Karnataka, Maharashtra, Gujarat and Orissa have taken the lead in mobilizing investment by national enterprises and multinational corporations, with control over sanctions to acquire land, buildings, power connections, telephones and other services. As the then Finance Minister, P. Chidambram, pointedly remarked, the push for economic reform no longer depends upon the uncertainties of party politics at the centre: 'Chief Ministers gather in Delhi to make policies for the central government. This is a most welcome development.' But the fact remains that economic reform is increasing disparities between states with the flow of domestic and foreign investment channelled to the relatively developed and stable states.

The formation of the United Front government in June 1996, comprising 13 regional and state-based parties, is a forceful demonstration of the shift of power to the states.[33] Dominated by regional parties, this conglomeration sealed the fate of the short-lived BJP government which was unable to secure the support of regional parties for the confidence vote sought by the BJP government in Parliament in May 1996.[34] The BJP had expected that once it was invited to form the government by the President, regional parties would simply gravitate towards the party at the prospect of participating in the BJP-led government, but this assumption clearly underrated the importance of the regional phenomena and misjudged the priorities of parties like the DMK, Telugu Desam, Assam Gana Parishad and Tamil Manila Congress who are socially rooted in regions and have their own regional agenda which run contrary to that of the BJP. Regardless of the BJP's efforts to demonstrate its federal face by making promises to revoke the arbitrary use of Article 356, the party favours a nationalized and unified organization which combines three dimensions: conflation of a strong state with a Hindu state, a highly centralized party apparatus, and links with the Rashtriya Swayamsevak Sangh (RSS) which is not accountable to Parliament or anyone.[35] The opposition to the BJP thus stems not only from a rejection of communalism, but also from the rejection of its notions of a monolithic and homogeneous India held together by a domineering centre.[36]

The appointment of Deve Gowda, a regional leader, as Prime Minister in 1996 signalled a most important moment in the regionalization process, because the crucial thing was not that regional leaders were playing an important role in the selection of the Prime Minister, but one of them had made it to the top job in the country. Gowda's selection marked the emergence of a new cluster of non-upper caste leadership with local roots and unwilling to be junior partners of national parties. Unable to speak Hindi, the official language of the Union, Gowda repeatedly emphasized the national relevance of Karnataka's development experience and his own political and administrative record as chief minister of that state. The process of replacing Gowda by Inder Kumar Gujral as the leader of the United Front in April 1997 was similarly controlled by regional leaders, notably by chief ministers of Andhra Pradesh, Tamil Nadu, Assam, West Bengal and Bihar. Again, no one was left in doubt of the enormity of transition from one-party dominance to regionally-driven coalition politics. Thus the United Front demonstrated the possibilities of regionally-driven coalition politics as a device for managing social and regional pluralism. The salience of both these aspects has grown as the Indian polity has become more participatory: for while regional leaders played a crucial role in the choice of successors to Jawaharlal Nehru in 1964 and Lal Bahadur Shastri in 1966, on both these occasions their role was not as decisive and conspicuous as it was in the operation of the United Front.

IV

It remains to be seen whether the new role played by chief ministers and regional parties signifies a substantial redistribution of power between states and centre, and more importantly, whether it will actually produce an alternative concept and structure of governance. So far little thought has been given to institutional arrangements which might provide mechanisms for communication between various parties involved in the coalition or between the centre and the states. Moreover, the crucial issue is not just a shift of power from centre to states but a change in the orientation of the state to build an institutional framework for a federal-democratic-secular state; to use the state actively to reconstitute society and maintain the balance in favour of unity and equity against incoherence and injustice. Undoubtedly, states have increased their relevance and significance, but this has happened mainly because of a regionalization of politics caused by Congress decline and the resulting redistribution of power, and not because of an energetic restructuring of the existing political system. Beyond this, the introduction of elections to municipal corporations and local panchayats, with statutory provisions for reservations to increase the participation of lower castes, dalits and women, has been used to institutionalize grassroots popular participation. Over time this has the greatest chance of heightening political consciousness and incorporating the demands of the newly mobilized and disadvantaged groups into the state and national policy-making process. Though the shape of political arrangements is not clear yet, none the less it is evident that we are witnessing a decisive movement in the power structure: the ascendancy of previously excluded and numerically large groups will be an enduring feature of the transition to a post-Congress polity and the regional and state-based parties will be the nodal points of democratic power.

Much of India's regional politics is not at odds with the centre or national economic development, rather state and regional parties have done well in states with the highest rates of growth. Among seven states ranked in 1996 as having had the highest rates of growth—Tamil

Nadu, Andhra Pradesh, Karnataka, Arunachal Pradesh, Maharashtra, Punjab and Assam—only Arunachal Pradesh was ruled by the Congress party and Karnataka by an officially designated national party, the Janata Dal.[37] Notwithstanding these positive trends, most importantly the increased participation of groups long considered marginal, there are serious problems of cohesion and unity of political parties in mobilizing support around issues of caste and religion that make it difficult to constitute stable alliances and governments at the state level. The complexities of these changes and the various tendencies at work is dramatized by the problems of ungovernability that confronted the United Front coalition and its short-lived collaboration with the Congress. The United Front's justification for cooperation with the Congress was to protect secularism, and, yet the Front was not able to prevent the BJP from coming to power in two states first as an ally of the Akali Dal in Punjab and then by making a deal with the Bahujan Samaj Party in Uttar Pradesh; what is more it was allowed to continue in power in the most crucial state even when the deal fell through in October 1997. In the event the coalition exhausted itself in mutual bickering with the Congress repeatedly threatening to withdraw its support from outside, thus discrediting the coalitional experiment. Clearly, there is a need to put in place institutional mechanisms to maintain coordination between political parties that provide support from outside for the effective working of coalition politics.

This brings me to the central point of this paper. Two conceptions of political identity—the inclusionary nationalism of the Congress and the exclusionary nationalism of the BJP have failed to either preserve or establish their supremacy across the length and breadth of the country. In utter contrast to the inclusiveness of the Congress, the BJP's attempts to privilege an exclusive Hindu identity and integrate all sections of society around an amorphous appeal of Hindutva has produced polarization and conflict, and thus compounded the problem of putting together an alternative agenda by exacerbating communal divisions. Neither of the centralized parties seem capable of dealing in any meaningful way with the increased competitiveness, rising assertiveness and mobilization of ever more segments of the population. At the same time, there is need to recognize that the Congress filled a space in Indian politics and continues to embody a shared imagination of the nation. The alternative in India, to the goal of creating a nation-state modelled on the unilingual states of Europe in which there is also a dominant culture and dominant religion, are the long-term tendencies represented by the transformative agenda of the Left parties in Kerala and West Bengal, and the social justice agenda of the secular parties of the lower and backward castes and the regional parties. Some of the issues in India's public life emanating from the tensions between centralizing and decentralizing tendencies, between nation and region and secularism and Hindu nationalism, have remained at the core of the evolution of our contemporary consciousness since the early decades of the twentieth century. Beneath the surface of the current struggles, however, lie a complex of changes in Indian society, which have as much to do with the evolution of different cultures and the uneven economic development of regions, as with the shifting ways in which regional and national identities are formed and reformed in response to structures of centralization and processes of politico-economic inclusion and exclusion.

NOTES

1. That Congress accepted the principle of unilingual states is evident from the fact that Congress branches from the early 1920s were known provincially by their linguistic divisions. Ashis Banerjee, 'Federalism and Nationalism', in Nirmal Mukharji and Balveer Arora (eds.), *Federalism in India: Origins and Development* (Delhi, 1992).
2. T.V. Satyamurthy, Introduction to vol. 3 in T.V. Satyamurthy (ed.), *Region, Religion, Caste, Gender and Culture in Contemporary India* (Delhi, 1996).
3. Granville Austin, *The Indian Constitution: Cornerstone of a Nation* (Oxford, 1966), p. 191.
4. For a recent account see Tilottama Misra and Udayan Misra, 'Movements for Autonomy in India's North-East', in T.V. Satyamurthy (ed.), *Region, Religion, Caste, Gender and Culture in Contemporary India* (Delhi, 1996).
5. This formed the core of the reform agenda of the 1970s. It was reflected in the terms of the Sarkaria Commission.
6. Regional insurgencies in Punjab, Kashmir and Assam have attracted much scholarly attention. There are a number of studies of the Punjab problem. See for example Rajiv Kapur, *Sikh Separatism: The Punjab Politics of Faith* (London, 1986), Paul Brass, 'The Punjab Crisis and the Unity of India' in Atul Kohli (ed.), *India's Democracy: An Analysis of Changing State-Society Relations* (Princeton, 1986). On Kashmir see M.J. Akbar, *Behind the Vale* (Delhi, 1991). On Assam see Jyotindra Dasguta, 'Ethnicity, Democracy and

Development in India: Assam in General Perspective', in Atul Kohli (ed.), *India's Democracy* (Delhi, 1991).

7. On this pattern see Achin Vanaik, *The Painful Transition: India's Bourgeois Democracy* (London, 1990).
8. On this see Paul Brass, 'Punjab Crisis and Unity of India', in Atul Kohli (ed.), *India's Democracy* (Delhi, 1991).
9. Together, the March 1971 parliamentary elections, the events in Bangladesh, the war with Pakistan, and the March 1972 assembly elections—all in the course of the one year—pushed towards the creation of a consensus on nation-building through a strong central government.
10. I have discussed some of these developments in my article 'The Prime Minister and the Left', in James Manor (ed.), *Nehru to the Nineties: the Changing Office of Prime Minister in India* (London, 1994).
11. In fact, the Congress itself—until the late sixties—was a cluster of regional power centres because the Congress organization in most states, except the northern states, functioned as an effective vehicle for regional participation, whereas after the 1977 elections it functioned as a national party but without strong roots in regional politics.
12. For the ruling party itself, centralization was premised on the assumption of a dichotomy between governance and polity and further that institutions at the state and district level embedded in the local polity were invariably weak, inefficient and unreliable and thus required the superior wisdom of the centre. This point is made by Balveer Arora and Nirmal Mukharji in their Introduction to *Federalism in India.*
13. For an analysis of centre-state relations in this period see Paul Brass, 'Pluralism, Regionalism and Decentralizing tendencies in Contemporary Indian Politics', A. Jayaratnam and Denis Dalton (eds.), *The States of South Asia: Problems of National Integration, Essays in Honour of W.J. Morris-Jones* (Delhi, 1982).
14. On the growth of the Telugu Desam see Atul Kohli, 'The NTR Phenomena in Andhra Pradesh: Political Change in a South Indian State', *Asian Survey*, October 1988.
15. 'Centre-State Relations: Changing Equations', *India Today*, 30 June 1996, p. 81.
16. Ibid.
17. Ibid., p. 81.
18. Ibid.
19. Balveer Arora, 'Adapting Federalism to India: Multilevel and Asymmetrical Innovations', in Balveer Arora and Douglas Verney (eds.), *Multiple Identities in a Single State: Indian Federalism in Comparative Perspective* (Delhi, 1995).
20. The 72nd Constitution Amendment Bill was unanimously passed on 22 December 1992. Although the Panchayat Act leaves the initiative to the states, it lays down a list of 29 subjects which must be transferred by the states to the panchayats.

21. Yogendra Yadav, 'How India Voted', *India Today,* 31 May 1996.
22. The BJP's vote share of 20 per cent hides the fact that the bulk of it comes from these five states where on an average its vote share is 36 per cent.
23. Yogendra Yadav, 'How India Voted', *India Today,* 31 May 1996.
24. For a detailed analysis of the pattern of party competition see Yogendra Yadav, 'Reconfiguration in Indian Politics: State Assembly Elections, 1993-95', *Economic and Political Weekly,* 13-20 January 1996, pp. 99-102.
25. Francine Frankel, 'The Problem', a symposium on emerging issues in centre-state relations, *Seminar, 459,* November 1997.
26. James Manor, 'Regional Parties in Federal Systems', in Balveer Arora and Douglas Verney (eds.), *Multiple Identities in a Single State,* p. 125.
27. Achin Vanaik, *The Painful Transition,* pp. 123-5.
28. Ibid., Chap., 3, pp. 130-1.
29. On this aspect see D.L. Sheth, 'The Great Language Debate: Politics of Metropolitan versus Vernacular India', in Upendra Baxi and Bhiku Parekh (eds.), *Crisis and Change in Contemporary India* (Delhi, 1995).
30. Sanjay Baru, 'Economic Policy and the Development of Capitalism in India: The Emerging Role of Regional Capitalists and Regional Political Parties', paper presented at the conference on 'Democracy and Transformation: India's Fifty Years after Independence', organized by the Centre for the Advanced Study of India, University of Pennsylvania, New Delhi, November 1997.
31. On the growing importance of the state as the leading arena of contestation see Atul Kohli, 'Power and Powerlessness', in Joel Migdal, Atul Kohli and Vivien Shue (eds.), *State Power and Social Forces: Domination and Transformation in the Third World* (Cambridge, 1995). Also see Yogendra Yadav, 'Reconfiguration of Indian Politics'.
32. Francine Frankel, 'The Problem', p. 14.
33. The combined strength of regional parties was greater than that of the Janata Dal: regional parties had 58 seats and Janata Dal 46 seats in the 1996 Parliament.
34. Although the BJP has allowed some flexibility to state units to adapt to specific political cultures of different states, the concerns of BJP's political discourse from Kashmir in the north to Karnataka and Kerala in the south are supra-regional. This is evident from the issues that form the staple of party's campaign for power at the centre—Ayodhya, uniform civil code, ban on cow slaughter, abolition of Article 370 which accords a special status to Kashmir.
35. While itself favouring a strong centralized state, it attacks the Congress for encouraging fissiparous tendencies and corruption, that in fact is a result of centralization. Tapan Basu, Pradip Datta, Sumit Sarkar, Tanika Sarkar, Sambuddha Sen, *Khaki Shorts, Saffron Flags* (Delhi, 1993), p. 114.
36. Mahesh Rangarajan, 'The Politics of Transition', *Seminar,* January 1997.
37. Francine Frankel, 'The Problem', pp. 13-15.

9

Behind the Verdict: Another Look at the Nation and the Regions

JAVEED ALAM

The purpose of examining the Indian electoral verdict of 1996 in this paper is not to provide a reading of the votes and seats and their statistical significance. This will only be a backdrop to some of the larger questions that I intend to examine: what kinds of notions of 'nation' are getting articulated in the way people have given expression to their political preferences during this and the previous election, and how these relate to the different linguistic-cultural regions of India.

As we look at the verdict and what lies behind it, I will try to show that while the BJP in 1996 emerged as the biggest party in terms of seats, it did not represent the nation. In fact, the idea of India that it has propagated with vehemence did not find acceptance in a large contiguous area of India. By sorting out the electoral data one can discern that the people are giving expression to two very different conceptions of India. It is not unimportant for them, given what they have been exposed to by the militant Hindu right-wing, to give a verdict on what it means to be an Indian.

Let me try to derive what I see as the emerging models of the nation called India behind the verdict. Of the states with more than two seats in Parliament, 13 already have a more or less clearly developed two-party system. (In talking of the two-party system it seems quite reasonable to treat stable coalitional patterns, like that in Kerala for instance, as part of this system.) Of these there are six states in which of the two parties that dominate the political scene, the BJP is one.

These are Himachal Pradesh, Delhi, Gujarat, Rajasthan, Maharashtra and Madhya Pradesh. In six of the other seven states with a two-party system the BJP is a minor presence polling 5-7 per cent of the vote. Only in Orissa has it a sizeable vote. There it polled 13.2 per cent of the votes and came in second in three of the twenty constituencies. In Andhra Pradesh, Punjab and Tamil Nadu one or the other regional party is dominant; in West Bengal, Tripura and Kerala the Left Front led by the Communist Party of India (Marxist) is the dominant force; only in Orissa are the two national secular parties the main contestants. In all the states where a two-party system has taken root, Congress continues to be a force to reckon with. Interestingly, in states like UP and Bihar, where Congress has disintegrated, there is a situation of intense multi-party competition and of confusion with fortunes changing along with shifting alliances. In Karnataka, Assam and Haryana the situation is one of multi-party competition but the direction is unclear. In UP the BJP has achieved a stable dominant position, enjoying the overwhelming support of the dominant castes, while in Karnataka, it has a stable sizeable presence with about a quarter of the vote over the last few election. But in Haryana its political fortunes have widely fluctuated (in 1996 it gained 24 per cent more vote than in 1991) depending on the sort of alliances it has managed to enter into. Whenever it has gone alone it has not done well. Finally in Assam, it has not managed to spread beyond a few pockets, with a vote around 15 per cent.

In spite of the fact that these verdicts at the state level are so unambiguous, they do not combine into any coherent pattern of majority for any party at the centre. It is not just a case of the federal nature of the political verdict (whatever be the nature of the constitutional scheme of power) but much more a case, I believe, of the manifestation of the 'national question' in India in a new form. A large number of Indian nationalities are now setting forth conditions on the terms in which the country or the Indian nation can be defined. No singular definition of a nation or the political requirements of unity based on that suffices any more for the people in these regions. Gone are the days when one type of leadership or party or centre could hustle people into accepting that India can only mean this and not that. Yet this, in itself, does not pose a threat to the unity of the country, as is suggested by BJP supporters. What does is the BJP's attempt to impose another monolithic definition, that of Hindu nation or what is also being referred to as cultural nationalism, inherited from the ruling class misconceptions about the nature of Indian society.

India can only be a voluntary union of nationalities; there is no way in which the latter can be coerced to be a part of an India arbitrarily defined from the top by the ruling classes in terms of the requirements of their rule. What seems to be happening today is not a questioning of India as a nation as such, but people representing the different linguistic-cultural zones and belonging to different communities coming forward to define India in terms of their experience of the nation over the last fifty years. It should be evident to any student of Indian society that in a country as diverse as India with histories of the people so different (and therefore the store of memories which people draw upon to make sense of politics also different), the sense of being Indian cannot obviously be the same everywhere if allowed democratic articulation. People are now freely articulating their experience of India and what it means to them to be called an Indian. The fear of being branded an 'enemy' of the nation or 'anti-national', which had gripped the country in the wake of partition, has now abated. And the danger lies not in this happening, because regions and people within these regions seem to be capable of sorting it out, but in the efforts of the BJP to foist on the voters another, more pernicious, monolithic definition of a nation and a morbid nationalism to go with it. BJP politics is simply an attempt to annul this emerging experience of the people which is leading to the democratization of the national question. It should, therefore, come as no surprise that none of the political parties representing the various nationality interests have responded to the BJP's appeals. They felt that what the BJP has come to represent is the diametric opposite of the experience that they have come to authenticate and actualize. Here is a very important popular base upon which to wage a long battle against Hindu nationalism and the fascist force that hides behind it.

In all the thirteen states where a two-party situation prevails, there has emerged, over the years, varying from state to state, a distinct political makeup centred around the linguistic-cultural specificity and/or history of the region and underpinned by the democratic movement there. This now seems to condition in a strong way the political preferences of the people of the states. How else do we explain the enduring persistence, in some of the states, of certain ideological trends and political parties or formations centred around these ideological trends? But within all this variation, if we look at the resemblances and approximations across the states in terms of their affinities, we find two broad patterns of national identity.

In an entire region covering almost the whole of southern India (barring Karnataka) and stretching over the eastern India into Assam and the north-eastern states, there is a clear absence of receptivity to something like Hindutva. Nationalism defined in Hindu religious-cultural terms has failed to gain a foothold in these regions. Not that religion is any less important here than in other regions. Far from it. But religion in the south and east does not seem to appeal so much to the political imagination of the people (or the popular consciousness). The overt, tangible and direct connection between politics and religion, and therefore the equation that follows between nation and religion among all shades of the militant Hindu right-wing, is lacking. In this region there is also a much clearer sense of distinct nationality make-up within each of linguistic-cultural groups or states. Let us therefore add that in this entire region the sense of nationality, together with the sense of being an Indian, is very strong. In other words, this means that the sense of being an Indian does not swamp strong local loyalties and that the diverse articulations are accepted as legitimate forms of political expression. Nevertheless, what seems to me to be quite clear is that a different notion of nation is being articulated in these regions. This is of some significance in understanding the emerging shape of India with the undermining of the monolithic nationalist centre that justified itself as the sole means of keeping India together.

Let us note, in passing, that in this entire region (let us also call it the anti-Hindutva India) there are something like 247 Parliamentary seats and the BJP in 1996 managed to win a mere 7, one in Assam and the rest in Karnataka. In all the other states it drew a blank. Only in Assam (16.5 per cent) and Orissa (13.2 per cent) could it poll a sizeable vote. We will look at the future prospects of the BJP a little later, but for now we can note that its chances of growing into a much bigger force in Assam and Orissa are good. From the mid-1980s the BJP's support base in both these states has steadily gone up. In Assam its vote went up from a mere 0.4 per cent in 1984 to 9.6 per cent in 1991 to 16.5 per cent in 1996. Likewise, in Orissa, it went up from 1.2 per cent in 1984 to 9.5 per cent in 1991 and 13.6 per cent in 1996. But in

Assam, unlike in Orissa, this growth of the BJP is strongly countered by a very articulate nationality movement which itself is facing demands of various smaller people with a clear national make-up. Nevertheless, the gain over the support level of 1991 is significant because those were times of unbridled communal frenzy.

The absence of support for the BJP in most parts of anti-Hindutva India entitles us to examine the claim of the BJP that it has a mandate to rule over India because it is the largest single party. What kind of largeness does 160 seats on the basis of an average 20 per cent vote and another 3 per cent for its smaller allies (and another 15 per cent for the Shiv Sena) represent in the largeness of India? It is representative territorially of less than half the country and has a winning capacity restricted as of now to about 330 seats. In any democratic understanding it should not matter from where one wins seats. No one will object if a certain party were to win its majority from only half the country in USA or Australia. Yet such a claim, if it were to be transferred to the Indian situation, would lead to an abstraction of democratic understanding from all its concrete specificities. No party in India can hold the country together for long in a situation like the one the BJP finds itself in. For all its bravado, the party knows itself to be in a very difficult position. To gain a national majority it will have to win a staggering 85 per cent of the seats from these 330 constituencies in those parts of the country where it finds itself acceptable. In 1996 the BJP contested 270 seats and won 59 per cent of them. Another 7 per cent of these were won by it allies, whose winning rate on these 90 seats was as low as 38 per cent. It therefore seems unlikely that the BJP in the near future will win a clear majority on its own.

To come back to the articulation of the notion of nation behind the choices of the people, let us consider a few more features of the BJP's 1996 performance. It won 74.37 per cent of its seats (119 out of 160) from the Hindi heartland. It won another 34 seats from Gujarat and Maharashtra. Therefore, 95.62 per cent of its seats came from three regions (153 of the 160 seats). It could only win 7 seats in the southern, eastern and north-eastern regions (out of 247 seats).

The above analysis suggests that there are clear limits to the further growth of the BJP. It has grown very fast in certain regions of the country, but slowly in others. For example, in Tamil Nadu it grew from 0.1 per cent in 1984 to 0.3 per cent in 1989 and from 1.6 per cent in

1991 to 2.9 per cent in 1996. In Kerala it rose from 1.8 per cent to 4.5 per cent and then from 4.6 per cent to 5.5 per cent over the same period. In Andhra Pradesh it got 2.2 per cent in 1984 and 2 per cent in 1989, 9.6 per cent in 1991 (contesting all but one of the state's 42 seats) and 5.1 per cent in 1996. In West Bengal its vote-share went up from 0.4 per cent (9 seats) in 1984 to 1.7 per cent (19 seats) in 1989 and to 11.7 per cent in 1991 (42 seats) but has come down to 7 per cent (42 seats) in 1996. Figures tell their own story but I want to point here two factors which seem likely to provide a check on the growth of the BJP in the foreseeable future.

The first has to do with the fact that in all these states/regions there is a powerful movement for state autonomy or a greater share of power within the federal system. Within this overall movement there is also a strong feeling in some regions of having been 'oppressed' by the centre. Assam, the north-eastern states and Tamil Nadu have often reversed the very principle of pan-Indian nationalism to argue that the centre has no right to dominate the nationalities. Any nationalist sentiment is made up, among other things, of the understanding that no power outside what constitutes that nation/nationality has a right to define the conditions of their existence—in the same way that India cannot be dominated by an outside force, Assamese cannot be dominated by Delhi or the Bodos by Assam. Such a sense of region and of the prerogative and exemptions it should enjoy goes counter to the notion of nation that is central to the BJP's understanding. This, I presume, is going to be a major obstacle in the path of BJP's growth in these regions.

To come to the second factor, let us ask what it is in the BJP version of nationalism or its conception of the nation that has an appeal for the people of certain regions? We have already talked of the Hindu equation of the nation in the BJP's conceptualization of it. What needs to be added here is the well known fact that since V.D. Savarkar in 1925 talked of Hinduizing nationalism and militarizing Hinduism, the Muslim as a suspect element within the Indian nation has been a constant refrain. Given this perception of Muslim mistrust and hatred, it seems possible to suggest that it is only in those regions of India where resistance to Muslim rule has been a feature of the political life and where the memories of this history have become a part of the collective consciousness, that the message of the militant Hindu right-wing has been well received. It is also interesting that the great Hindu cult figures, which were historically elaborated and hammered into the popular consciousness beginning in the latter half of the nineteenth century are also all drawn from these regions. They are now part of the regional historical legend. It is not that there was no Muslim rule in southern or eastern India. The Muslim rulers of Bengal and the Tipus and Nizams of south are testimony to that. But the fact of the matter is that while in these regions Muslim rule was resisted at different times, resistance did not become legendary history and did not give rise to cult heroes. On the contrary, some of the Muslim rulers from these regions like Siraj ud-Daula in Bengal or Tipu Sultan in what is now Karnataka themselves became symbols of national resurgence or anti-colonial heroism and remain so today in spite of all the efforts of Hindu communalists. All this is in sharp contrast to what happened in northern or western India.

It seems to me that the notion of India as *a* 'nation' with a certain cultural mooring has had a very uneven refraction across different regions of the country. If we now try to spatially plot this spread, we may find from the so-called heartland, the dissemination of the idea of the nation as 'Hindu' moves down towards the western side of the country into Gujarat and Maharashtra and related cultural belts without any serious impediments or political resistance; it is only recently that Other Backward Castes (OBCs), with their politics of empowerment, have put up a resistance to the Hindutva wave. But as one heads south or east one cannot help discern a different pattern, with a much greater insistence on being recognized as a distinct 'national identity'. There are demands for autonomy or muted voices for recognition as different nationalities (strident in the tribal belt of Jharkand). I do not want to suggest that the boundaries between the two contiguous belts (south and east) are rigid or even well formed. There is a lot of communication across the boundaries. Yet it cannot be questioned that the notion of India as it exists in the different cultural belts of India is certainly not of one kind. For building a lasting, voluntary union of the people it is a bare minimum requirement to recognize this reality and resist the imposition of any one notion of India on all.

Here, then, is the primary question we encounter in the wake of the 1996 election: is India a multi-national state?

Unlike the nationalists who view India as single nation in a unqualified way, the Marxists and Communists subscribe to the notion of

India being a 'multi-national state' rather than a nation in the sense in which Egypt or Sweden are.[1] This at once may suggest that its national peculiarities, made up as these are of a large number of cultural-linguistic formations, put it together with countries like Switzerland or the erstwhile USSR, and so on, and that the options for politically unifying the people, as in Italy or Portugal or Japan, are not feasible in India. There is nothing in this to be ashamed or afraid of. What they have to clearly specify, however, is the sense in which India is, if at all, multinational. It is indeed here that the Marxists can be seen not to have done their homework properly, and it is also on this point that the argument I made in an earlier article is inadequate.[2] Vanaik in fact cites this as one of the examples of the uncritical nature of Indian Marxist scholarship on the national question. Till now, none of the Marxists have identified features within the evolution of the Indian social formation capable of providing a basis for making formulations or reaching conclusions about the 'national question' in India in the way that E.M.S. Namboodripad does in his study of *The National Question in Kerala*.

It is of some importance at this point to note that the Marxist analyses of the nation have generally failed to go into the intricacies of the social formation within which the nation is situated and out of which it acquires its characteristics. It has more often than not concerned itself with relating the nation to the question of the state. An unwelcome result has been to emphasize common denominators; on deeper analysis these would have to be revealed as superficial similarities. I am therefore somewhat sceptical of the re-evaluatory works like those of Prakash Karat or Ajit Roy or Irfan Habib.[3] A more long-term damaging consequence of this has been a tendency to reductionism—to deduce from conclusions reached in another situation (as in Lenin's writings). In reaching knowledge about human affairs you can not, *per se*, treat a conclusion as a premise.

The fact that the different linguistic-cultural groups in India could never be held together in a single state through conquest is, it seems to me, of consequence. The relatively high degree of structural uniformity and varying levels of cultural unity that Indian achieved in history has not been a result of state-induced coercion or forced incorporation as happened in Tsarist Russia or the Austro-Hungarian empire. Rather, they slowly came closer together through a framework of social action and a set of philosophical presuppositions. The philosophical presuppositions—notions and expectations entailed in concepts like *karma*, *varna*, *maya*, *moksha* and so on—slowly spread across the country under Brahmanical auspices and became coterminous with what is now called the Indian subcontinent.

The pronounced variations between regions and the affinities across these (such that we can notice certain 'belts' as discussed earlier) have been the result of number of features, but chief among these are: the compromises that Brahmanism entered into as it expanded; the history of colonial transformation; and the subsequent trajectories of the democratic movement. One may be tempted here to compare this to the spread of Christianity in Europe. But this is different as it was also supplemented by the spread of the same occupational principles and organizational forms of social structure having strong scriptural sanction and therefore enjoying deep legitimacy. The *varna* philosophy and the ideology of *jati* sanctified in scriptural legitimacy provided, in spite of all regional and local variations, a basis of a lasting social uniformity. All this without a central authority, religious or secular.

It is important to emphasize that this was not limited just to the dominant classes. It created a common reference-world and framework of meanings in terms of which exploited and illiterate people could not only be drawn into the world of Hinduism but could relate spontaneously to the sphere of secular activity. How these came to acquire a deep-rooted social acceptance is a long and complex story. Suffice it to note here that in India there neither was a state in the accepted sense nor an organized Church to enforce centrally supervised compliance. Hundreds of locally-based, village-centred modes of enforcing compliance do not induce a feeling of oppression by an external force; local chieftains may have played an important role but they cannot be considered as the key element in this system of compliance. The state as a centralized institution, in any case, was an episodic presence, enjoying (as all new-born in India do) a high level of infant mortality. This *mode of creation* of a common or similar cultural network and philosophical systems and social practices embedded in them is something very much an Indian specificity. The Church and the state were central to the Christian experience in Europe and so was the state the chief instrument in making Confucianism the hegemonic force in China.

This civilizational inheritance does not imply, however, that there existed anything like an Indian nation as claimed by revivalists and Hindu fanatics today. The presence of such a civilizational uniformity does not anywhere get automatically translated into a sense of national community or political unity. This can be easily seen in the trajectory of developments in the Arabic-speaking Muslim world or Spanish-speaking Catholic-Christian Latin America. It may only facilitate—given the emergence of a common market and a transregional bourgeoisie and a regionally mobile elite—the growth of a supra-national nationalism and give a certain content to it when conditions emerge for a national awakening. Civilization and nation are relations of non-identity. Anyway, it was into this pre-existing uniformity/unity that innumerable migrations took place. All such migrations got, with time, assimilated into Hinduism.

Let me at this point disturb the narrative of civilizational unity. While assimilation was the overall pattern, it broke down when Muslims started coming to South Asia in large numbers from the eleventh century. Muslims were the first outside people who could not be assimilated into the pre-existing civilizational pattern. The reverse of this is also equally true. India is one of the very few places where Muslims, after the conquest and the establishment of their prolonged, centralized rule, could not convert the entire indigenous religious communities to Islam. Nevertheless, Islam did spread both through coercion and via numerous mystic movements—but not everywhere. Muslims became an overwhelming majority only in certain belts of north-western India. Further to the east of these region, in Punjab and in Bengal, they acquired a majority without an overwhelming advantage. In the rest of the country they did not constitute anywhere much more than a fifth of the population. Such a pattern of development had a profound impact on the evolution of the national question with the distorted development of capitalism under colonial patronage. It also created considerable confusion among the Indian nationalists in drawing up a clear-cut national programme in the face of the growth of Muslim 'separatism' and the demand for Pakistan.[4]

Given this complexity and difference what do we say of the issue of India as national or multinational? I think an answer one way or the other would land us into too categorial a position which is not warranted by the nature of our national inheritance or in the way social reality is evolving, as we have seen above. It would very much depend on where we view India from and who does the viewing. The 'discourse' about India as a *nation* seems to have seeped down into popular consciousness over a large geographical space from the north to the west, whereas it has failed to do so in an unqualified way in the east, north-east and south, an equally large geographical expanse. In an extended belt comprising many regions the discourse and process correspond, while in the other belt the 'discourse' and the process sharply diverge.[5] Viewed in one way India is clearly not multinational; but the same country viewed another way has indeed many features, including the perceptual ones, that we consider multinational.

The Marxists were wrong to call India multinational. What we need is a much more nuanced analysis of the 'national' reality of India than has been forthcoming from any ideological or intellectual perspective. A proper theorization of the national question can follow only around attempts to arrive at detailed concrete analyses. While this requires time, a beginning at the level of policy initiatives has to be made.

Left and democratic political understanding has concentrated on the question of state autonomy and on decentralization as a remedy for the multi-nation dilemma. But I think that things have moved far beyond that as a solution to the crisis of the country. It does not seem likely to me that the affected regions are going to accept constitutional solutions in the conventional sense of something doled out from above. The main democratic political currents in India must prepare the general public opinion in the country to be ready to reach out towards a *radical re-negotiation* of Indian federalism. Whatever we do in terms of fiscal and related reforms, the fact will remain that the federalism was created from above and the states and regions made to subscribe to it. As against this, in working out the new we will have to rework the federal scheme in such a way that the states and regions feel that they have voluntarily come together and given shape to a new centre.

Will this decentralization threaten national unity? This prospect seems to me to be not groundless but exaggerated. Centralization and the bureaucratized views of the nation have not insured against secessionist movements. We are today witness to the unwelcome spectacle of continuous military deployment to hold India together. Can anything worse than this be contemplated?

Nevertheless two serious anxieties within the democratic forces have to be addressed. One pertains to the genuine fear that, given this degree of freedom, some States or regions may choose to secede. In view of the prevailing mood in certain parts of the country, this can very well be foreseen as a possibility. But what is the alternative? To hold such areas forever by force of arms? And for how long? Can the democratic opinion be confident that in five or ten years things will get sorted out and so coercion, however unpleasant, is going to be a very transitory phenomenon? It is difficult to think that the retarded capitalism we have in India will provide the social wherewithal to handle such problems; against the current only powerful Left and democratic movements can. Moreover, to have a high estimation of possibilities is to credit the bourgeois-landlord leadership with democratic propensities which it simply does not possess. Taking into view the range of possibilities in the given situation, the one option that the Left and democratic forces ought to keep in view is to prepare popular opinion for a fight to grant to these regions a very high degree of autonomy, high enough to allow the people of the region to feel that they are the masters in their areas. This is the price we will have to pay if we want to avoid the militarization of society that is fast taking place and the consequent brutalization of the life of ordinary people.

NOTES

1. Achin Vanaik, *Painful Transitions: Bourgeois Democracy in India* (London, 1991).
2. Javeed Alam, 'Capitalist Transformation and National Crystallisation', *Economic and Political Weekly*, 29 January 1983.
3. See *Social Scientist* (special issue on the 'National Question'), No. 37, August 1975.
4. See Javeed Alam, 'Nation: Discourse and Intervention by the Communists in India' in T.V. Sathyamurthy (ed.), *State and Nation in the Context of Social Change,* vol. 1 (Delhi, 1994).
5. From what I have analysed as the historical process in the making of India and its various discursive dimensions—how it is talked of and conceived—in the different regions/belts of the country, it follows that India as we have it today cannot essentially be a discursive formation. It is clear that the refraction of the idea of India in diferent regions/belts is so different that in spite of a strong common denominator it cannot be the same discursive entity. India as one and whole will have to have an intellecutally demarcated

discursive field for a similar discourse to prevail. Mutually distinct discursive fields cannot constitute a single discourse because the flow of discourse across these regionally specific discursive fields will be impeded. There can, in situations as of modern-day India only be so *many* different discursive formations of nation. I am therefore not convinced of the seemingly persuasive and erudite analysis of Sudipto Kaviraj, 'The Imaginary Institution of India', *Subaltern Studies*, II, 1993. The logical flaw in the argument is to extend in an impermissible manner and in an intellectually imperious way the discourse features from one region like Bengal at a point of historical time to the whole of India as it has evolved to what it is today. The making of India is much more, as it was in its earlier phases too, in the non-discursive and often imperceptible processes, as we have seen, for one breezy moment, behind the verdict for the 1996 Lok Sabha elections.

10

The Two Nations: Indian Federalism in the Rip Tide of Debt and Globalism

PETER MAYER

INTRODUCTION

The rip tide of globalism is coursing along the coastal borders of virtually every nation. According to many observers, it is the integrity of national sovereignty itself which is being eroded by that swift current. In their popular *The Third Wave*, the Tofflers offer an alternative image of the impact upon the state which is being wrought by worldwide economic change:

> As the Third Wave thunders across the earth, the nation-state—the key political unit of the Second Wave era—is being squeezed by vice like pressures from above and below. One set of forces seeks to transfer power downwards from the nation-state to subnational regions and groups. The others seek to shift power upwards from the nation to transnational agencies and organizations. Together they are leading to a crack-up of the high-technology nations into smaller and less powerful units. . . .[1]

In this paper I argue that the currents of globalism have also begun to sweep India along with them and that the implications for Indian federalism are likely to be profound. Let me begin to trace what those currents are by looking at an aspect of centre-state relations which has strong resonance in Australia and no doubt elsewhere: the 'black hole' of national finances.

BUDGETS

The financial crisis of 1991 which was coincidental with the assassination of Rajiv Gandhi, precipitated the newly installed Congress leader P.V. Narasimha Rao into the unlikely role of economic reformer. That crisis was largely one caused in the short run by an acute shortage of foreign exchange; India was down to a few week's foreign reserves and was forced to turn to the International Monetary Fund (IMF) for assistance, which came, as it always does, at a price. Almost beyond any hope, the measures of liberalization adopted by Rao and his Finance Minister Manmohan Singh, turned around the crisis in foreign exchange. Although in subsequent years imports have still exceeded exports, capital inflows have been such that the rupee has been remarkably steady as it comes closer to full convertibility.

But it possible to argue that underlying the foreign exchange crisis is a financial situation—a 'black hole' to adopt the overblown rhetoric of Australian politics—which will drive relations in India's federal system as strongly as it does Australia's. In the aftermath of the mid-1991 crisis, measures were taken to increase receipts from taxation and to cut expenditures. Although that has had the effect of restraining a run-away deficit, it has not ended it. And there are strong currents still running.

A consistent trend since 1987 in the budget figures has been the growing share of central revenues which has had to be allocated to repayment of interest.

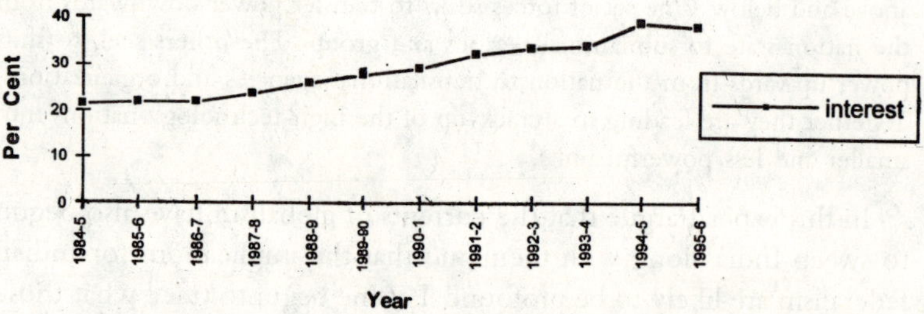

SOURCE: Economic Division, Ministry of Finance, Government of India, *Economic Survey*, 1988-9, 1992-3, 1994-5, Gosh *et al.* (1995).

FIGURE 1: INTEREST AS PERCENTAGE OF CENTRAL REVENUE EXPENDITURE

As Figure 1 indicates, payments of interest as a percentage of revenue expenditure have nearly doubled, rising from just over 21 per cent in 1984-5 to nearly 39 per cent in 1995-6. It appears that interest payments have largley been financed in recent years by fresh borrowing. Figure 2 indicates that interest payments and borrowings have tended to be nearly equal.

As India has begun to open up its economy, it has had to begin to lower its very high levels of tariff protection. Following the 1991 crisis, the highest level of protection was 'reduced' to 110 per cent.[2] Two years later the peak level of protection had come down to 65 per cent.[3] One relatively unnoticed consequence has been that the share of revenue derived from tariffs has fallen by 7 per cent.[4] More broadly, reforms to indirect taxation in 1994-5 were estimated to lead to a revenue loss of Rs. 3604 crore (roughly A$1.6 billion).

One of the principal casualties of the growing burden of interest repayments has been spending on capital investment. Figure 3 shows that capital spending has fallen from 30 per cent of total expenditure in the late 1980s to just about 20 per cent in recent years. This decline appears to hold serious consequences as the speed of Indian development depends crucially on infrastructure investment, especially in electric power.

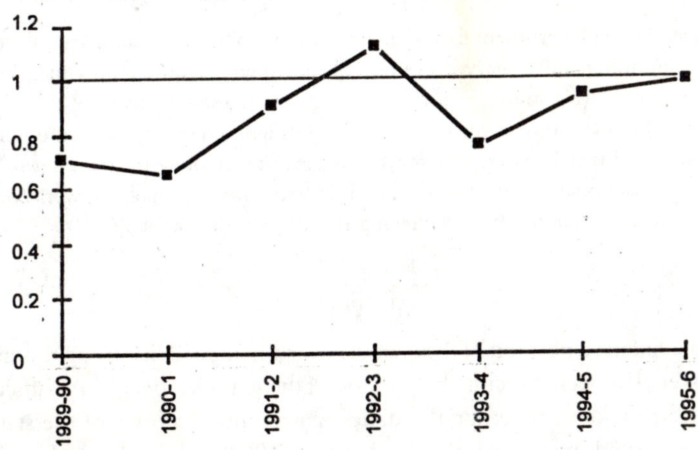

SOURCE: *Economic Survey*, 1994-5.

FIGURE 2: INTEREST PAYMENTS AS A FRACTION OF BORROWING

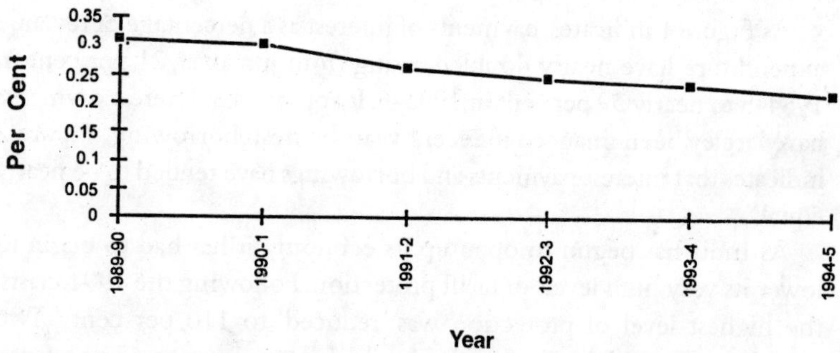

SOURCE: *Economic Survey*, 1994-5.

FIGURE 3: CAPITAL EXPENDITURE AS A FRACTION OF TOTAL EXPENDITURE

It is possible to take a more positive view of the budget figures. For example, while interest payments as a percentage of total government revenue have risen from 17.4 per cent in 1989-90 to 27.4 per cent in 1994-5, as a share of Gross Domestic Product (GDP) they have tended to remain in the 4-5 per cent band. Similarly, while the revenue deficit as a percentage of government revenue expenditure has risen from around 22 per cent in 1989-90 to as high as 45 per cent in 1993-4, relative to GDP it has remained in the 3.5-4.5 per cent band.

Overall, the *Economic Survey* for 1994-5 offers a sober assessment:

> The Central Government fiscal deficit continues to be high and this is reflected in continuing inflationary pressure. The borrowing requirements of a high fiscal deficit are a source of pressure on interest rates and adversely affect the availability of resources for productive investment, especially at a time when a strong industrial recovery has resuscitated private sector demand for investible funds. Inadequate supply of quality infrastructure, especially power, could prevent the economy from achieving its full growth potential.[5]

STATE FINANCES

If the financial position of the central government, with its strong revenue powers, has been difficult, the position of the states has been very difficult indeed. Taken altogether, the deficit on revenue account of the states has persisted since 1987-8, rising between 1994-5 and 1995-6 alone by 36 per cent to Rs. 10,462 crore (roughly A$4.6 billion).[6] The principal causes of the sharply increasing deficits are unavoidable commitments such as pensions and interest payments as well as major programmes in education and social welfare. In addition, expenditure on other items of administrative expenditure and on energy have also increased.[7] What is more, the 73rd and 74th Amendments to the Constitution will require devolution of state funds to local bodies. As Figure 4 shows, debt as a percentage of total state receipts is at or above 15 per cent for all states; a decade earlier the ratio was less than 9 per cent.[8]

The income of the states has, at best, remained static. Transfers from the central government, which form about 42 per cent of the overall spending of the states, appear to have remained constant in real terms.[9] As in Australia, the UK and elsewhere, the only area of growth in the finances of states appears to arise from gambling. Reliance on receipts from gambling (lotteries) has increased by over 70 per cent.[10]

Inevitably, for the states, as for the centre, the growing fiscal deficit has meant that they have less to spend on economic development. Only Maharashtra was able to increase its capital outlays.[11] Ironically, in late 1996 it was reported that Maharashtra was on the brink of bankruptcy and that, unless it too cut back on its spending plans its cheques would start to bounce.[12] To meet non-development commitments, especially interest payments, the states have increasingly had to resort to borrowing—which of course only adds to the eventual burden of interest repayments. The majority of the states thus appear superficially to be in the position of the poor peasant who is falling into a downward spiral of indebtedness to the local money-lender. Only two are in a relatively favourable position, Goa and Karnataka. Five (Kerala, Orissa, Tamil Nadu, UP and WB) are borrowing mainly

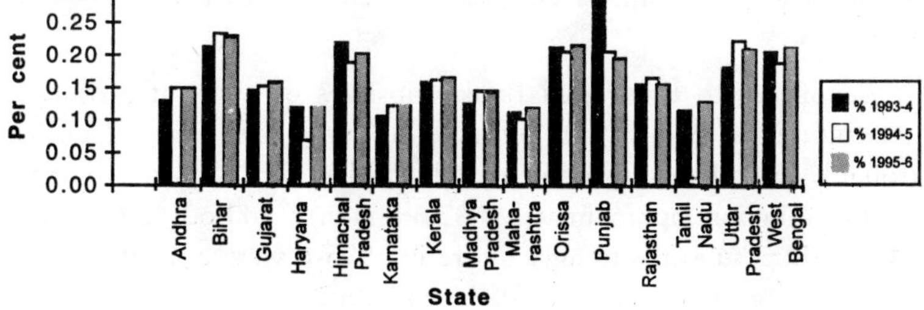

FIGURE 4: INTEREST AS A PROPORTION OF STATE RECEIPTS

to meet current expenditures. The share of development expenditure is falling in most states, Kerala and West Bengal being the exceptions.[13]

Politics and populism lie at the heart of many of the revenue deficits of the state governments. The situation of the State Electricity Boards (SEBs) is relatively well known and is symptomatic of the general problem. The SEBs occupy a pivotal position in India's efforts at development. They generate 75 per cent of the nation's electricity and distribute 95 per cent of it.[14] Power shortages have become a crippling constraint on economic growth. As Jishnu notes

> Maharashtra and Gujarat, powerhouses of the country's industrial drive, have been halted in their tracks with as many [as] six major grid failures in the last three months of 1995. Maharashtra has announced load shedding of up to 500 mw daily till June; in Gujarat, high tension (HT) industries are staggering under a 25% power cut, in addition to a weekly 'power holiday'.[14]

Energy shortages are estimated to run at around 9 per cent on average and at 20 per cent at times of peak demand (a figure which reaches 46 per cent in some states).[16]

At the core of the difficulties of SEBs are the unremunerative electricity charges which they can levy, especially upon agriculture. According to a World Bank study, India's electricity charges are the second lowest in the world. Average tariffs in Argentina are US$.099/kWh; those in Indonesia are US$.071/kWh; Pakistanis are charged US$.048/kWh. The average charge to Indian consumers in US$.038/kWh. According to the Bank:

> Broadly, utilities need retail tariffs in the region of 8 cents to 9 cents per kwh for financial viability. India's overall tariff is less than half of this amount. If agricultural supply is excluded, the average rises to about 5 cents, still well below the level needed for sound financial management and attracting new investment.[18]

According to the World Bank, subsidies on sales of power to agriculture for 1995-6 were estimated to amount to Rs. 112 billion (roughly A$4 billion) and unrecovered subsidies were estimated to come to Rs. 74 billion (approximately A$2.6 billion).[19] In both Gujarat and Maharashtra, subsidies to agriculture in 1995-6 were estimated to be about Rs. 1450 crore (about A$400 million).[20]

Targeted increases in power generation capacity projected in the Eighth Plan (1992-7), initially of 48,000 mW, later reduced to

30,000 mW, are unlikely to be met because of the reduced sums available for capital spending.[21] Jishnu quotes Power Secretary P. Abraham as saying: 'It is now expected that we may not be able to achieve more than 19,000 mW, including 3,600 mW of new capacity during 1996-97.'[22] The result of the failure to invest in infrastructure has been that firms at all levels of the economy have had to purchase their own generators—'captive power'—to allow their operations to continue. The cost to the economy of irregular power supply is very high, perhaps as much as high as 3.5 per cent of GDP.[23]

GLOBALISM

I would like now to turn away from the particularly dismal corner of the dismal science that is public finance and consider the second force which I believe will play a major part in giving a structure to Indian federalism in the coming decade, namely globalism. As noted, it was the foreign exchange crisis of 1991 which forced India to make major changes in its relationship with the international economy. Although that process is still very much in its early days, we can already see that it will have important implications for the nature of Indian federalism. One area where these changes are already evident is in the competition which has emerged between states to secure investment in manufacturing, especially foreign investment. One of the consequences of the ongoing difficulties which the BJP-Shiv Sena government in Maharashtra have raised for the US-based ENRON Corporation's power station in Dabhol (and for Kentucky Fried Chicken) has been that investors have been deciding to place headquarters and plants outside Maharashtra.[24] Strong competition is emerging in petrochemicals from Gujarat and in automotive manufacturing from Tamil Nadu. The decisions of Serlite, Ford-Mahindra and Thapar-DuPont to place their investments in Tamil Nadu are symptomatic of the increasing tempo of interstate competition.[25] In the words of Rohit Saran and his colleagues:

> A bustling market for corporate investment is emerging, with state governments as the sellers and corporates planning new projects . . . as the buyers. Like the Indian economy, it is becoming an unprotected, competitive arena, where only the smartest customers can make the best deals.[26]

At the same time, the patterns of industrialization and foreign investment are likely to accentuate existing regional inequalities. One measure of the existing inequalities is given by the per capita value added by industries in 1990-1 (Table 1).

TABLE 1: PER CAPITA VALUE ADDED BY INDUSTRIES, INDIA, 1990-1

State	Value Added per Capita	*Business Today* Investment Index
Maharashtra	1536	119.9
Gujarat	1089	58.9
Tamil Nadu	1043	7.4
Haryana	1004	1.09
Punjab	922	1.05
Himachal Pradesh	735	.10
Karnataka	620	6.37
West Bengal	474	-3.27
Madhya Pradesh	459	2.85
Andhra Pradesh	452	-.61
Kerala	422	-.67
Orissa	367	-.039
Rajasthan	357	.81
Uttar Pradesh	335	-5.36
Bihar	303	-31.58

SOURCES: Tata Services Ltd., December 1995, p. 10 and Saran, 7-21 June 1996, p. 81.

The 'Big Three' (Maharashtra, Gujarat and Tamil Nadu) account for just under 40 per cent of all of the value-added by factories in India.[27] These three states are indicative of a broader trend: that much of the industrial investment and much of the most rapid economic growth in India is—and is likely to be—concentrated in a handful of states which already have moderate-to-well-developed infrastructure (Andhra Pradesh, Gujarat, Haryana, Delhi, Karnataka, Kerala, Punjab, Tamil Nadu, West Bengal). A recent index of the 'best states to invest in' compiled by *Business Today*, produced a very comparable ranking.

CONCLUSION: THE 'TWO NATIONS'?

One way to interpret these trends is to argue that what Ashish Bose has termed the BIMARU states—an acronym which describes the Hindi-speaking states of Bihar, Madhya Pradesh, Rajasthan and Uttar Pradesh, plus Orissa and the smaller, mountainous states—are likely to fall further behind as India's economic development gains pace.

This interpretation is certainly sound, but I think that approaching the data from a comparative perspective offers another possibility. I would like to suggest that we can gain much from examining the experience of China which is arguably about ten years ahead of India in its growth trajectory. Gerald Segal notes that one of the most conspicuous results of China's recent industrialization has been both increased regional inequality and external orientation. He accepts Womack's delineation of three regional groups in terms of their external orientation: coastal provinces, border provinces and inland provinces.[28] These divisions appear to map reasonably well onto India. Maharashtra corresponds, for argument's sake, to Guandong which in 1990 accounted for 22 per cent of all Chinese exports, while Tamil Nadu may be an incipient Shanghai.[29] Whether cross-border smuggling qualifies the Punjab and Haryana for border state status is perhaps more doubtful. Least affected by globalism are the inland provinces like Shaanxi, Anhui, Gansu and Qinghai. Segal notes that it is the coastal provinces, and to a lesser extent, the border provinces, which are increasingly dependent upon, and hence increasingly affected by, external trade.

One conspicuous feature of the growing interdependence of the coastal provinces on the global economy has been their growing independence from the central government in Beijing. Increasingly, the crucial economic decisions in China are being taken at the provincial and at the township level.[30] Interprovincial competition, as was manifested by the 'fibre wars' of the late 1980s, is symptomatic of the process.[31] And as increasing power is given to markets, the control of the central government over crucial aspects of foreign policy is also being eroded.[32]

What appears to be happening in China, Segal suggests, is that Natural Economic Territories (NETS) are taking shape which transcend national borders. The two which have most developed are the southern Chinese region which links Guangdong, Fujian, Hainan and their hinterlands with Hong Kong and Taiwan. A second region includes Liaoning and possibly Shandong with Japan and South Korea. Is it too far fetched to think about Mumbai, with its adjacent hinterlands of Maharashtra, Gujarat, Madhya Pradesh and Rajasthan, as well as its external economic links with the states of the Gulf and East and South Africa as a Natural

Economic Territory? There are similar, if weaker, linkages between Chennai, Singapore and Malaysia. And Karnataka is poised in some sense as a bridge between these incipient international aggregations.

These emerging NETs suggest that we can foresee a broader geography of prosperity and stagnation, one with profound consequences for India. If one places these zones on a map it suggests that these global trends are tending to divide the subcontinent along a vertical axis, roughly stretching from Moradabad to Hyderabad. Except for Kerala (and as we know, it is the *dharma* of Kerala ever to be an exception!) most of India's development in the coming decade is likely to occur to the west of this line. Those areas which lie to the west of the axis have every likelihood in the next decade of reaching the levels of prosperity enjoyed by present-day South-East Asia. And the future for that 'other nation' which lies to the east of the axis, appears to be one of relative stagnation.

Like the 'sunbelts' and 'rust belts' of the United States and Australia, globalism appears to be amplifying existing regional inequalities in South Asia at a time when the redistributive capabilities of the central government are greatly diminished. As states are forced to become increasingly reliant upon their own efforts to secure development investment, we can expect that the competition for foreign investment between states and regions will become increasingly aggressive. All the signs are most of that investment will flow to the existing 'growth magnets' and little to the states on the eastern periphery.

One does not need to accept fully Alvin Toffler's image of the vice jaws of globalism tearing apart the existing nation-state to see that major long-term economic forces are at work which will profoundly alter the existing balance of forces in the Indian federal system.

NOTES

1. Alvin Toffler, *The Third Wave* (London, 1981), p. 322.
2. *Economic Survey*, 1992-3, p. 35.
3. *Economic Survey*, 1994-5, p. 27.
4. Ibid., p. 25.
5. *Economic Survey*, 1994-5, p. 1.
6. *Reserve Bank of India Bulletin* (*RBIB*), December 1995, p. 989.
7. Ibid., pp. 989-91.

8. World Bank, 1995, *Economic Developments in India: Achievements and Challenges* (Washington, 1995), p. 40.
9. *RBIB*, December 1995, p. 990. This is my own rough estimate. Transfers to the states, as a proportion of GDP, have remained nearly constant since 1989.
10. *RBIB*, December 1995, p. 991.
11. Ibid.
12. Mahesh, 1996b.
13. *RBIB*, December 1995, p. 997.
14. World Bank, 1995, p. 62.
15. Latha Jishnu, 'Struggle for power', *Business World*, 1996, pp. 35-6.
16. Ibid., p. 35.
17. Mahesh, 1996a.
18. Bodhisatva Ganguli and Tushar Pania, 'The Anatomy of a Controversial Deal', *Business India*, 24 April-27 May 1995, pp. 58-9.
19. World Bank, 1995, p. 63.
20. Jishnu, p. 37.
21. Ibid. and World Bank, 1995, p. 63.
22. Jishnu, p. 38.
23. Ibid., p. 41.
24. I have summarized the events surrounding both the ENRON and KFC investments in 'We Are All Reformers Now: Reform and Resistance in South Asia', paper presented to the 'Economic Change, Political Pluralism and Democratic Reform in the Asian Region' Symposium, University of Adelaide, 20-1 April 1996.
25. Charudatta Desphande, Mayank Bhatt and Merle Almeida, 'Is Maharashtra Losing Out?' *Business India*, 25 March-26 April 1996, p. 64.
26. Rohit Saran *et al.*, 'The Best States to Invest In', *Business Today*, 7-21 June 1996, p. 87.
27. Tata Services Ltd., *Statistical Survey of India*, 1995-6, p. 81.
28. G. Segal, 'Deconstructing Foreign Relations', in D.S.G. Goodman and G. Segal (eds.), *China Deconstructs: Politics, Trade and Regionalism* (London, 1994), p. 323.
29. I am grateful to Andrew Watson for drawing Goodman and Segal's work to my attention. Unlike China where data for provincial exports is readily available, I have not been able to locate disaggregated export statistics for India. T.M. Thomas Isaac notes that 'The major reason for the failure to incorporate trade flows into [my] regional analysis has been the virtual non-availability of the relevant data. Even with respect to international trade accurate region-wise figures are not available' [Tim Isaac, 'The Trend are Pattern of External Trade of Kerala', in B.A. Prakash (ed.), *Kerala's Economy: Performance, Problems, Prospects* (New Delhi, 1994), p. 368]. I am indebted to Marika Vicziany for drawing Isaac's work to my attention.

30. Segal, p. 342.
31. See Peter Mayer, Christopher Findlay and Andrew Watson 'Fighting Over Fleece: Economic Reform, Regional Conflict and Terms of Trade in China (A Case Study of Wool Production and Processing in Yulin Prefecture, Shaanxi)', paper presented to the Politics Department Staff Seminar, September 1989.
32. Segal, p. 343.

11

Did the People Make Laws?

STUART MACINTYRE

Australians have long had an ambiguous relationship to their federal Commonwealth and the means whereby it was created. Its creators regarded their work sometimes reverentially and sometimes as the outcome of a series of necessary compromises, the best outcome that could be obtained from fairly intractable material.

Thus we have Alfred Deakin's retrospective reflection on the final success of the federal movement. From the first moment to the last, he observed, there were interruptions that might have marred its accomplishment, the ulterior objects of those 'public men' who supported the scheme as well as those who opposed it, and the appeal of both to the selfish interests of the electors. As one who watched its inner workings, followed its progress, prayed for it and lived the life of devotion to it day by day, Deakin attributed its success to the idealism of the young and imaginative patriots who sustained enthusiasm for the union for a full decade, from the initial conference of the colonial representatives 1890 through to the final passage of the Commonwealth Constitution Bill in 1900, at times when it might otherwise have stalled. His *Federal Story* is a providential account of how by a series of miracles something noble emanated from the ignoble processes of colonial public life.[1] For George Reid, on the other hand, federation was an arrangement subject to keen negotiation, an issue that lent itself to political manoeuvre, something that might be necessary but to which he felt little personal attachment.

A similar ambivalence marks the historical interpretation of Australian federation. For a number of decades it was the affirmative account of the participants that prevailed. Robert Garran, secretary to the drafting committee of the conventions, and John Quick, the convention delegate who claimed to have devised the procedure that made their work possible, provided a narrative history of Australian federation as early as 1901 that regarded the Commonwealth Constitution as the zenith of liberty, the culmination of national progress. Ernest Scott, a reporter of the Adelaide convention, drummed the same interpretation into school-children in successive editions of his *Short History*, first published in 1916. Garran reiterated it in his chapter of the Australian volume of the 1933 *Cambridge History of the British Empire*, and again, as late as 1958, in his book *Prosper the Commonwealth*.

But already this celebratory version was under attack from the academics. After the Second World War a new generation of university-based historians and political scientists reoriented their disciplines. Applying far more explicit methodologies to closely-defined research topics, they set out to formulate and test explanatory hypotheses about political behaviour. These academics paid considerable initial attention to federation as a formative moment of the nation's history and institutional structure, but they were impatient with the 'cheerful romance' left by its celebrants. Thus in an early number of *Historical Studies* R.S. Parker analysed the voting patterns of the federal referenda according to the economic interests of the voters.[2] In what would become the standard textbook of Australian politics, Fin Crisp similarly interpreted the Constitution as a conservative instrument reflecting the interests of its makers—a view which he derived from an occupational analysis.

Subsequently, for reasons that need not concern us here, interest in such political history waned. John La Nauze's study of *The Making of the Australian Constitution 1919-72* is prefaced by the unduly modest explanation that it was meant to assist the future author of a 'much-needed general history of the 'federal movement'.[3] That history has yet to appear.

The fifth volume of Manning Clark's *History of Australia* (1981) therefore remains one of the most substantial and influential accounts of the subject. The title of that volume, 'The People Make Laws', indicates the centrality of federation and the subsequent work of the early Commonwealth parliaments. Portraits of Parker, Barton, Griffith, Reid, Kingston and the other central figures of federation dominate the book. Clark saw the federal movement, the work of the conventions and the creation of the Commonwealth as narrowly constrained, the noble rhetoric of national and democratic fulfilment belied by the ignoble motives and actions of the Federal Fathers. Against a threatening background of depression, strikes and class turmoil, federation operates in his history as a means whereby the people could be restrained and the dangers averted. In his own words, 'Federation was one of those constitutional devices recommended by apologists for bourgeois democracy for containing political equality, and stigmatising all radical change as something outside the constitutional powers. . . .'[4]

More recently, this critical account of federation has itself been challenged as the nation and its past once more become the object of celebration. Again, the reasons for the altered temper—from challenging to rebuilding national self-esteem—fall outside the compass of this paper. They seem to me to lie in the decline of alternative ideologies, the fragmentation of the social movements, and the desire for a past that will serve the new needs of the present. The degree of consensus should not be exaggerated: there are major differences between academic Geoffrey Blainey's denunciation of the 'black armband' view of history and Prime Minister Paul Keating's self-styled post-colonial maturity of a people coming to terms with who they are, to take just two influential expositors of the new mood. No doubt his successor, John Howard, will develop his own predilections.

Perhaps the most cogent statement of the post-revisionist interpretation of federation is advanced by John Hirst, partly in his *Republican Manifesto* and partly in correspondence between us. Three years ago I sent him a copy of a paper I had delivered to mark the centenary of the Corowa Conference. This Conference was an unofficial gathering summoned to rescue the federal movement from paralysis in 1893, when the colonial parliaments were unable to move beyond vague support for union. It devised the crucial mechanism, usually attributed to John Quick, that hit upon the solution.

A brief summary of the antecedent and subsequent chain of events may be helpful. Representatives of the seven Colonies, New Zealand as well as the six Australian ones, had met in conference in Melbourne in 1890. They had then sent parliamentary delegations to a convention in Sydney in 1891 that drafted a federal constitution to be submitted to the various legislatures. That process failed because of disagreement, opposition and apathy. The unofficial meeting at Corowa in 1893 therefore proposed an alternative procedure to revive the federal movement: direct election of delegates to prepare a new constitution that would then be submitted directly to the voters. The procedure was adopted by four of the Australian premiers in Hobart early in 1895 and necessary enabling legislation was enacted by 1896; the new federal convention met in Adelaide, Sydney and Melbourne during 1897 and 1898; five of the six Colonies carried the Bill in 1899; Western Australia came in a year later; and the British parliament enacted the Constitution in 1900.

The significance of Corowa for Hirst is that it initiated a particularly strong form of popular sovereignty as the very basis of the federal constitution: the people themselves elected its authors, the people themselves adopted it and the people themselves were inscribed in its preamble and included in the provisions for its amendment. This was a unique achievement—unparalleled in other federal schemes of Europe and north America—and the adoption of the scheme worked out at Corowa was in his opinion 'the greatest miracle of Australian political history.[5]

My examination tied the events at Corowa to the strategies of organized pressure groups who sought to mobilize popular support for federation. I observed how the organization that actually initiated the Corowa Conference, the Australasian Federal League, was concerned to present itself as 'an organization of citizens owning no class distinction or party influence', but was in fact linked closely to leading politicians in New South Wales and Victoria, the very politicians who would be elected to the conventions. I recounted the efforts of these organizers to exclude republicans and socialists, and suggested that the rubric 'no class distinction or party influence' was aimed at excluding those radical alternative versions of the nations' meaning and form.

I tried also to draw out the dichotomous pairing of the politicians and the people, which was used to characterize federation as a popular movement rather than a political process. The depreciation of politics and the validation of the popular, the juxtaposition of the self-serving dissembler and his long-suffering victims are rhetorical forms that are all about us—much of the language of the Australian gun lobby, for example, pits unreliable unscrupulous politicians against the people. These formulations are so deeply embedded in the public discourse that we seldom notice their historical formation. I argued in my paper that the forms of representative government that were established in nineteenth-century Australia combined principles of popular sovereignty with the habits of utilitarian liberalism.

The Australian colonists made the state serve their needs with roads and bridges, land grants and comfortable billets, and despised the patterns of flattery and jobbery that characterized their civic life. The politicians, having impugned their own calling, called forth a voice that could restore its legitimacy: they reinstated the people as a disembodied presence capable of an altruism that they themselves could not achieve.

The people were inscribed as a redemptive agency without class distinctions or party loyalties, gender, race or other potentially divisive identities: they spoke at the command of the politicians and then fell silent as the business of government was subsumed into the Commonwealth that this act of ventriloquism brought into being.[6]

These arguments are by no means irrelevant to the present arguments over how the Australian Constitution might be revised to meet present needs and values. We saw it in the Liberal/National Party Coalition's scheme for a new convention, misnamed a popular convention because it consisted in part of elected representatives—the original popular conventions were so-called because they were unofficial. We saw it again in the insistence of some that the elected delegates should not belong to parties, or should in some way be free from politics. From the other side of the coin, you see it in the call by the Prime Minister's speechwriter, Christopher Person, for safeguards against precipitate implementation of the scheme. But you seldom see any reference back to the events of the 1890s and the lessons they might provide.

Why is it that Australians are so ambivalent about the history of their federation? Part of the reason lies, I think, in the sort of reservations expressed by Manning Clark. Australian federation is associated with hierarchies of class, race and gender that we find uncomfortable. It institutionalized certain sorts of preferences—a mixed form of representation, with the federal nature of the upper house compromising the majoritarian form of the lower one; a carefully limited set of Commonwealth powers more concerned with defence and business than social reform; constitutional monarchy and imperial loyalty rather than republican independence.

This last aspect is perhaps the greatest present obstacle to a stronger attachment to the federal heritage. It is hard for us to understand the amalgam of Australian and imperial patriotism that was axiomatic to the federalists of the 1890s. Bernhard Wise entitled his history of *The Making of the Australian Commonwealth,* 'A Stage in the Growth of the Empire'. It is equally hard for the present-day Australian to understand that this imperial loyalty was by no means uncritical or unreflective. It had both practical and emotional force, combining the hardheaded appreciation of strategic and economic interest with a fervent, almost mystical reverence that we associate now with such crackpots as Lionel Curtis, John Buchan and Rudyard Kipling. While it is possible to show how those geopolitical considerations and emotional identifications worked on figures such as Deakin, or later Robert Menzies and his imaginary England, it is even harder to appreciate that they had popular purchase. This makes the role of the people all the more elusive.

Finally, there is an important corollary. Federation involved no act of rebellion, such as characterized the American union, no post-colonial experience such as other former British colonies have embedded in their national formation. Consequently, for much of the twentieth century Australians have lived with a legacy they have found increasingly difficult to understand—we do not know whether our Commonwealth represents a continuation or a new beginning, for we have no moment of independence.

NOTES

1. Stuart Macintyre (ed.), *'And Be One People': Alfred Deakin's Federal Story* (Melbourne, 1995), p. 173.
2. John Hirst, 'Can Subjects Be Citizens', unpublished paper, 1993, pp. 5-6; R.S. Parker, 'Australian Federation: The Influence of Economic Interests', *Historical Studies Australia and New Zealand,* 1949, 3(13).
3. La Nauze, p. v.
4. Clark, vol. 5, p. 139.
5. John Hirst, *A Republican Manifesto* (Melbourne, 1984), p. 35.
6. Stuart Macintyre, 'Corowa and the Voice of the People', *Canberra Historical Journal,* n.s. 33, March 1994, pp. 2-8.

12

Federalism and Australian Citizenship[1]

BRIAN GALLIGAN and JOHN CHESTERMAN

Australian citizenship is currently the subject of considerable public and academic interest and there have been many suggestions as to how it might be enhanced. These include comparing our citizenship practices with the best in the world, inculcating citizenship knowledge and values in young Australians through education in schools, and raising community knowledge and appreciation of the Constitution generally in the lead up to the constitutional centenary.

It is important that efforts to enhance Australian citizenship take proper account of its institutional structure and historical development. That means appreciating four key features. The first is that the Constitution did not include a core definition of citizenship or enumerate citizen rights and privileges. Rather, it used the notion of 'subject' and left citizen rights and privileges to be legislated by the Commonwealth and States. The second key feature which flows from the basic federal structure of the Constitution is that Australian citizenship is essentially federal. Federalism creates a system of limited national government and multiple state governments and divides powers, including powers over citizenship matters, between them. Such a system entails dual citizenship, where people are citizens of the nation and of their regional state, and have rights and privileges as well as duties in both spheres of government. The third attribute of citizenship follows from the other two: that in order to study Australian citizenship we need to look at the legislative and administrative arrangements in both Commonwealth and state spheres of government. The fourth is the historical exclusion of 'aboriginal natives', which was a major part of

Australia's citizenship regime at both the Commonwealth and state level until the 1960s. The negative definition of citizenship and the administrative policing of exclusionary citizenship boundaries form a significant part of our citizenship history. They cast a dim light over our heritage.

Australian citizenship did not become a legal reality until 1948, when an Act of Parliament outlined the basis on which one could become an Australian citizen. But even in this Act the rights of the citizen were not spelt out. One became citizen, for instance, by being born in Australia, but not all people born in Australia shared the same citizenship rights. This is most clearly evident when one looks at the citizenship status of Aborigines. After 1948 Aborigines were Australian citizens, according to citizenship legislation, but they had no right to vote in Queensland, the Northern Territory, Western Australia or federally. Their rights to social security were extremely limited, and they were subject to a range of powers not applicable to other Australians. Citizenship in name was not citizenship in practice.

Australia's federal system of government has enabled such diverse treatment of people at the Commonwealth and state level. Commonwealth franchise and social security laws have clearly impacted upon the citizenship rights of Australians. Equally, however, the states have retained power over a range of key citizenship areas, such as the conduct of criminal and civil trials, education, the use of land, and the state electoral franchise. For a proper picture of Australian citizenship we need to look at both levels of government.

In this paper we address two main questions: why has there been no core statement of what it means to be an Australian citizen? And how have the states and Commonwealth set about establishing a *de facto* citizenship regime? Federalism is a major part of the answer to the first question, and it provides the basis for formulating a response to the second. We begin with the most important starting point, the Australian Constitution.

In 1898, during the debates that led to the adoption of the Australian Constitution, the convention delegates turned their attention to the question of citizenship. What should the Constitution say about citizenship? Should the rights of Australian citizens be spelt out? Some, like the South Australian premier, argued that the Constitution should define citizenship and that the states should be prevented from encroaching upon the rights of Australian citizenship. But this was the minority view. Other delegates thought that such provisions would 'be very mischievous' because they would unduly limit the right of the states to determine their own citizenship regimes.

The majority of delegates even objected to the use of the word 'citizen' in the Constitution. Indeed the word appears only in Section 44, where citizens of foreign countries are prohibited from holding parliamentary office. The concern about using 'citizen' was twofold. First, 'citizen', as it had been used in the American and French revolutions, had republican overtones. It had been used to describe the position of people who participated in the violent overthrow of monarchic regimes. The republican connotations attached to the word were considered inappropriate for Australia, a country that sought to affirm its constitutional links with the British monarch. Second, delegates were concerned that if 'citizen' appeared in the Constitution, there would be confusion as to whether it referred to citizenship in the states or in the Commonwealth. Most delegates did not want references to citizens of the Commonwealth for fear that this might lead to a limitation of state power to deal with citizenship matters.

So concerned were delegates not to abridge the rights of states, that a complex provision, Section 41, was adopted which ensured a Commonwealth vote for all of the voters in the states. This was complex because at the time of federation women had the vote only in South Australia and Western Australia, and Aborigines were not permitted to vote in Queensland and Western Australia. While convention delegates did not want to say exactly who the Commonwealth should enfranchise when it passed its first electoral law, they ensured that the Commonwealth could not disfranchise anyone who already had a state vote.

Thus, although the Constitution was responsible for establishing the Commonwealth government and for dividing power between it and the states, it did not contain any statement of the rights of Australian citizenship. Instead, these rights were left to be decided by legislative and administrative action. Since Australia was a federal nation, with powers divided between the states and the Commonwealth, the rights of citizenship were to be decided at not one but two levels of government. To understand citizenship in Australia, one must understand its binary nature.

De Facto Citizenship

In addition to there being no constitutional statement about Australian citizenship, there has been no substantive Commonwealth or state legislative statement about the meaning of Australian citizenship. To discover what it entails we must first establish the rights and duties of citizenship, and then examine how particular laws impact upon these.

An uncontentious understanding of Australian citizenship would include such basic rights as the right to vote, the right to receive a minimum level of social security, the right to move freely, and the right to enjoy the equal protection of the law.

Franchise

Generally speaking, the States have been responsible for establishing their own franchise laws, as has the Commonwealth. By the turn of the twentieth century all States had their own franchise laws. Two groups featured prominently in being excluded from the State vote. Women were initially excluded from the vote in all jurisdictions, but gradually this exclusion was overturned. South Australian women were the first to get the vote, in 1894, and Victorian women were the last to be enfranchised, in 1908. Aborigines were expressly denied the vote in Queensland and Western Australia and later in the Northern Territory, and these exclusions more or less stayed in place until the 1960s. Meanwhile other States, like New South Wales and Victoria, denied the vote to people deemed to be in receipt of charitable aid. Aboriginal residents of government stations were generally considered to come within this category.

At the federal level, the 1902 *Commonwealth Franchise Act* established the new federal franchise. Hailed appropriately for giving most Australian women the vote, the Act also expressly denied the vote to Aborigines. Aborigines had not been excluded in an early draft of the Act, but a handful of parliamentarians argued that Aborigines in Western Australia were not worthy of the vote and that they might be led astray by unscrupulous people in their exercise of it. This was enough to convince others to exclude Aborigines from the vote.

Section 41 of the Constitution, which we discussed earlier, caused a complex relationship to exist between state and federal franchise laws.

In short, Section 41 meant that anyone with a state vote at the time of federation could not be denied a federal vote. This had repercussions for those excluded from the federal franchise. Section 41 initially had been designed to protect the vote of women who had gained it in the states, but it was rendered superfluous in this regard when the Commonwealth enfranchised women. However, the provision remained relevant to Aborigines.

An example, drawn from documents in the Australian Archives, serves to highlight the complex relationship between state and federal laws on this key citizenship issue. As mentioned earlier, Aborigines in New South Wales were not specifically prevented from voting, but they and anyone else in receipt of charitable aid could not vote. A significant number of them, both men and women, living in the Riveriana area of southern New South Wales voted in the 1903 federal election. As the correspondence from one divisional returning officer in 1904 indicates, these Aborigines, who resided on a government station, subsequently lost the vote at both state and federal levels. Referring to a group of Aborigines living on a mission, who were on the federal roll and had been on the state roll, the divisional officer reported: 'these electors have been struck off the State Electoral Roll by a recent State Revision Court on the grounds that they are in receipt of continuous State aid—they are therefore not entitled to be on the Commonwealth Roll.[2] For these Aborigines, the loss of the State vote meant the loss of the federal vote.

Social security

The Commonwealth's first pieces of social security legislation made one exception to the entitlement to benefits. In 1908 the legislation governing invalid and old-age pensions stated that the pensions were not payable to 'aboriginal natives'. Likewise in 1912, the maternity allowance was not payable to 'aboriginal natives'. This situation largely prevailed until 1959, when most of the restrictions that prevented Aborigines from receiving social security were removed. In announcing the 1959 changes, the Minister for Social Services said:

> An additional £1,000,000 will be paid towards the welfare of Australia's aborigines as evidence of the Commonwealth Government's intention to give

them equality with other Australians in the field of social services. Unless they are nomadic or primitive, aborigines will in future qualify for age, invalid and widows' pensions, and maternity allowances, on the same basis as other members of the community.[3]

Until 1959 Aborigines largely had been denied social security, on the basis that they were not part of the Australian polity. Even after 1959 those who were 'nomadic or primitive' were still denied access to one of the fundamental elements of citizenship. The citizenship legislation passed eleven years earlier clearly had no impact on this key aspect of citizenship.

Movement

Another indicator of citizenship status is the existence of laws restricting one's movement. Again, the one group of people who most notably and consistently have been the victims of laws regulating movement have been Aborigines. With the exception of Tasmania, which endorsed the historical fiction that it had no Aborigines, all states between 1869 and 1911 enacted 'protection' regimes that enabled administrators and police to force Aborigines to reside on reserves. Not until the 1960s were these powers finally repealed.

In the Northern Territory, for example, local protectors exercised large amounts of power over Aborigines. They had power to move an Aboriginal camp or 'proposed camp', they could authorize the removal of Aborigines from one district to another, or between reserves and institutions, and they could arrest without warrant any person suspected of committing an offence against the protection legislation. Other restrictions prevented Aborigines from entering hotels or other areas declared 'prohibited'. In addition, the Northern Territory Administrator held broad regulatory power and could order that Aboriginal children be detained in schools or institutions.

Regulations made in 1919 clarified the way Northern Territory Aborigines were restricted in their movement. Aborigines living on employers' properties, or on reserves within certain town districts, could not be 'at large' in towns one hour after sunset without written permission. Those who were 'at large' faced one month's imprisonment. Ten years later this situation still prevailed, and the argument that Aborigines were aliens in their own land was strengthened by new regulations that enabled Aborigines to go into prohibited areas only after being issued with a permit. Aborigines virtually required passports to go to some parts of their own country.

Meanwhile, in Western Australia, an amendment in 1941 to its protection Act spoke volumes for the view held by the West Australian government as to the citizenship rights of Aborigines. In a move to prevent the spread of leprosy, the government legislated to prevent any Aboriginal living north of twentieth parallel—which roughly crosses Port Hedland—to come south of the parallel. The only permissible exceptions to this were when an Aboriginal needed specialist medical attention, when legal proceedings required an Aboriginal's attendance, or when an Aboriginal's employer held a special permit to take the Aboriginal to the south.

These examples are representative of many of the restrictions that affected Aborigines at the State and Territory level. Such were these restrictions that even if the Commonwealth had enfranchised Aborigines and deleted all other discriminatory provisions over which it had power, the existence of restrictive State laws still meant that Aborigines would not have been citizens in any true sense of word.

Equal Protection of the Law

The final of our rudimentary citizenship rights is the right to the equal protection of the law. In all States, until relatively recently, uncorroborated Aboriginal evidence was unlikely to result in the conviction of a white defendant. In addition, the reality has been that the enforcers of the law, the police and the judiciary, historically have not dealt with crimes involving Aborigines as they have other crimes.

The extent to which Aborigines have not enjoyed the equal protection of the law is exemplified by a High Court case that followed the murder of a police officer in 1933 on Woodah Island, off the coast of the Northern Territory. The murderer was allegedly an Aboriginal man. After missionaries had acted as go-betweens, a Mr Tuckiar agreed to come to Darwin on what he thought was to be a peace mission. Tuckiar was convicted of murdering the policeman and sentenced to death.

The evidence used to convict Tuckiar, who spoke no English, included two statements he had made to Aboriginal witnesses, which the Court took to be contradictory. Tuckiar's statement to the first Aboriginal witness suggested that he had murdered the policeman. His statement to the second witness indicated that he had acted more in self defence. Both stories made reference to the dead policeman taking away one or more of Tuckiar's wives, the second story indicating that the policeman had had sex with one of Tuckiar's wives. Commentators at the time, and since, have accepted Tuckiar's statements, both of which were interpreted by different people, may well have been complementary rather than contradictory. Nevertheless, Tuckiar's counsel put it to him that one of his statements had to be worng. At this stage, Tuckiar withdrew the second story, a fact which Tuckiar's counsel communicated to the judge in chambers. In charging the jury, the judge all but told them which story they should believe, saying that the first of Tuckiar's statements was highly probable and that the other was an obvious fabrication. He added that the jury could draw any inference it liked from Tuckiar's failure to give evidence.

As the famous anthropologist A.P. Elkin argued, the fact that Tuckiar through an interpreter and then through his counsel, withdrew the self-defence version, did not indicate he did not believe it. He, had been kept for weeks in jail in Darwin, and was then told that one of his statements was a lie. His only choice was to withdraw one of the 'contradictory' statements so that the trial could end and he could receive the freedom he believed he would then enjoy. Further, as C.D. Rowley argues in *The Destruction of Aboriginal Society*, the death sentence received by Tuckiar could only be explained by the fact that a white man had been the victim of the crime. Only a short time earlier the same Judge had ordered the imprisonment of Aboriginal men who had killed several Japanese fishermen.

Tuckiar was subsequently acquitted by the High Court, which ruled that the trial judge had erred in a number of fundamental respects. Included amongst these errors were his comments on Tuckiar's failure to give evidence, and his charge to the jury, during which he had said that a verdict of not guilty would denigrate the deceased policeman. So concerned had the trial judge been to clear the policeman's name that he admitted evidence as to his character, a matter irrelevant to the trial. So Tuckiar was cleared by the High Court and allowed to go home. But he never made it home, and is commonly understood to have been murdered en route.[4]

The fact that Tuckiar seems in the end to have been the victim of a revenge killing makes the legal rights, which the High Court declared him to have, seem somewhat fantastic. Tuckiar had to go to the High Court to have his fairly rudimentary legal rights judicially acknowledged. And even then, when formal justice finally supported him, informal justice claimed him.

Negative Citizenship

A definite pattern emerges from an investigation into state and federal laws on various citizenship criteria. The state and Commonwealth laws that have governed people's rights to vote, to receive social security, to move freely and to be equally protected by the law, have excluded certain people from these rights. Indeed it is fair to say that more attention had been paid to excluding certain people from the rights of citizenship, than has been paid to establishing a positive conception of the rights of, and entitlement to, citizenship. Foremost amongst those excluded have been the Aborigines.

The piece of legislation that most clearly displayed this negative citizenship practice was Western Australia's *Natives (Citizenship Rights) Act 1944*. This extraordinary Act enabled an Aboriginal to apply for a Certificate of Citizenship, which, if granted, meant that he or she would 'be deemed to be no longer a native or aborigine and shall have all the rights, privileges and immunities and shall be subject to the duties and liabilities of a natural born or naturalized subject of His Majesty'.

The notion that Aborigines could thus gain and lose citizenship status made a mockery of the inherent or abiding 'rights' terminology. Aborigines, according to the West Australian government, clearly did not have citizenship rights. Indeed the Act was the clearest legislative statement ever made that, as a general rule, Aborigines could not be citizens. All that Aborigines gained through the legislation was the ability to be exempted from the citizenship exclusion that otherwise affected all of them.

Moreover, reinforcing the dual nature of citizenship in federal Australia, one's exemption from state exclusionary regimes did not exempt one from federal disadvantages. The 1961 federal Select Committee on the Voting Rights of Aborigines was advised that

> The grant of a State Certificate of Citizenship, with the effect of giving full civil rights under the law of the State, does not, and was not intended to, trench in any way upon the status of an aboriginal as an Australian citizen by

virtue of the Commonwealth Nationality and Citizenship Act, or upon any rights or duties arising under any other law of the Commonwealth. State law could not have such an effect.[5]

So a West Australian Aboriginal who in 1945 was exempted from restrictive state laws still had no right to the federal vote, or to receive social security. This fact was brought home in 1959 to a group of Aborigines in Western Australia. Twenty-four Aborigines, who resided at one West Australian mission and who all held certificates exempting them from protection legislation, submitted claims for social security. The Department of Social Services rejected twenty-one of their claims, on the basis that 'only three of the claimants were sufficiently advanced to receive pensions'.[6]

This confusing and illogical state of affairs was summed up most succinctly in 1959 by Attorney-General Garfield Barwick, in response to a letter from Mr Sandy McDonald. McDonald had written to Paul Hasluck, the Minister for Territories, saying that he was regarded as a citizen in the Northern Territory, but that when he crossed the border into Western Australia he was regarded as an Aboriginal. Hasluck sought Barwick's opinion, commenting that while McDonald could obtain a passport and could thus be recognized as an Australian citizen in every foreign country, the passport would apparently have no meaning for him in Western Australia. Barwick advised the following:

> Mr McDonald is an Australian citizen wherever he may be in Australia and this citizenship is not lost on his passing from one State or Territory to another. But this does not mean that he is necessarily entitled to all the rights enjoyable by a non-aboriginal Australian citizen throughout Australia.[7]

McDonald was thus a citizen who was not entitled to the rights held by non-Aboriginal Australian citizens. He could not vote at state level and was liable to have his employment and movement regulated in ways that white West Australians were not.

During the 1960s Aborigines slowly gained formal citizenship at the state and Commonwealth levels. The legislation that had restricted their rights was repealed, and the 1967 referendum—wrongly seen by many to have granted citizenship to Aborigines—gave the Commonwealth the power to make laws for Aborigines and ensured that they would be counted in census statistics.

Federalism and Citizenship

We have focused on the ignoble side of Australian citizenship, the exclusion of Aborigines from normal citizenship rights and privileges by both the Commonwealth and the States. Obviously, this is only part of a larger story in which white Australians and certain immigrants have enjoyed the enormous benefits of easy citizenship in an affluent liberal democratic nation. However, it is a vital part of the story which is often overlooked and which partly explains why citizenship was structured the way it was. The term citizen and any positive definition of citizen rights and privileges were deliberately excluded from the Constitution for federal as well as monarchic reasons. The states were to be left with considerable discretion over citizenship definition so they could discriminate against certain groups of people. The history of Australian citizenship has involved substantial state discrimination against Aboriginal people.

This is not to suggest that federalism was to blame, or that things would have been better under a unitary regime. Indeed any argument that the Constitution was to blame for the treatment of Aborigines is ill-founded. For it is fair to say that the existence of a specific Commonwealth power to make laws with respect to Aborigines would have made little difference to their status before the 1960s. Such a power would have been used, if at all, to reinforce the policies of the day over which both the Commonwealth and the States were in broad agreement. Indeed, the Commonwealth's administration of Aboriginal affairs in the Northern Territory from 1911 was entirely consistent with the most oppressive state practices.

The actual treatment of Aboriginal people depended on the ongoing legislative and administrative regimes of the Commonwealth and the states: it was a matter of political will rather than institutional design or constitutional necessity. This can be shown by reference to the positive story of women's suffrage. Even though only two States, South Australia and Western Australia, had implemented women's suffrage at the time, the 1902 *Commonwealth Franchise Act* adopted the most progressive state practice and enfranchized all white women. This provided a significant impetus to the other states, all of which soon adopted female suffrage. In the very Act which granted female suffrage, however, an amendment was carried barring any 'aboriginal native' from the vote. This was championed by parliamentarians from Western Australia and Queensland, states which had relatively large numbers of Aboriginal people and which excluded them from voting.

By enshrining the exclusionary practice of those two states at the national level, the Commonwealth reinforced and legitimated the basic denial of citizenship rights to Aborigines at the state level. Had the Commonwealth passed the earlier version of the Franchise Bill that did not exclude Australian Aborigines, Aboriginal voters may have caused their shameful treatment to have been arrested sometime earlier than 1962, the year when they were belatedly and uniformly enfranchized.

Australian governments, rather than outlining who is entitled to citizenship, have concentrated instead on who is not entitled to citizenship. In piecemeal fashion, in a range of laws, governments have drawn up negative rather than positive citizenship criteria. We know who is an Australian citizen only by knowing who is not.

NOTES

1. An earlier version of this paper was published in S. Rufus Davis (ed.), *Citizenship in Australia: Democracy, Law and Society* (Constitutional Century Foundation), 1996.
2. See documents in A101, B1904/4739, Australian Archives, Canberra.
3. Minister's statement at R254, IA/467, Queensland State Archives.
4. See C.D. Rowley, *The Destruction of Aboriginal Society* (Ringwood), 1972, pp. 290-7.
5. See p. 48 of the Committee's report, in *Commonwealth Parliamentary Papers*, 1961, vol. 2.
6. A432/70, 1967/3321, Part 1, Australian Archives, Canberra.
7. A342/81, 1966/3171, Australian Archives, Canberra.

13

Fictions of Citizenship and Community: The Experience of Federation in Novels of Salman Rushdie, Rohinton Mistry, Peter Carey and Sam Watson

JOHN McLAREN

Although political scientists, historians and literary scholars have all been involved in recent years in studying issues of citizenship and the state, the different disciplines have tended to emphasize different aspects of the question. Political scientists have been interested in rights and obligations, historians in the development of the national state and nationalism, and literary theorists in questions of identity. In this paper I am contending that issues of identity underlie political forms, and that, although they are always historically situated, they can be usefully examined in the fictional narratives that embody the responses of individuals to the possibilities and denials of community in which their particular histories involve them.

A starting point for the paper is Zygmunt Bauman's proposition that the traditional community depends on the distinction between friends and enemies, whereas the modern nation state is challenged by strangers who cannot be accommodated in either category. This challenge can only be met by a form of nationalism based on an open community. The ideal of Commonwealth gives political and legal form to this concept, but to function effectively it must nurture a community that exists in the lived experience of its citizens. The two Indian novels I examine are both by writers who have chosen to become expatriates, or strangers abroad, in part because they have been made strangers at home. They both come from the English-speaking elite of Bombay (Mumbai), but both belong to minority groups, and their novels trace the process by which the Indian community has been destroyed from within as a monolithic conception of nationalism has been imposed. The Australian novels, by contrast, show a Commonwealth that has failed to establish a community because it has failed to resists outside domination and because it is itself grounded in a denial of the conditions that brought a settler society into existence on the continent.

The boundaries of modern India are themselves a response to a failure to distinguish between strangers and enemies, while its federal and secular constitution is an attempt to accommodate linguistic and cultural difference without generating enmity. The continuing separatist struggles in Kashmir and the Punjab show the geographic limitations of this attempt in its geographic dimension, while the substantial vote garnered by the Bharatiya Janata Party (BJP) in the last two elections demonstrates the weakening of the secular ideal and the persistence of the urge to force those who are different—the strangers—into the binary categories of friends or enemies. This attempt is the more violent because the strangers have lived within the boundaries of the present state for hundreds or even thousands of years. Mughal and earlier Indian rulers, and their successors under the Raj, were able to accommodate this diversity, not necessarily peacefully, because their rule depended on various combinations of client relationships and military power rather than on any national ideology. The modern state, however, demands both territorial integrity and the allegiance, rather than the acquiescence, of those living within its boundaries. It must, in other words, be a commonwealth, a community in which all its citizens feel they have a stake. Both Salman Rushdie and Rohinton Mistry chronicle the way in which this sense of community through diversity has been eroded, and, with it, the basis in individual experience of the political forms of the federal state.

The movement that produced the political structures of the Australian Commonwealth was based on a perception that the white inhabitants of the six Colonies were not strangers to each other, and therefore should be friends rather than enemies. The reality behind this perception can be demonstrated at a number of levels, not least being the common variety of English that seems to have developed from the earliest days of settlement, the free movement of settlers and itinerant workers between the colonies, and the wide circulation of journals like *The Bulletin*, with its radical nationalist aspirations. The motto of *The Bulletin*, 'Australia for the white man', is one example of the way the colonists' recognition of each other as friends was strengthened by their rejection of blacks and coloureds as enemies. Like the *Bulletin's* creed of mateship, Australian nationalism was as much a refuge for the weak and fearful as it was a declaration of strength. The Commonwealth that it produced was a compromise between colonial rivalry and the assertion of common identity. Its separation of powers did not so much encourage regional differences as allow citizens direct access to government on those matters that most concerned them. Implicit in the framework of authority given to the Commonwealth, as well as the matters left to the states, is the assumption that the role of government is to serve a common weal. The absence of a Bill of Rights is testimony to the belief that government is to work for its electorate, as opposed to the assumption of the United States Constitution that the citizen is to be protected from government. Yet the adherence to the ideal of a secular state, through the prohibition on the Commonwealth's making any laws to establish religion, impose religious observance, inhibit the free exercise of religion or impose religious tests on office-holders, points to a desire that private differences should not breach communality. This is very different from the elements of the United States Constitution that encourage a more active role for citizens, but may be responsible for the tolerance, noted by John Hirst, that has enabled the Australian Commonwealth in the past fifty years to absorb the great numbers of immigrant strangers who have become part of the community and enabled it, to a considerable extent, to transcend the racial hostilities that gave it its earlier coherence. Nevertheless, the legal differences it recognizes are geographic rather than social or cultural. Unlike India, the cultural distinctions between regions are not great, and consequently the Australian Constitution acts as an obstacle rather than a framework for resolving the disputes that do arise. Peter Carey's *Tristam Smith* is an allegory of an Australia that is disintegrating, culturally and socially, along with its powerful friend and overlord. In the struggle for power, community is destroyed. In *The Kadaitcha Sung*, on the other hand, Sam Watson shows how the present of the Commonwealth is destroyed by its failure from its beginning to incorporate the strangers whose territory it has usurped.

RUSHDIE'S *MIDNIGHT'S CHILDREN*

New nations, in particular, need a founding mythology. India, which did not exist until the midnight that ushered in 15 August 1947, occupied a space that had never been ruled by a single authority, and had neither common language, race, religion or culture. It was held together in what J.K. Galbraith has called 'functioning anarchy' by the myths of the struggle against the British, *satyagraha*—the form of non-violence practised by Mahatma Gandhi—and the inclusive secular state embodied in the Indian National Congress and symbolized by the English-educated and Anglophilic Jawaharlal Nehru. On Independence, as Congress became a political party, the violence of partition, culminating in the assassination of Gandhi, shattered the hopes of peaceful transition, and the failure to resolve the succession in Kashmir destroyed Nehru's hopes of national unity. Over the next half century, the seeds of violence, disunity and religious zealotry that were then sown have produced monstrous fruit as new mythologies have flourished on the basis of division and exclusivity. Salman Rushdie's *Midnight's Children* is, amongst other things, a record of the way the generation born to the new state remade its past to suit its present purposes, using memory as its tool.[1] By making the teller of the story, Saleem, an unreliable narrator who gets wrong even elementary facts of history, such as the name of the general who received the surrender of the Pakistani army at the end of the Bangladesh war, Rushdie demonstrates the partiality of the memory and experience from which we construct our mythologies. Thus, in the case of India, the myth of religion comes to overpower the founding myths of secularity and diversity.

Rushdie tells us that he started to write *Midnight's Children* with the Proustian ambition of recreating without filter that past which is a different country, only to realize in the process of writing that the past is in fact the present in which we live, shaped by the filters of language and memory. Various forms of filter appear throughout the novel, as husbands and wives filter their thoughts to each other, and impose filters between their partners and the world, and as members of different religious and linguistic communities variously filter the messages and noise coming to them from the turbulent stream of events. The children born at the midnight of the new nation at first seem able to bypass these filters and achieve direct communication, but as their commonwealth—itself a metaphor for the nation—develops, so they impose their own filters, first of personality, later of politics. But the novel's central metaphor for the nation is not this mystical community between the custodians of the national ideal, but the sheet with the seven-inch hole through which Dr Aadam Aziz, grandfather of the narrator, is allowed to view the woman who eventually becomes his wife. As he diagnoses her successive illnesses through this hole in the sheet, he falls in love with her several parts, seeing her fully only on the night of their marriage. Yet the marriage is not successful, as the two parties are unable to accept each other fully—their love remains confined to the parts that do not add up to a sum. Similarly, their daughter Muntaz, or Amina as she becomes known—the mother of the narrator, Saleem Sinai—wills herself to love her husband by concentrating separately on each of his attributes—so falling in love intellectually as her father had sensually. Both father and daughter are capable of selfless courage in emergency, transcending social boundaries to save the lives of fugitives from the law or the mob. They are unable to transcend the boundaries within themselves to establish a community within their marriages. This failure is allegorical of India's failure to knit its separate parts into harmony.

The central image of *Midnight's Children* is the midnight conference through which Saleem brings together the 581 survivors of the 1001 children born in the first hour of Independence on 15 August 1947. The conference is a metaphor for the divided, confused yet hopeful India that came into existence on that date when, in Saleem's words, 'history . . . entered a new phase'. However, the longer view of Hindu cosmology, he reminds us, suggests the alternative view that date is 'no more than one fleeting instant in the Age of Darkness . . . in which the cow of morality has been reduced to standing, teetering, on a single log . . . on the losing throw in our national dice game (p. 144). This doubleness enters into the structure of the novel. Saleem's parents and grandparents are couples in conflict, between reason and faith, modernity and tradition, withdrawal and engagement. The children of that momentous midnight are each endowed with some remarkable quality—physical, intellectual or magical—which makes it easy for them to be brilliant, but at the same time they are 'always confused about being good'.[2] Centrally, the two boys who are born on the stroke of midnight, Saleem and Siva, represent the intellectual and the physical, the idealistic and the exploitative, yet are joined in a common destiny not only by the hour of their birth but because they are changelings, switched at birth by a midwife trying to remedy the injustice of fate. Their unity in division continues to the end of the novel. Saleem's son, the pragmatist born at the moment the Emergency is declared, and in fact fathered by Siva, in turn is destroyed by the violence he has cultivated, yet survives to redress both the idealism and the violence of his fathers.

Although the conference of midnight's children is the central conceit of the novel, a metaphor—in its diversity and its hope—for the new federal nation, it is itself the heir of the traditions and the family histories that have gone into this nation. The conference does not convene until almost half-way through the novel, and before that Saleem has summed up for us everything that has gone into its making:

> There were rubies and diamonds . . . there were blind landowners and lady wrestlers . . . my inheritance grows, because I now have the mythical golden teeth of the boatman Tai, and his brandy bottle which foretold my father's alcoholic djinns; I have Ilse Lubin for suicide and pickled snakes for virility; I have Tai-for-changelessness opposed to Aadam-for-progress; and I have, too, the odours of the unwashed boatman which drove my grandparents south, and made Bombay a possibility.
>
> How many things people notions we bring with us into the world, how many possibilities and also restrictions of possibility!—Because all of these were the parents of the child born that midnight, and for every one of the children there were as many more. Among the parents of midnight: the failure of the Cabinet Mission scheme; the determination of M.A. Jinnah, who was dying and wanted to see Pakistan formed in his lifetime, and would have done anything to ensure it— . . . and more and more—Red Fort and Old Fort, monkeys and vultures dropping hands, and white transvestites, and bone-setters and mongoose trainers and Shri Ramrath Seth who made too much prophecy. And my father's dream of rearranging the Quran has its place; and the burning of a godown which turned him into a man of property and not leathercloth; and the piece of Ahmed which Amina could not love. To understand just one life, you have to swallow the world. I told you that.[3]

The combination of public and private, act and aspiration, contingent and determinate, concrete and abstract, typifies the book and its understanding of history. Although each of the characters is shown to be responsible for their actions, even Saleem's gift of entering into the minds of others does not enable him to understand enough to be responsible for his fate. His unreliability as a narrator symbolizes the unreliability of all the characters in telling either private or public histories, and therefore the necessary unreliability of their policies and actions. The midnight conference eventually falls apart because of the failures of its members, but even more because, like India, it is unable to withstand the blows of history, the machinations, of Siva or the Widow, the violence of the 1971 with Pakistan war, or the betrayal of the Emergency.

MISTRY'S *SUCH A LONG JOURNEY*

Like Rushdie, Rohinton Mistry sets his novel against the background of the war in Bangladesh. Yet, while Rushdie constructs an epic tale that Saleem explicitly compares with the *Ramayana*, Mistry focuses on a few months in the life of a Parsi family in the compound of a Bombay block of flats.

> The first light of morning barely illumined the sky as Gustad Noble faced eastward to offer his orisons to Ahura Mazda. The hour was approaching six, and up in the compound's solitary tree the sparrows began to call. Gustad listened to their chirping every morning while reciting his *kusti* prayers. There was something reassuring about it. Always, the sparrows were first; the cawing of the crows came later.[4]

On returning to this paragraph after reading the whole book, the reference to the crows may appear ominous, but on first reading the emphasis is clearly on the reassurance of domestic routine and humble life. From this opening, the author widens his focus to take in first the neighbouring women, buying their milk from the vendor, then Gustad's flat and his family, and eventually Bombay and the whole of India.

In the only long physical journey taken in the novel, Gustad travels, in a wonderfully confused manner, by train to Delhi, where he discovers and in part resolves the cause of the disquiet that has been troubling him. This reverses the normal political perspective, which starts with the capital and traces the lines of authority by which it exerts its influence over the state. The reversal, placing the domestic at the centre, emphasizes the fact that the nation, as opposed to the state, exists only insofar as it lives within the everyday reality of its citizens. The other journey in the novel, the long metaphysical journey which provides its linear movement, takes Gustad away from the comfort of the opening scene, and the simple pride he takes in his family, his friends and his nation, to the point where that early commonwealth has disintegrated and he has to rebuild his community from the most basic relationships.

The sense of unease that builds up on this journey begins early. The compound is at once a refuge for its inhabitants and a microcosm of the nation. Certainly, its inhabitants are all Parsis, but they have a secure place in the larger world and enjoy easy relationships with their neighbours and with the world that passes in a constant stream outside their walls. Yet from the beginning there are signs that their world is crumbling. The petty squabbles among the tenants of the flats do not matter so much—they are contained within the community. But their circumstances are becoming straitened. The water comes through the pipes for only two hours a day, the vendor waters the milk he sells, the families can no longer afford to buy higher quality milk from the shops. In Gustad's own family, his pride at his son's success in passing the entrance examination for the Indian Institute of Technology is undermined by the son's lack of enthusiasm, and his eventual refusal to take up a place. This disappointment reinforces Gustad's long grieving for his father's loss of his bookselling business and his own sense of failure to provide for his children the same rich environment he had enjoyed as a child. Deepest of all, however, is his sense of wounding and betrayal by his neighbour and old friend, Major Bilimoria, an heroic character who could have stepped out of Kipling. Having first left the flats without farewell or explanation, the major has now written to Gustad calling on him as a friend to assist him in a transaction which, as it turns out, is not only illegal but threatens Gustad's own job at the bank, and thus the precarious security he has built for himself and his family.

Gustad's attempt to escape from his troubles by staging a party that will re-create the domestic comforts of his youth prove a failure, and he is precipitated against his will into active engagement with the present. He brings an artist to paint the wall of the compound as celebration of all the world's religions. He accepts the mission for Major Bilimoria when he is persuaded that it is a patriotic endeavour, and this in turn revives old friendships. Yet each of these ventures leads to eventual disaster. His loss of temper on the night of his party seems to bring death into his house, and although he saves his daughter's life he loses his remaining friend and guest. The municipality moves to destroy the artist's wall to make way for a wider road, and in the ensuing riot the cripple whom Gustad has protected, whose life has become a symbol of Gustad's charity in the face of prejudice, is killed. And the Major's patriotic scheme turns out to be a fraud perpetrated on him by Indira Gandhi for her own purposes, and leads to the Major's incarceration and death. Yet the novel ends positively as Gustad removes the black-out papers that have shrouded his flat for the nine years since the Indo-Chinese war destroyed Nehru's idealism and blighted the hopes of those who, like Gustad, had trusted him to lead them to a brighter future. The political structures of the nation may have been hopelessly corrupted, but the ideals survive in the simple strength of people like Gustad, his neighbours and friends. The title of the book, taken from Eliot's 'The Journey of the Magi', offers hope as well as sadness.

CAREY'S *THE UNUSUAL LIFE OF TRISTAN SMITH*

While these Indian novels describe the destruction of the hopes of the nation from within, Peter Carey's *The Unusual Life of Tristan Smith* describes the way a nation can succumb to external influences. Unlike Rushdie, who is a fantasist, or Mistry, who is a realist, Carey works in the mode of allegory, but post-modern allegory, where the world of the novel corresponds in general rather than specific terms to the world we experience. He takes care to provide both geographical and linguistic obstacles that prevent his readers precisely identifying the two major countries of his novel, Efica and Voorstand, with the Australia and United States to which, in cultural and political terms, they correspond. Efica is an archipelago, and its French origins and vocabulary associate it with Canada as well as Australia. Voorstand is in its cultural identity and dominance the United States of America, but its Dutch origins and vocabulary also lend it a passing resemblance to South Africa. For the purposes of this paper, however, the problems of its Efica are those of Australia.

The novel opens, in Tristan Smith's narration, with the day of his birth to a Voorstandish mother who provides the essential artistic and financial support for the Feu Follet Collective, 'a small radical theatre group which was always in trouble with the authorities for its opposition to the country of her birth'.[5] Like the hero of Gunter Grass' *The Tin Drum*, Tristan Smith is a dwarf, but his stature is not a moral gesture against his times so much as a metaphor for his standing, and that of his native country, in the wider world. In an echo of Rushdie's *Shame*, where one of the major characters has three mothers, Tristan Smith has three fathers. But whereas in Rushdie's novel this multiple parenting suggests an overdetermination of care, in Carey's work the triplicated fathers represent three different elements in Efican society. The natural father is proud of his achievement but dodges responsibility as he heads off to Voorstand in search of his own fame and fortune. His mother's patron cares for him as a way to his mother's affections. And the adoptive father, the man who actually cares for Tristan and brings him up, is discarded at the critical moment. In cultural terms, these fathers represent the three aspects of colonialism—the imperative of the cringe, the desire for economic independence, and the ingrained sense of inferiority. Finally, it is only when Tristan takes control of his own fate and escapes from the spheres of both Efica and Voorstand that he finds a hope of survival.

The second part of the novel, Tristan's travels in Voorstand, does not concern us now, except insofar as it shows the way in which extreme individualism has destroyed the possibility of commonwealth and provided the facade behind which absolute state power can operate. Voorstand, like the United States, offers refuge for people from the whole globe, yet it offers it on terms that keep them as outsiders, subject to constant surveillance, unable to contribute to society because they are precluded from membership of the community. The forms of democracy provide the means of tyranny. The rhetoric of defending a free society excuses control and enables exploitation. In Efica, on the other hand, the little theatre of Feu Follet offers a genuine prospect of commonwealth through creative activity. In a direct parallel with Australia, however—or with Canada—this attempt is impeded by its own economic marginality and by the cultural imperialism of the dominant power. It eventually falls apart, like so many artistic endeavours, as a consequence of personal jealousies, but its failure to regroup, to build anew, is a direct consequence of lethal political interference by the agents of Voorstand. The assassination of Tristan's mother by the agent of an ally may have no direct historical counterpart, but is a logical extension of Carey's analysis of the cultural and political situation of a country like Australia. Commonwealth requires a community that cannot exist in a global economy. Even in Voorstand, the folk myth of Bruder Rabbit has been suppressed in favour of a commercial simulacrum that entertains without empowering. Tristan Smith, for all his diminutive stature, threatens this commercial order by removing his own mask.

WATSON'S *THE KADAITCHA*

Peter Carey, like Salman Rushdie and Rohinton Mistry, is an expatriate. All three show a deep attachment to their native country, as well as something approaching despair about its chances of realizing its potential. Sam Watson, by contrast, is an exile in his own country, an Aboriginal political activist who has still to change the commonwealth to find room for his own people.

While both Rushdie and Mistry demonstrate the conflict between tradition and present imperatives, Watson uses mythology to explain the present. His book opens with a question asked of his own people: where did we go wrong to be inflicted with such suffering? His answer goes back to the Aboriginal creation myth, and to the failure of succeeding generations to keep the covenant that they entered then and which bound them as custodians of the land. The struggle in the present then is between those who seek to rediscover this relationship and those who accept the exploitative ideologies of the white settlers. The novel, set in contemporary Brisbane, is brutally realistic, anticipating grunge fiction in its portrayal of hatred, systematic violence and exploitative sex, but its mythological framework gives it both an interpretative and a moral force. The conflict it portrays is not merely over power and survival, but over the recovery of a community that will value people both for what they are and for what they offer to each other and the land. It stands out from much black writing both in locating the source of the problem among blacks themselves, and in seeing their achievement of a solution as a necessary step towards the renewal of a community that will give legitimacy to white settlement.

Watson however offers no suggestion that this community will be won easily. His hero, Tommy Gubba, carries both white and black blood, but he identifies with the Aborigines, just as his opponent, the Kadaitcha who has broken the faith, identifies with the whites. But in restoring the balance, Tommy exacts vengeance on the whites, and for this his god, Biamee, exacts retribution, so that the novel ends with Tommy's hanging for the death of a white policeman he had never seen. However, in his words from the dock he pronounces sentence on the whites who have usurped his ancestors' lands and taken his people's lives:

> . . . you are like empty shells. You do not have any substance or guts. I have my strength and my history in my heart and in my soul. I carry them all the time. You do not have that. My land and my spirit are in me and they are me. That is the way of the people and that is the way of my law.
>
> And you cannot take this thing away from me. Because I am the dirt. I am the rock and the tree. I am the land. And I say this to you migloo: you will be doomed to the end of time to wear the blood of my people.
>
> You will carry that scar on your mind and on your body, and you will not be able to wash it away. The blood is upon the land until the end of time, and it is upon you until the end of time.[6]

The language is that of biblical prophecy, which has the function not of foretelling the future but of revealing the truth of the present. It is not the language of guilt but of responsibility, calling on the migloo, the whites, to recognize the price paid by the first dwellers for our possession of the land, and to recognize what is needed to make this possession legitimate.

But these are not the last words of the novel. When Tommy, the last initiated Kadaitcha, is hanged—ironically on Christmas day—his fellows go north, back to their tribal lands, taking with them Tommy's partner and his unborn child: a symbol of a possible reconciliation based on a union of the peoples and an acceptance of responsibility for each other and the land.

Manning Clark has said that humanity can be divided between those who believe that just institutions will produce good people and remove evil from the world, and those who believe that evil comes from the devil in the human heart. These four novels separately demonstrate the way political institutions and the hope of commonwealth are corrupted by human fear, greed, hatred and the drive for power over others. Yet each also shows the capacity of humans for compassion and for such simple virtues as friendship and loyalty. Without strong governmental institutions and national independence these capacities will be thwarted, leaving us with the sordid anarchy of Carey's Voorstand. Where the institutions do not allow room for diversity, they will be corrupted in the way shown in the novels by Rushdie and Mistry, and community will degenerate into its deadly opposite, communalism based on religious, linguistic and cultural exclusion. Where, as in Australia, the constitution of the commonwealth fails to recognize the conditions of its existence, its order will be maintained only by violence directed at the minority in order to repress the insecurity of the majority. Yet even in the midst of this violence and denial, Watson shows the capacity for love and sharing that can provide the basis for community. The challenge to the law-makers is to build the institutions that will allow the realization of this potential.

NOTES

1. Salman Rushdie, ' "Errata", or, Unreliable Narration in *Midnight's Children*', in *Imaginary Homelands: Essays and Criticism 1981-1991* (London and New York, 1991), p. 24.
2. Salman Rushdie, *Midnight's Children* (London, 1982), p. 200.
3. Ibid., pp. 107-9.
4. Rohinton Mistry, *Such a Long Journey* (London and Boston, 1991), p. 1.
5. P. Carey, *The Unusual Life of Tristan Smith* (St Lucia, 1995), p. 6.
6. S. Watson, *The Kadaitcha Survey* (Ringwood, 1990), p. 31.

14

From Confrontation to Cooperation: Australian Commonwealth-State Relations in the 1980s and 1990s

J.C. BANNON

Despite the clear rejection of a unitary state in favour of a federation in the convention and subsequent referendums that adopted the Australian Constitution in the last decade of the nineteenth century, there has been ongoing and inevitable tension between the state and federal levels of government. It has mainly expressed itself in economic and fiscal matters, and contrary to the understanding of nearly all involved in the making of the Constitution, Australia has shown increasingly centralist tendencies particularly under the impact of war or economic depression.

The expiry of the income guarantee (the so-called Braddon Blot) after ten years[1] saw the Commonwealth increasing its power of the purse and the states becoming increasingly dependent. The creation of the Loan Council in 1928, the Premiers' Plan to tackle the depression of the 1930s, and the dismissal of a state government not toeing the line in financial matters were important demonstrations of Commonwealth supremacy. This was consolidated in the Second World War when the sweeping use of the defence power allowed the Commonwealth to bring about the surrender of the states' income-taxing power in 1942, inaugurating so-called 'coercive federalism'[2] and created the basic element of the system we have today where the Commonwealth collects most taxes centrally and distributes them to the states by agreed and negotiated formulas.

The twenty-three years of conservative government (1949-72) did little to change the balance established under Labor during the war. The Gorton Coalition (1967-71) and the Whitlam Labor (1972-5) governments took this process much further by the use of specific purpose payments—payments made to the states under Section 96 of the Constitution. The period saw them grow from 30 to 40 per cent of Commonwealth outlays and from 18 to 33 per cent of state budget expenditure. Such programmes, theoretically negotiated with the states, greatly increased the ability of the Commonwealth to determine priorities in areas where their jurisdiction was shared or excluded. Confronted with the 'take it or leave it' offer of money for specific programmes, the states invariably took it.

Fraser's (1975-83) 'New Federalism', which proposed returning the power of income tax to the states (something which they did not want at this time), was a failure, and the advent of the Hawke Labor government in March 1983 promised a new deal of cooperation. In its first years this was delivered. There was a growth in financial support to the states, in both general and special purpose payments, and there was less bite in the traditional grizzles of the premiers at their annual conference with the prime minister and treasurer. But from the 1985-6 financial year there was a marked change in federal policy, and reductions in payments, which by 1992-3 amounted to 15 per cent. This was accompanied by limits on the loan raisings of the states, an agreed total public sector borrowing requirement being established and shared (and in some cases traded) between the states.

At first the effect of this squeeze was masked as the economy boomed and property market transactions in particular brought big revenue increases to the states. The Commonwealth produced its first surplus budget. Little attention was paid to the fact that most of the savings were achieved at the expense of grants to the states. While Commonwealth payments to the states declined, its 'own-purpose' payments actually increased. With the drop in state-sourced revenue as the economy contracted, and the consequent reduction in services, there was greater acrimony between the two levels of government. This was heightened by the tension among the states, as Victoria and New South Wales challenged fiscal equalization with a view to increasing their share of the Commonwealth monies at the expense of the smaller states.

The procedure of the Premiers Conference, virtually unchanged for four decades, was proving unable to cope with the new pressures. In fact, it worked against the settlement of financial disputes, and gave little scope to deal with any other major issues. The pattern was as follows:

- first, the notional agenda on which the parochial and essentially bilateral concerns of the states were added to the financial and other major national issues;
- second, the pre-conference media briefing as the premiers flew to Canberra;
- third, the behind-the-scenes lobbying;
- fourth, the Commonwealth offer pushed under the hotel door on the morning of the conference;
- fifth, the public meeting where all parties postured;
- sixth, the private meeting in the Cabinet Room where the posturing was only slightly modified and the deals were done;
- seventh, the post conference media announcements as each leader interpreted the results.

All this came to a head in 1990 with results I will outline shortly. But before doing so, it is interesting to note that with one or two rare exceptions (the tax summit, the housing summit) the heads of the Australian governments did not meet together, except in this way and no more than once a year. Meanwhile ministers from all states and territories, usually including New Zealand and sometimes Papua-New Guinea as well, were meeting frequently over the year in exotic and interesting places. In the smaller states where ministers hold a number of portfolios an individual could attend an almost continuous series of ministerial meetings, many of them being formalized as councils. Cooperative federalism was flourishing, but at a level that only dealt with issues in a particular and piecemeal fashion—often attempting to pre-empt Cabinet consideration, and always running the risk of being overruled because of the lack of authority.

Against this background, the June 1990 Premiers Conference resulted in a stand-off. In 1990 the language used was more vigorous than it had ever been but the disagreements went much deeper. Everything pointed to a fundamental breakdown in federal-state relations, despite the many macro- and micro-reforms that were needed and the clear inability to get them moving without cooperation between governments. All participants understood that a meeting of that kind must not happen again. Accordingly, in July 1990, Prime Minister Hawke wrote to the premiers calling a Special Premiers Conference to discuss cooperative arrangements. He specifically acknowledged the federal nature of the Constitution and suggested a broad agenda that would include the financial arrangements. He established a joint Steering Committee which, among other things, revived a languishing process of examination of duplication of services and functions between levels of government. For the first time since 1982 the heads of government were to meet outside the destructive ritual of the Annual Conference and Loan Council meeting to discuss a wide range of general issues and procedures. More importantly, the meeting was envisaged to be the start of a series of meetings to address the problems of federation on an ongoing basis.

A number of factors were operating at that time which gave the initiative a greater measure of goodwill and higher chance of success than it might have done:[3]

- the federation centenary decade gave a focus to the fundamentals of the Australian Commonwealth;
- Prime Minister Hawke was looking for a landmark reform in his fourth term of government;
- five state Labor governments were acting as a balance to federal Labor's centralist tendency;
- one of the great barriers to cooperative federalism, Queensland Premier Joh Bjelke Petersen, had left the scene and the government had changed in Queensland for the first time in thirty-two years;
- the only Liberal premier, Nick Greiner, had an active agenda of reducing vertical fiscal imbalance and more precise definition of respective powers;
- there was a real identity of purpose among the leaders who, apart from the prime minister and the South Australian premier, were new and impatient with the inadequate system;
- the financial squeeze on the states had become unbearable as the recession deepened; and
- no government was due to go to election before 1992—an unusual 'election free zone' was available to develop new approaches without distraction.

The first Special Premiers Conference was held not in Canberra but in Brisbane in October 1990 and was most productive in identifying issues and procedures. To those of us participating it was a refreshing change, with the opportunity to discuss the Premiers Conference procedures and financial arrangements and other matters in a less pressured atmosphere for the first time. As with other Premiers Conferences, the agenda was long, but all the items were actually considered—from general questions such as regulatory reform, the environment, and duplication of services to specific matters such as a national rail freight system and electricity generation. Although there were still complaints by the states that old Commonwealth habits continued (such as taking over the agenda and communique rather than treating it as a meeting of equals in terms of their respective responsibilities) the meeting concluded with a range of studies commissioned and areas of agreement identified.

The psychological difference between the Special Premiers Conference (and its later manifestation), and the annual haggle over financial shares and grants is most important. In the latter, the Commonwealth is firmly in charge, having the last say and most of the sanctions. In the former, in many areas, as Patrick Weller puts it

> the Commonwealth responsibility is small, with the States the principal actors. Even in areas where the Commonwealth may be able to act unilaterally, it may still need the support, and preferably the cooperation of the States. . . . It could take the high moral ground of good national policy but needed assistance to implement it.[4]

Another critical factor was that for the first time there was a head of government equivalent to the burgeoning Ministerial Councils and Committees mentioned above. To quote Patrick Weller again, 'There had been no equivalent forum for the centre of governments. . . . It allowed Premiers to strengthen Cabinet processes by using COAG to corral ministers.'[5]

Plans were made to meet again in early 1991. Unfortunately a lot of the impetus was lost when the calling of an early election by Greiner in New South Wales forced its postponement to the end of July. Nevertheless considerable progress was made at that meeting, including the establishment of the National Rail Corporation, an agreement on a national heavy vehicle registration and regulation scheme, the establishment of an electricity National Grid Management Council, an agreement on the respective responsibility for each level of government on disability services, and progress on a range of welfare, health and urban cooperative issues. A further conference was scheduled for later in the year. Before it could be convened, though, the prime minister and treasurer were embroiled in a leadership battle. The issue of state tax share and power got caught up in this and the next attempt to meet, in Perth in late 1991, failed, as the prime minister's negotiating power had been severely constrained by his colleagues in the federal caucus.

Rather than compromise on a half-baked meeting, the premiers determined to go ahead without the Commonwealth, and met in Adelaide in late November. Much to the surprise of cynics and even possibly of the participants, considerable progress was made. A statement of the principles of the Australian federal system was adopted, which is still the point of reference today. The four principles were:

- *The Australian Nation Principle*: All governments in Australia recognize the social, political and economic imperatives of nationhood and will work cooperatively to ensure that national issues are resolved in the interests of Australia as a whole;
- *The Subsidiary Principle*: Responsibilities for the regulation and for allocation of public goods and services should be devolved to the maximum extent possible consistent with the national interest so that government is accessible and accountable to those affected by its decisions;
- *The Structural Effeciency Principle*: Increased competitiveness and flexibility of the Australian economy require structural reform in the public sector to complement private sector reform: inefficient Commonwealth-State divisions of functions can no longer be tolerated;
- *The Accountability Principle*: The structure of intergovernmental arrangements should promote democratic accountability and the transparency of government to the electorate.[6]

A formal agreement on mutual recognition of standards and the elimination of impediments to a national market of goods and services was signed; there was an in-principle discussion to establish national standards if agreed to by at least six of the jurisdictions; a formal agreement was released on the prudential supervision of state-based building societies and credit unions, and uniform road rules; a light vehicles national register was agreed to; there was agreement on finalizing an intergovernmental protocol on the environment with the Commonwealth; a National Environment Protection Authority was established and an agreement on gun control and anti-violence measures was put in place. On the contentious issue of finance and vertical fiscal imbalance the leaders reiterated their support for a national income tax-sharing scheme. A wide range of other matters was dealt with and outlined in the twenty-three-page communique issued following the meeting and a number of letters containing the specific proposals were sent to the prime minister. Of particular note was the call for the establishment of what was to be called the Council of the Federation, which the prime minister was to be invited to chair.[7]

The value of a meeting of state leaders, joined in this instance by local government representatives, was clear. It demonstrated that such meetings had been long overdue and that even in the absence of the Commonwealth considerable progress could be made on matters of national significance. It also acknowledged that, while a number of things were not possible without Commonwealth involvement, in addressing most issues that did not involve the financial arrangements, the Commonwealth was simply another partner in the process—in a national Council of Federation it could not dominate the agenda or dictate the outcome. Perhaps the success of the independent venture hastened the demise of prime minister Hawke. Certainly the change of prime minister occurred in the midst of follow-up negotiations. Unfortunately the change of national leader also foreshadowed that the process might end.

In fact, Prime Minister Keating was keen to promote a reform agenda and saw the value of the vehicle which had been created and more importantly the need to have state action and cooperation to make things happen. Heads of government met again with the Commonwealth on reform matters in May 1992, a month before the regular Premiers Conference and Loan Council meeting of that year. Agreement was reached on accelerating the reform of the rail systems and the development of national occupational health and safety standards; a Mutual Recognition Agreement was signed which was given legislative force in all jurisdictions; and discussions took place which led to the establishment of the Australia National Training Authority Agreement in July 1992. Most importantly, agreement was reached to establish the Council of Australian Governments and a new acronym, COAG, was born.

The momentum was unstoppable. This was demonstrated when a meeting in Darwin to consider the Hilmer proposals for reform ended in the old acrimony, but separate meetings of state leaders and another Council reached agreement soon afterwards.

This progress in interstate transport, common standards, electricity grids and so on continues. One of the subjects considered by the meeting of premiers and chief ministers in 1991 was gun control and anti-violence measures. Nine points of agreement were reached on gun control based on an earlier police ministers' meeting—it was the starting point for national consideration of this issue. The goodwill created by the on-going COAG process was fundamental to the achievement of the 1996 agreement on gun laws.

There is no question that economic and social change in Australia is putting a strain on federal-state relations. The discrepancy in size between the states becomes more important in a free economy. The pace of development and population on the north-eastern seaboard, the disaffection of an expanding Western Australia, the threat to fiscal equalization, and the impact of industry restructuring has created great competitive tensions among the states.

In analysing how the new process got away to its successful start in 1990, I identified eight factors which were critical. On looking at the current situation I believe that three of those factors are working more powerfully than in 1990, four are just as strong, albeit in different ways, and only one could be seen as weaker. In summary the stronger factors include:

- the imperatives of the approaching centenary of Federation, now so close that landmark activities are urgent;
- new leadership at State and Federal level, with senior leader having held office for only three years;
- and the financial squeeze on government at all levels which if anything is greater than in 1990.

Factors remaining unchanged include:

- the prime minister's commitment, where John Howard is driven by the same imperatives as his predecessors, albeit with a different philosophy;

- the political complexion of the governments and their attitudes to federalism, which is a mirror image of 1990, with all governments being from the conservative side of politics (and perhaps less centralist in philosophy) and NSW the only state government not of the coalition parties.

There is not the same 'election-free' zone to encourage statesmanlike rather than expedient decisions, although with only two of the states due to face an election in 1997 the factor is still present.

This, together with the record of success so far, is a cause for optimism that the process of COAG, state leaders meetings and reform of inter-government relations will continue. To be sure, the first Premiers Conference of the new federal government did make this assessment look a little optimistic. The reversion to the classic stand-off and unacceptable bargaining methods that occurred in May 1996 was a tragedy. Six years' hard work seemed to be undone in the dispute over sales tax on government vehicles. It was not just in the implications of the proposal but the way it was presented. Yet the swift demonstration by the states that they had political if not financial clout may have got the process back on the rails—and again would not have been possible without the confidence and solidarity that the new processes of COAG and leaders meetings has brought.

NOTES

1. See Sec. 87 of the Constitution of the Commonwealth of Australia.
2. See Dennis W. James, *Intergovernmental Financial Relations in Australia* (Sydney, 1992).
3. See J.C. Bannon, *Cooperative Federalism Good Policy and Good Government,* Discussion Paper No. 16, Federalism Research Centre (Canberra, 1992).
4. Patrick Weller, *Commonwealth State Reform Processes, Report to the Department of the Prime Minister and Cabinet* (1995), p. 5.
5. Weller, p. 13.
6. Attachment to *Communique of Premiers and Chief Ministers Meeting,* Adelaide, 21-2 November 1991.
7. *Communique of Premiers and Chief Ministers Meeting,* Adelaide, 21-2 November 1991, pp. 14-15.

15

Federalism and Fiscal Equalization: Should India Follow the Australian Path?

BHAJAN S. GREWAL

In most federations, the intergovernmental financial transfers are based on the principle that relatively weaker jurisdictions (in fiscal terms) receive more resources per capita than the other jurisdictions, although not every country has put in place a systematic approach to the application of this principle, and the practice differs from one case to another. In Australia, Canada and Germany, relatively more formal and systematic approaches are adopted for this purpose, even though there are important differences in each country's coverage of fiscal equalization and the associated institutional arrangements. In India too, there is a strong redistributive element in the distribution of central government grants to the States, but the approach is again different from that in the other countries.

Not only do Australia and India share the objective of geographic redistribution, but in recent years suggestions have been made that India modify some features of her grant distribution; this, if implemented, would bring the two countries' approaches closer. In particular, this would be the case if the work of the Finance Commission were to cover the entire revenue budget of the states, not just the non-plan revenue budgets, and if the Finance Commission were to be either made a permanent body or serviced by a permanent secretariat. The Finance Commission could then become an organization similar to the Commonwealth Grants Commission in Australia in terms of its coverage and tenure. Even then, however, important differences will remain in what each commission is required to do and how it approaches its brief. Focusing on these substantive differences, the paper considers whether or not they should be maintained in future.

FISCAL EQUALIZATION IN AUSTRALIA

The Grants Commission was established in 1933 in response to the increasing concerns of the less populous states about the adverse effects on their public finances arising from the financial provisions of the federation, in particular the effects of the tariff policy, the conciliation and arbitration system, the Navigation Act, as well as the differential effects of the Great Depression of 1930. Based on its recommendations, special grants (the equalization-driven assistance) were made between 1934-5 and 1980-1 to those states which applied for such assistance. From time to time, the so-called claimant states those receiving special grants) included Western Australia, South Australia, Tasmania and Queensland, although not all of them at the same time. Throughout this period, there was at least one claimant state receiving special grants; in earlier years, two or three had been in this category at the same time but Queensland was the only claimant from 1976-7 onwards, when the other states withdrew from the fiscal equalization framework in favour of direct (bilateral) arrangements with the Commonwealth for special financial assistance.

In broad terms, the aim of the special grants was to equalize per capita revenue-raising capacity and unit costs of government services in a claimant state to the standard per capita revenue-raising capacity and unit costs. The 'standard' was derived from the average of the relevant variables in New South Wales and Victoria (initially Queensland was also part of the standard for a few years).

Special grants during this period were funded out of the Commonwealth budget and did not directly affect Commonwealth grants for New South Wales and Victoria. Typically, special grants also remained a small proportion of total outlays of either the claimant states or of the Commonwealth. It is not surprising, therefore, that during this period of benign fiscal equalization neither of the two larger States took much notice of the principle on methodology of the Grants Commission or of its possible implications for their own public finances.

The benign form of fiscal equalization changed dramatically from 1982-3, when, as a result of an agreement reached at the 1982 Premiers'

Conference, the Grants Commission's procedures began to determine the distribution of the entire pool of tax-sharing grants (subsequently called financial assistance grants or general revenue grants), and thereby started to impact on the budgetary position of *all* states. Some received more than the equal per capita share of the grants while others received less. Thus, for the first time, the Australian system became a truly horizontal equalization because the equalization payments to the weaker states were effectively funded by the other states, not by the Commonwealth government.

Predictably, this drew opposition from the larger states and was challenged on both theoretical and practical grounds. These challenges were disputed, equally predictably, by the less populous states and, where the Commission's procedures were in question, by the Commonwealth Grants Commission also. These controversies led to a formal inquiry into the Commission's methodology in 1989-90 (which was somewhat anomalously also conducted by the Commission itself[1] because the Commonwealth and states could not agree on any other suitable organization), several specialized studies commissioned by the various parties to focus on specific issues, and a report by the heads of treasuries of Commonwealth, state and territories.[2]

Since 1982-3, therefore, Australia has adopted arguably the most elaborate and comprehensive approach to horizontal fiscal equalization (HFE) in the world. The distribution of practically all revenue grants, including those for specific purposes, is directly or indirectly subjected to the criteria of HFE. State per capita relativities are assessed by the Commonwealth Grants Commission on the basis of comparisons of not only revenue-raising capacities but also unit costs of public services provided by the states and territories. Virtually the whole of the recurrent budgets of the states are included in the assessments of the standards and the (assessed) needs. Since 1988, a major review of the whole methodology is conducted every five years in which all states participate vigorously. These assessments are also updated each year. Finally, a somewhat less rigorous approach is also applied to the distribution of Commonwealth funds for local government authorities; in this case the state Grants Commission assesses the relativities. From 1984 onwards, the Commonwealth has also conducted inquiries into the appropriate levels of Commonwealth funding for the Cocos and Christmas Island communities.[3]

TABLE 1: SOME INDICATORS OF THE IMPACT OF FISCAL EQUALIZATION

State	Distribution of General Revenue Grants $m (1)	Equal per Capita Distribution $m (2)	Difference (1)-(2) $m (3)	Distribution using Income Tax Collected (a) $m (4)	Difference (1)-(4) $m (5)
New South Wales	5046	5916	-870	6117	-1071
Victoria	3658	4386	-728	4805	-1147
Queensland	3367	3085	282	2507	860
Western Australia	1842	1651	191	1581	261
South Australia	1752	1437	315	1315	437
Tasmania	686	464	222	395	291
Northern Territory	795	166	629	144	651
Australian Capital Territory	255	295	-40	537	-282
Total	17401	17400	1	17401	0

NOTES: Distribution based on data from 1990-1; Australian Taxation Statistics, 1990-1.

SOURCE: Heads of Treasuries (1994).

The extent of fiscal equalization in Australia can be gauged from Table 1 which shows that in 1993-4, when a grants pool totalling $17,400 million was distributed, New South Wales, Victoria and the Australian Capital Territory received less than equal per capita distribution while the other states and the Northern Territory received more than their equal per capita shares. A total of $1.64 billion, or a little less than 10 per cent of the total pool, was redistributed in that year due to fiscal equalization.

The entitlement of a state for these grants is basically the sum of its per capita share of the available pool *plus* its revenue need *plus* its expenditure need. If a state has above-average revenue-raising capacity, its revenue need is assessed as negative; for a state with below average capacity, revenue need is positive. Similarly, expenditure need is positive if a state is assessed to have above standard demand for, or unit costs of, a government service and negative if the opposite is the case. Revenue needs are assessed separately for 19 categories of tax and non-tax revenue (at one time there were 31 categories). Accordingly, it is not uncommon for a state to have positive revenue needs for some categories and negative needs for the others. But it is the sum of such needs across

TABLE 2: DISTRIBUTION OF GENERAL REVENUE GRANTS, 1993-4

State	Equal per Capita Share of General Revenue $pc (1)	Revenue Needs (a) $pc (2)	Expenditure Needs (b) $pc (3)	Adjustment for Receipt of Other Commonwealth Payments (c) $pc (4)	General Revenue Grant Requirement Sum of (1) to (4) $pc (5)	Per Capita Relativities (d) (5)/(1) (6)
New South Wales	980	-91	-66	13	836	0.853
Victoria	980	23	-203	17	818	0.834
Queensland	980	35	46	9	1070	1.092
Western Australia	980	-95	247	-39	1094	1.116
South Australia	980	203	40	-28	1196	1.219
Tasmania	980	335	177	-44	1449	1.478
Northern Territory	980	-4	4064	-356	4685	4.778
Australian Capital Territory	980	141	-296	21	847	0.864
Average	980	0	0	0	980	1.000

NOTES: (a) Negative revenue needs means above-average revenue-raising capacity, and *vice versa*.

(b) Negative expenditure needs means below-average expenditure requirements, and *vice versa*.

(c) Negative adjustment means above-average receipt of relevant payments.

(d) These relativities differ slightly from the Premiers' Conference relativities due to a minor technical adjustment.

pc: per capita.

SOURCE: Heads of Treasuries (1994).

the 19 categories which represents its aggregate revenue need. In the same way, expenditure need is the sum of separate assessments across 41 categories of expenditure (once there were 70 of them). A final adjustment is made to these entitlements to account for the differences in the receipt of specific purpose grants by the states. This means that if a state had received more (less) than its per capita share of these grants, its entitlement for general revenue grant is correspondingly reduced (increased). The result of this procedure for 1993-4 is shown in Table 2.

Fiscal Equalization in India: An Overview

The institutional framework for intergovernmental grants and revenue sharing in India is quite different. It consists of two separate bodies, the Finance Commission and the Planning Commission. Initially, there was some confusion, and even some tension, about the respective roles of the two Commissions in the field of federal finance, as exemplified by the Third Finance Commission's unsuccessful attempt to extend its role into the 'plan' finance.[4] But the two Commissions have operated alongside each other for nearly half a century, their roles separated by the distinction between plan and non-plan outlays.

The states in India receive a share of the revenue raised by the central government from a variety of taxes, including income tax, central excise duties and a number of other taxes. The distribution of their collective shares from each of these taxes is determined by the central government after considering the recommendations of the Finance Commission. The revenue from each shared tax is distributed on the basis of a different formula, with the result that there are several formulas impacting upon the interstate distribution of shared revenues. Each formula often consists of several criteria, increasing correspondingly the number of factors entering into the determination of state shares. For example, the shared revenue from income tax is distributed according to a formula in which:

- 20 per cent weight is assigned to a State's share of the total population;
- 60 per cent weight is assigned to per capita income relative to that of the richest state;
- 10 per cent weight is assigned to relative tax effort;
- 5 per cent weight is assigned to the area of a state.

The Constitution of India (Article 280) provides for the establishment of a Finance Commission at least once every five years to make recommendations in regard to: (a) the distribution between the centre and the states of the net proceeds of taxes which are to be, or may be, divided between them and the allocation between the states of the respective shares of such proceeds; (b) the principles which should govern the grants-in-aid of the revenue of the states out of the Consolidated Fund of India; and (c) any other matter referred to the Commission by the President in the interest of sound finance. Each Finance Commission's normal tenure of office is approximately one year and expires after the completion of its report. There have been ten Finance Commissions between 1950 and 1994.

The states are also heavily dependent on the centre for the financing of their programmes of development embodied in annual and five-year plans. On average, more than two-thirds of their plan outlay, which includes capital and recurrent expenditure on 'plan schemes', is met through central assistance. This assistance is based on the recommendations of the Planning Commission, established by a resolution of the Cabinet in 1950, which has no standing in the Constitution.

The two Commissions work independently within their respective spheres and the lack of coordination between them, together with the consequential absence of a unified or coherent approach to inter-governmental financial transfers has often been criticized as a shortcoming of India's institutional framework. Recently, the Tenth Finance Commission (1994) added to the continuing commentary on these issues by claiming that 'the present artificial distinction between plan and non-plan expenditures, which runs across revenue and capital budgets shall be replaced by the simpler and conventionally well recognized distinction between revenue and capital', and that in future 'Finance Commissions may be required to examine the aggregate requirements on revenue accounts and recommend means to bridge the revenue gaps' (para 15.11). In the event this does happen, the Finance Commission's task will become similar to that performed in Australia by the Commonwealth Grants Commission, which deals with the entire revenue budgets of the states.

The multiplicity of separate pools of funds which are distributed on the basis of different formulas, consisting of multiple factors, makes the approach of the Finance Commission complex and rather diffused (in contrast to the Commonwealth Grants Commission's approach). In principle, the lack of a sharp focus must also impact adversely on the effectiveness of the Commission's approach in achieving its objectives. In practice, however, it is not possible to assess the extent of such loss of effectiveness simply because there is no well-defined target for the Finance Commission to achieve. In other words, unlike the target of fiscal capacity defined by the Commonwealth Grants Commission for equalization, there is no single target or set of variables which the Finance Commission seeks to equalize.

In recent years, however, a consensus has been developing in India for replacing the multiple separate pools with one pool consisting of a stipulated share (around 25 per cent) of the centre's total tax receipts. The Chelliah Committee on Tax Reform (1991), the Tenth Finance Commission (1994), the Central Government's Ministry of Finance and many of the states favour such a change. It is widely acknowledged that the current situation, in which as much as 85 per cent of the income tax receipts must be passed on to the states, creates a strong disincentive for the central government to fully exploit the revenue potential of this tax. Similar reasoning applies to other shared taxes also. A major advantage of the proposed change is considered to be the removal of any such disincentives from the formulation of the central government's taxation policy. The states also expect to benefit from the added certainty of the annual flow of funds from the centre, once their percentage share is known in advance. The stipulated share of the states would remain unchanged for fifteen to twenty years before being reviewed. The proposed replacement of the multiple revenue pools with one consolidated pool might also open the way eventually for the application of a more coherent and targeted approach to the distribution of the pool among the states. In view of the special features of Australia's approach to fiscal equalization noted above, it would be natural to consider its relevance for developing a more targeted approach for India. The short-term tenure of the Finance Commission has also been generally regarded as another shortcoming of the institutional framework of fiscal federalism in India. Proposals for addressing this issue have ranged from the establishment of a permanent Finance Commission[5] to the setting up of a permanent secretariat for the Finance Commission (for example, Tenth Finance Commission, 1994, which also cites a similar proposal made by the Eighth Finance Commission).

The Ninth Finance Commission made an attempt, for the first time, to estimate capacities and needs of the states for determining their entitlements for financial transfers. This could be another important pointer towards greater potential similarities between the two countries as measurement and comparisons of revenue-raising capacities and expenditure needs of the states is a key feature of Australia's approach.

It is against this background that Australia's recent experience with fiscal equalization is considered in the following section.

THE AUSTRALIAN APPROACH UNDER THE SPOTLIGHT

As noted above, the entry of fiscal equalization to the centre stage in Australia was not smooth. The first report of the Commonwealth Grants Commission in which relativities were assessed for the distribution of the entire pool of tax-sharing grants was considered by the 1981 Premiers' Conference. The Commission had found that as the less populous states were receiving more than their equalization-based shares, there needed to be a redistribution from these states to the larger states of New South Wales and Victoria. Following opposition from the four states that stood to lose funds if the 1981 report was implemented, the Commonwealth decided not to act on it and instead asked the Commission to prepare another report for the 1982 Premiers' Conference, to be based on a slightly longer period of four years data—instead of three years as in the 1981 report. The 1982 report also recommended the same direction of redistribution, although this time involving a smaller amount to be redistributed.

For the first time, tax-sharing grants were distributed in 1982-3 on the basis largely of an equalization-based formula, although the Commonwealth government gave certain guarantees of minimum growth to the states, which diluted the effect of fiscal equalization. Following the 1985 review of state relativities, the Commonwealth adopted the assessments of the Commission as virtually the only basis for the distribution of what were then called financial assistance grants.[6]

The extended application of the fiscal equalization principle also occurred at a time when the Commonwealth government was pursuing a vigorous policy of budget deficit reduction, primarily through cutbacks in grants to the states. New South Wales and Victoria found themselves to be losing Commonwealth grants on two fronts; first, to the Commonwealth (as the pool of general revenue grants available for the states was shrinking in real terms), and second to the less populous states (as the application of fiscal equalization was further reducing their shares of that shrinking pool). Spurred partly by the effect of these factors on their finances, and partly by their concerns about the opportunity costs of fiscal equalization (awareness of which was lacking in the political process which considered the CGC's assessments), the two states challenged the theoretical and operational aspects of fiscal equalization. As the questions raised in the ensuing debates were progressively refined, the Commonwealth Treasury also joined them on some of the issues. The other states predictably rallied to the defence of fiscal equalization and of the Commission's procedures.

In 1989, the Commonwealth government initiated a special inquiry into certain issues relating to the methodology used by the Commonwealth Grants Commission in its *Report on General Revenue Grant Relativities 1988*. Given the background and the purpose of that inquiry, it was, as noted above, unusual that the centre asked the Commonwealth Grants Commission itself to conduct the inquiry. Nevertheless, the Commission conducted the inquiry with a characteristically high standard of professionalism, and presented a report in 1990 which is a valuable source of information.

In spite of the Commission's best efforts, and of the other parties involved, the issues raised in these debates remained largely unresolved. In 1992, in recognition of the importance of the unresolved questions, the Premiers' Conference issued a reference to a Heads of Treasuries Working Party to undertake a review of the 'adequacy of the current fiscal equalization scope and methodology, and the principles on which it is based'.[7] At the same time, these debates raised the general level of awareness about the issues in the country and the subject of fiscal equalization attracted comments from the Industry Commission (1993), the National Commission of Audit (1996), and many others.

The major issues raised in these reviews included the relationship between fiscal equalization and allocative efficiency, interpersonal equity, and the complexity of the Commission's model and assessment procedures. These will now discussed in some detail.

The possible loss of efficiency was raised as an issue arising from the equalization of the costs of government services. It was argued by the government of Victoria in 1988 that any differences in unit costs of government services should, as they normally would in the absence of fiscal equalization, cause the governments to find ways of economizing on the provision of such services or to invest in alternative (lower-cost) technologies or to reduce expenditure in some other areas if the demand for the high-cost services was for some reason inelastic. In other words, the cost differences normally serve as price signals for governments to react to, and when they are equalized, the argument ran, the price signals would be distorted and the state governments will be responding not to the true costs, but the shadow costs (i.e. costs affected by equalization). Shadow costs would be lower (higher) than the true cost if a particular state is assessed to have a disability (an advantage) *vis-a-vis* the standard. It was argued that loss of efficiency would occur for the states on both sides of the equalization equation (i.e. the gainers as well as the losers).

Counter-arguments were made by some of the less populous states (and by the Commission), arguing that as the equalization grants were unconditional payments, they did not affect relative costs, and that there was no empirical evidence of such distortions actually occurring.

Three separate studies attempted to estimate the efficiency cost to the national economy of equalizing the so-called location-based factors (for example, dispersion of population, and diseconomies of small scale provision). The first study was commissioned by the Commonwealth Grants Commission and it put the estimated loss of efficiency at 0.008 per cent of GDP or $30 million a year. This was regarded by all concerned as insignificant. A second estimate was made in a study commissioned by Victoria's Treasury, and put the loss of efficiency at $500 million a year. A third estimate, made by the same group of consultants which conducted the first study (but this time commissioned jointly by New South Wales and Victoria), put the efficiency cost at around $920 million, or about 0.23 per cent of GDP a year. It is remarkable that all these empirical studies confirmed the existence of a conflict between allocative efficiency and fiscal equalization, although the magnitude of the estimated loss (and hence their significance for future policy) varied widely.

However, the less populous states continue to deny any possible conflict between allocative efficiency and fiscal equalization. Thus, in a submission made to the Industry Commission, which considered the regional effects of fiscal equalization in 1993, one state argued that without fiscal equalization, locational decisions would be distorted due to the fact that tax rates would differ across the states on account of factors other than differences in costs, such as differences in taxable capacity or relatively higher demand for services due to demographic differences. Another suggested that fiscal equalization assists efficiency by keeping low the congestion costs of large cities like Sydney and Melbourne. A third state noted that the issue of any efficiency costs arising from fiscal equalization was a very minor area of concern in comparison with the potential gains to efficiency from reducing vertical fiscal imbalance (between the Commonwealth on the one hand and the States on the other).

However, the Industry Commission and the Commonwealth Grants Commission also acknowledged that 'the consensus to have emerged to date from these attempts is that the equalization transfers *must* be having some effect on population between states and between regions within states'.[8]

The high degree of complexity of the Grants Commission's procedures has been a major target of criticism. The main source of the complexity is the so-called factor assessment method, which is applied by the Commission to assess relative disabilities for each of the 19 revenue categories and 41 expenditure categories for each state. As noted earlier, these assessments are used for determining revenue and expenditure needs. Each of these assessments requires detailed information about policy and non-policy factors impacting on a state's revenue base and/or expenditure levels. For expenditure equalization, the impact of each of the several disability factors (such as dispersion, diseconomies of scale, urbanization, physical environment, age-sex composition of population) on the demand for and the cost of public services is assessed. This lengthy and detailed procedure is repeated over each category and for each state.

Objective information is not always available or sufficient and the Commission often relies on its own 'broad judgement' in arriving at final assessments. The reliance on broad judgment has been a feature of the Commission's work since its establishment in the 1930s and was acknowledged by Giblin in his candid evidence in 1938 before the Canadian Royal Commission on Dominion Provincial Relations:

> The thing is dressed up in arithmetical terms as much as possible, and that perhaps is politically useful. But it must be admitted that in a good many instances the actual decision as to how much allowance must be made for this or that depends not on the strictly arithmetical computation, but on the broad judgment of the Commissioners as to what is a reasonable figure. . . . I believe that the calculations . . . do indicate the figure, but with a fairly wide margin of error.[9]

In spite of considerable improvements in the availability of relevant data since the days of Giblin, outsiders often find it difficult to understand or replicate the Commission's assessments. A former prime minister is reported to have described the Commission's model as a 'black box'.

The Heads of Treasuries Working Party in 1994 also noted that the complex nature of these procedures had restricted their accessibility to those who could afford to invest a considerable time and effort in making use of the available information. It said that there is considerable ignorance about these processes even in government, and that there is a perception that 'elements of the Commission's calculations are based on dubious assumptions, poor data and a substantial element of judgement. In the same vein, the Commission's approach to fiscal equalization is said by some to be, at times, inconsistent.'

These and many other similar observations suggest that the desire, on the part of the Grants Commission, to put in place the most comprehensive system of assessing revenue and expenditure needs, category by category, has resulted in less simplicity and transparency and in some cases has even undermined the credibility of its assessments.

The category by category assessment of needs also makes it possible that a state's grant entitlement could be affected appreciably by a reclassification of an item of revenue or expenditure from one category to another. A recent example of such an affect is that a state's share of general revenue grant increased by $8 million when the non-inpatient expenditure of another state was reclassified by the Commission from the 'Community Health Services' to the 'Hospital Services' category.[10] This example also indicates the scope for a state to influence the size of its grant by either persuading the Commission to adopt a particular classification or by concentrating on expenditure or revenue in some categories and not in others. A study commissioned by New South Wales and Victoria claimed that this particular aspect of the Commission's model encouraged a state to over-provide services for which the cost structure was relatively expensive and to under-provide those services in which it had a relative cost advantage.[11]

The relationship between horizontal equity and fiscal equalization, or more appropriately the absence of any relationship between the two, has been the focus of critical comment in the Australian debates, although no clear workable solutions have emerged so far. In the theoretical literature on fiscal federalism, the case for horizontal fiscal equalization follows Buchanan's articulation that if per capita income levels of the subnational units in a federation were unequal, the principle of equal fiscal treatment of equals would be violated, unless corrective actions were taken (1950). Possible corrective actions included a discriminatory income tax (which would be impracticable in any federation) or unconditional intergovernmental, rather than interpersonal, grants to the states with lower incomes. Indeed, a similar argument was made in Australia in 1925 by Giblin and others for the Tasmanian Disabilities Committee and was the basis of a recommendation for differential per capita grants from the Commonwealth to the states.[12]

Achievement of interpersonal equity is not an objective of the fiscal equalization schemes in Australia or India. In both countries as elsewhere wherever horizontal fiscal equalization is applied, the objective is to remove some of the effects of income differences on the public finances of the states. The conceptual basis of the fiscal equalization scheme in Australia is that 'each State should be given the capacity to provide the average standard of State-type public services, assuming it does so at an average level of operational level of efficiency and makes an average effort to raise revenue from its own sources'.[13] Over the years, the precise statement of the principle has been refined but its central idea has remained essentially intact. As explained by Mathews:

> . . . under fiscal capacity equalization, governments are merely put into a position where they may provide services on a standard scale whilst imposing taxes and other charges at standard severity. They *are not obliged* to match the standard revenue effort; indeed governments receiving equalization payments are free to impose below-standard services, or conversely to combine above-standard taxes and above standard services. (emphasis added)

It has been pointed out by the critics that such an approach to fiscal equalization does not address what ought to be the ultimate concern of such a scheme—the interpersonal equity across the states. If interpersonal equity were indeed the concern of an equalization scheme, the distribution model would need to deal with issues such as effective tax rates in the states, interstate shifting and the patterns of incidence of taxation and of Commonwealth policies which affected differentially the disposable incomes in the states. The Commonwealth Grants Commission's response to these criticisms has been that interpersonal equity should be advanced through the taxation-transfer system.[14]

At the theoretical level, a solution was suggested by Dimasi who argued that equal fiscal treatment of equals could be achieved in a federation without the need for intergovernmental grants if the central government included the (differential) fiscal net benefits of the individuals in their taxable income for personal income taxation. In recent paper, it has been claimed that:

> In the Dimasi framework, not only are like individuals treated equally at the federal level, but at the same time the fundamental weakness in the Buchanan justification for fiscal equalization is revealed. There is no case for subsidizing particular *States* via equalization grants. . . .[15]

At the practical level, however, turning the focus of a fiscal equalization scheme towards interpersonal equity appears to be extremely problematic, involving as it would the computation of net fiscal benefits for all individuals over all taxes and public expenditures. As most participants in the Australian debates realized the limited practical value of such proposals, the missing link between equity and equalization has not been a major issue in the latest discussions. Nevertheless, the fact remains that fiscal equalization is only an imperfect and inadequate response to the problem of horizontal inequity. The capacity equalization approach adopted in Australia also allows the disconcerting possibility that a poor taxpayer living in a high-income state could well be subsidizing a rich taxpayer living in a low-income state, as equalization grants may well be used by the government of the latter to reduce taxes of, or increase the level of services consumed by, the well-off taxpayers. Capacity equalization is not concerned with equality in the actual provision of services.

The Report of the Heads of Treasuries Working Party in 1994 canvassed several options for reform of fiscal equalization. Two major themes dominate its report. One is the sentiment that some commitment to horizontal fiscal equalization must be maintained. This sentiment has been important in Australia since the 1920s when, thanks to the work of Giblin, Brigden and others, it was accepted that special grants to some states were justified, not as a compensation for the disabilities caused by federation but because every member state in the federation had a legal and moral obligation to conform to the general standard, or at least not to fall seriously below it.[16] The same sentiment was echoed recently by Mathews when he described horizontal fiscal equalization as the linchpin of the Australian federation. Conscious, however, of the fact that fiscal equalization might entail efficiency costs, it was recognized that the scope of fiscal equalization might be restricted to those states which really needed to be helped.

The second theme is the strong desire to simplify the procedures of fiscal equalization, which are, as noted above, widely regarded to be too complex. Among the options considered by the Working Party is a possible discounting of the relativities assessed by the Grants Commission by combining them with equal per capita distribution, on 80/20 or some other similar basis. Considering the substantial redistribution this might lead to, a phasing-in of the new relativities has been suggested as a means of softening the impact on the losing states. Another option involves the exclusion of cost equalization which, the report notes, would align the Australian approach with that of Canada and, with some exceptions, Germany. Such an approach would restrict the process to revenue equalization, and could either continue to be based on the current procedures (involving tax by tax assessment of needs) or move to some global measure of revenue capacity (for example, Gross State Product). A partial per capita distribution approach is also considered, which would allow fiscal equalization to be targeted at the most needy states of South Australia, Tasmania and the Northern Territory. Under this option, the available grants pool would be distributed first among these states according to the Commission's relativities and then between the other states on equal per capita basis. Needless to say, each of these options would involve a departure from full fiscal equalization and the Premiers' Conference did not take any action in response to the report.

Is Fiscal Equalization a Cure or a Palliative?

Whether or not fiscal equalization contributes to the narrowing of interstate economic disparities over time is one issue that has not been debated in recent times in Australia. But it is a valid question for consideration in any country, especially if fiscal equalization is assigned a role in removing from state public sectors the effects of unequal state per capita incomes (or revenue-raising capacities).

In the 1920s, when the seeds of fiscal equalization were sown in Australia, this issue was debated at length, particularly around 1925 in the context of determining the real nature of Tasmania's claims of disability. A good account of these deliberations is provided by May, who says:

The view that the small States could overcome their difficulties if only they could reach a take-off stage had, of course, been suggested by Lockyer and it was not without supporters in Tasmania. The British Economic Mission of 1929 revealed a similar attitude when, in commenting on special grants, it said, 'These subsidies, however, can only be regarded as palliatives of a system with which something is amiss.'[17]

At the 1926 Premiers' Conference, where the problem of the small states was discussed in some detail, the Commonwealth similarly concluded that 'the mere making of a money grant is not the solution to the problem. . . . The true principle . . . is to discover the causes of the financial difficulties and to seek to provide means for their removal. . . .[18]

In India, there is greater explicit concern about interstate income inequality insofar as it figures as an important factor in the Finance Commission's distribution scheme. The so-called distance criterion (given 60 per cent weight by the Tenth Finance Commission, 1994) and the infrastructure index (5 per cent weight) can be regarded as indications of this concern. In Australia's fiscal equalization approach, there is no recognition of any role that special grants might play in the process of the removal of the 'causes' of fiscal disabilities, instead of the fiscal disabilities *per se*. In neither country, however, has there been an attempt made to examine and assess the effectiveness of fiscal equalization in reducing interstate income inequalities.

A recent study of the Australian states has, however, reported that between 1977-8 and 1991-2, Queensland, South Australia and Tasmania had below average real GDP at factor cost per head in all 15 years, Tasmania had the lowest real GDP at factor cost per head for 14 out of the 15 years. This raises the question why these states failed, in spite of being the recipients of fiscal equalization grants for many years, first under the special grants arrangements and since 1982-3 under the current arrangements, in lifting the rates of real per capita output to above average levels, even for some years of this period. In this context, it appears unwise to continue with the current system of fiscal equalization, arguably at a cost to national output, regardless of its impact on interstate economic disparities.

It should be clear from the above that by any account, all is not well with fiscal equalization in Australia. It remains an equity-based principle whose contribution to inter-personal equity remains unconvincing and is, at best, rather weak. Nevertheless at least the Australian experience confirms that there is an element of truth about the binding power of fiscal equalization in a federation. Even in the midst of the vigorous debates over this issue, a certain commitment to assist the weaker units of the federation has always been acknowledged in this country.

The problem, however, is that this commitment does not automatically translate well into a practical approach to fiscal equalization. One lesson of the Australian experience is that, beyond a certain point, the desire for detail and comprehensiveness is likely to turn into complexity. The equalization process then becomes a liability, as it detracts from the crucial virtues of simplicity and ease of understanding.

Another lesson is that the costs of fiscal equalization to particular states as well as to the national economy, cannot be ignored. The recent debate about the nature and the magnitude of such costs in Australia leaves little doubt that fiscal equalization comes at a price; perhaps this realization is Australia's unique contribution to the wider literature on fiscal equalization. How big that price is depends upon the specific features of a country's approach and its economic structure.

A separate point made in this paper, although not much debated so far even in Australia, is that the effectiveness of an approach to fiscal equalization needs to be judged, at least in part, in terms of its contribution, over time, to the narrowing of interstate economic disparities. For otherwise, the principle of fiscal equalization simply becomes an inert response to the symptoms of the problem (of economic disparities) rather than addressing its root cause.

In relation to the institutional framework, the issue of the temporary tenure of the Finance Commission in India was noted above. While the establishment of a permanent secretariat will no doubt facilitate the ongoing monitoring of and research into state finances which is clearly beyond the capacity of a Finance Commission at present, the Australian experience suggests that the benefits of the creation of a permanent commission are not altogether clear. Permanency of tenure will certainly add to the continuity of the Commission's work but there is also a risk that the establishment of a permanent body could create a strong stakeholder in the equalization process, preventing critical scrutiny and injection of fresh perspectives into the process. One advantage of the current situation in India is that there is a regular turnover of personnel who can bring fresh perspectives and new ideas to bear upon the issues. This type of dynamism may be lost under a permanent Finance Commission, especially if the same members are able to hold office for long periods.

Finally, there seems to be no reason for India to venture towards the Australian model of fiscal equalization. Indeed, it is clear from the recent debates on this subject that in Australia, momentum is building up for retreating towards a less ambitious, simple and, importantly, an affordable approach to fiscal equalization. A question which both countries need to rigorously examine, in this context is whether interstate redistribution of grants makes a lasting contribution to the growth rates of the weaker States' economies; at this stage, there is no evidence that it does so.

NOTES

1. Commonwealth Grants Commission, *Report on Issues in Fiscal Equalization*, vols. I and II (Canberra, 1990).
2. Heads of Treasuries, *Horizontal Fiscal Equalization* (Canberra, 1994).
3. Commonwealth Grants Commission, *Report on General Revenue Grant Relativities: 1995 Update* (Canberra, 1995).
4. B.G. Grewal, *Centre-State Financial Relations in India* (Patiala, 1975).
5. See M.G. Rao and R.J. Chelliah, *Fiscal Federalism in India* (New Delhi, 1996).
6. See R. Mathews and B. Grewal, *Fiscal Federalism in Australia: From Whitlam to Keating*, CSEA Working Paper No. 1, Centre for Strategic Economic Studies, Victoria University (Melbourne, 1995).
7. Heads of Treasuries 1994.
8. CGC quoted in Industry Commission *Taxation and Financial Policy Impacts on Urban Settlement: Report on Impediments to Regional Industry Adjustment* (Canberra, 1993), p. 327 (original emphasis).
9. Cited in R.J. May, *Financing the Small States in Australian Federalism* (Melbourne, 1971), p. 70.
10. Commonwealth Grants Commission, *Report on General Revenue Grant Relativities: 1996 Update* (Canberra, 1996), p. 29.
11. P.L. Swan and G.T. Garvey, *The Equity and Efficiency Implications of Fiscal Equalization* (Sydney, 1996), p. ii.
12. R.L. Mathews and W.R. Jay, *Federal Finance* (Melbourne, 1972).
13. Commonwealth Grants Commission 1995.

14. Commonwealth Grants Commission 1990.
15. Swan and Garvey, pp. 39-40 (original emphasis).
16. May, *Financing the Small States*; see also Mathews and Jay, *Federal Finance* (1972).
17. May, p. 17.
18. Ibid.

16

Federalism and Fiscal Autonomy of States: The Indian Experience

ROKKAM S. RAO

Fiscal autonomy is one of the most important dimensions of federalism. Political autonomy is a myth without adequate fiscal autonomy of the federating units, especially in a developing country like India. The Indian federation has been experiencing both vertical and horizontal fiscal imbalances. The states which are responsible for discharging many public functions cannot deliver the goods at the optimum level due to a paucity of funds. They have to depend largely on the central government for financial resources. The centre in turn has been assisting the states with several kinds of fiscal transfers. The missing link in the process is fiscal autonomy. Fiscal dependence on the part of the states needs to be reduced, if not ended altogether. Healthy relations between the centre and states can only be ensured if the states enjoy something like fiscal autonomy.

A federation is formed either by aggregation of erstwhile sovereign independent states or by disaggregation of a union into several regional governments. Public finance operations in a federal structure are altogether different from those of a unitary type of structure, hence the importance of fiscal federalism. Oates defined federalism as 'a public sector with both centralized and decentralized levels of decision-making in which choices made at each level concerning the provisions of public services are determined largely by the demands for these services of the residents of the respective jurisdictions'.[1] This calls for a division of available resources and responsibilities between the two levels of government. Another definition of a federation is a political entity formed by several units of government surrendering their powers and functions while retaining a measure of internal autonomy. Here, 'internal autonomy' refers to both political and fiscal autonomy. Indeed, political autonomy is a myth without fiscal autonomy.

What they do we mean by fiscal autonomy? Fiscal autonomy may be defined as the exercise of fiscal powers and functions without intervention or direction from another level of government. Fiscal autonomy depends to a large extent on the amount of revenues governments raise relative to their expenditure commitments. If the total revenue expenditure is financed by a unit with its own revenues, fiscal autonomy is said to be absolute. If the local revenues fall short of expenditure, the government has to depend upon fiscal transfers. If the proportion of fiscal transfers is higher, the fiscal dependence of the unit will be higher (and *vice versa*). However, all types of fiscal transfers do not affect the fiscal autonomy of the states equally. Fiscal transfers which are envisaged in the constitution or are provided for in federal-state agreements will not erode fiscal autonomy even though there exists a convention of fiscal dependence. But fiscal transfers which are made through bargaining and which are not mandatory and statutory *will* lead to an erosion of *fiscal* autonomy of the units. Apart from fiscal transfers, the decision-making of the federal government and its encroachment upon the states' constitutional rights relating to fiscal aspects will also lead to an erosion of fiscal autonomy. This is a common feature in all federations.

The Federal Fiscal System in India

India is usually considered to be a federation though the word federation has not been used in its Constitution. At present the Indian federation consists of 25 States and 7 Union Territories. The fiscal powers and functions have been divided between the central and state governments as is the case in any federation.

The division of functions is enumerated in the Union List, the State List, and the Concurrent List in the Seventh Schedule of the Constitution. The Union List contains all functions of national importance such as defence, railways, national highways, navigation, atomic energy, and posts and telegraphs. Ninety-seven items have been entrusted to the central government; sixty-six items of local interest such as law and order, public health, agriculture, irrigation, power, rural and community development, fisheries and forests have been entrusted to the state governments; forty-seven items such as industrial and commercial monopolies, economic and social planning, labour welfare and social justice, have been enumerated in the Concurrent List over which both centre and states can make legislation. However, in case of a conflict between the centre and states, federal laws prevail.

Taxing powers are distributed in the Constitution between the two levels of government. The states have been given exclusive tax powers in respect of land revenue, taxes on agricultural income, duties in respect of succession to agricultural land, estate duty in respect of agricultural land, taxes on land and buildings, taxes on mineral rights, excise duties on goods containing alcoholic liquors for human consumption, opium, Indian hemp and other narcotic drugs and narcotics, taxes on the entry of goods into local areas, taxes on the consumption or sale of electricity, taxes on the sale or purchase of goods other than newspapers, taxes on advertisements other than advertisements published in newspaper and broadcast by radio and television, taxes on goods and passengers carried by road or inland waterways, taxes on animals and boats, taxes on vehicles, tolls, taxes on professions, trades, callings and employment, capitation taxes, taxes on luxuries including taxes on entertainment, amusements, betting and gambling, and rates of stamp duty in respect of documents other than those specified in the Union List. The centre, by contrast, has fewer tax sources but they include, potentially, those with the widest economic base.

The centre has powers in respect of taxes on income other than agricultural income, customs duties, excise duties on tobacco and other goods manufactured or produced in India (except alcoholic liquor for human consumption, opium, Indian hemp and other narcotic drugs and narcotics, but including medicinal and toilet preparations containing alcohol), corporation tax, taxes on capital values, estate duty in respect of property other than agricultural land, duties in respect of succession to property other than agricultural land, terminal taxes on goods or passengers carried by railway, sea or air; taxes on railway passenger fares and freights, taxes other than stamp duties on transactions in stock exchanges and futures markets, rates of stamp duty in respect of bills of exchange, cheques, promissory notes, bills of landing, letters of credit, policies of insurance, transfer of shares, debentures, proxies and receipts, taxes on sale or purchase of newspapers and on advertisements published therein, taxes on the sale and purchase of goods other than newpapers, where such sale or purchase takes place in course of interstate trade or commerce, and taxes on the consignment of goods where such consignment takes place in the course in interstate trade or commerce.

However, the centre does not get revenue from all the thirteen items mentioned earlier. They can be divided into four categories on the basis of levy, administration and the accrual of revenue.

(i) Taxes that are levied, collected and retained by the central government—corporation tax and customs duties.
(ii) Taxes that are levied and collected by the centre but may be shared with the states—the net proceeds from income tax under Article 270 and the net proceeds from union excise duties under Article 272 respectively.
(iii) Taxes that are levied and collected by the union but whose net proceeds are assigned to the states—all the eight items under Article 269 of the Constitution such as estate duty, taxes on railway passenger fares and freights, consignment tax.
(iv) Taxes levied by the centre but collected and appropriated by states—such as excise duties on medicinal and toilet preparations, etc.

Apart from the division of tax powers between the centre and states, powers of borrowing have been also set out in the Constitution. Article 292 empowers the centre to borrow funds within and outside the country as per the limits imposed by the Parliament. Article 293(3) empowers the states to borrow funds within India; while Article 293(2) empowers the centre to give loans to any state subject to the conditions as laid down by Parliament. A state, in practice, cannot raise any loan without the prior permission of the centre or if there is an outstanding loan from the centre to the state or an outstanding loan for which the centre has given a guarantee.

It is evident from the constitutional-fiscal arrangements outlined above that fiscal imbalances are inevitable in India, since most of the productive and elastic taxes are entrusted to the central government, whereas the most expensive functions are given to the states. The division of resources and functions leads to a vertical federal fiscal imbalance while the differences in the endowment position of economic resources cause a horizontal federal fiscal imbalance. The Constitution, however, anticipated this. It incorporated a mechanism of fiscal adjustment by way of federal fiscal transfers. Provisions were made in the Constitution under Article 280(3) for setting up of a Finance Commission with the following functions:

(a) the distribution of net proceeds from income tax under Article 270 and the permissive distribution of net proceeds from union excise duties under Article 272 between the union and states and the allocation between the states of the respective shares of such proceeds;
(b) the allocation of grants-in-aid under Article 275(1) to be made to states in need; and
(c) any other matter referred to the Commission by the president in the interest of sound finance.

So far, ten Finance Commissions have been appointed. Their recommendations relate to shareable taxes, grants-in-aid, debt relief, financing of state relief projects and transfer of fiscal resources to the states.

The Planning Commission

Even though constitutional provision was made only for a Finance Commission, the Government of India constituted another agency—the Planning Commission—in March 1950. This non-statutory body, of which the prime minister is the chairman, was set up by executive order. Originally established to look after the formulation and evaluation of Five Year Plans, the Planning Commission has entered into every fiscal aspect of the nation. Using Article 282 of the Constitution, it recommended grants for financing states' plans, central sector schemes and centrally sponsored schemes in addition to loans. In the course of time it overtook the statutory body (the Finance Commission) in recommending fiscal resources in bulk amounts. The overwhelming influence of the Planning Commission in the sphere of centre-state financial relations has downgraded the Finance Commission's role in the process of fiscal adjustment. Thus the functioning of the Planning Commission has an important bearing on the states' fiscal position.

In addition to the transfers made through the two Commissions, grants and loans are transferred to the states by central ministries. Known as Non-Plan Non-Statutory Transfers or Discretionary Transfers, these transactions are made to finance programmes like relief and rehabilitation, procurement of food and road repairs which are not covered under the fiscal adjustment scheme of the two Commissions. This type of assistance also influences the fiscal autonomy of the states.

Centralization of revenue and/or expenditure can be taken as an indicator of fiscal dominance. Various measures have been used to measure the concentration of revenue or expenditure at a particular level of government in a federation. Musgrave[2] and Oates[3] measured revenue concentration in India by proportion of revenues collected by the central government in the combined revenues of the centre and states. Similarly, expenditure concentration is calculated by the proportion of central government expenditure in the current combined expenditures of centre and states. Several studies have examined the trends and the level of concentration of revenue and expenditure relating to the Indian federation. Pillai and Krishnan,[4] Ansari,[5] the National Institute of Public Finance and Policy (NIPFP),[6] Chellaiah,[7] Bajaj, Sinha and Agarwal[8] have found an increasing trend toward centralization. The different periods of their respective studies range between 1950-1 to 1980-1. But the World Bank study[9] found no evidence of increasing centralization of expenditures or revenues during the period 1950-1 to 1978-9 while the NIPFP found no consistent trend of centralization of revenue expenditure during the period of study.

Nevertheless, the question is worth re-examining. To this end, data have been gathered on Indian governmental revenue and expenditure for the period 1961-2 to 1994-5. Revised estimates have been taken for the year 1994-5 as the actual revenue and expenditure figures are not available. Revenue concentration is measured by the proportion of states' own revenues in the combined revenues of centre and states. If the proportion of the states' own revenues in the combined revenues of centre and states is higher, centralization will be less. Conversely, it will be more if the ratio is less. In the same way, a high proportion of states' revenue expenditure in the combined revenue expenditures of the centre and states indicates a lower expenditure centralization and a low proportion indicates a higher level of centralization. Revenue centralization during 1961-2 to 1994-5 in the Indian federation is

TABLE 1. REVENUE CENTRALIZATION IN THE INDIAN FEDERATION 1961-95

(Rs. in crores)

Year (1)	States' Own Revenue (2)	States' Total Revenue (3)	Combined Revenues of Centre & States (4)	Col. 2 as % of Col. 4 (5)	Col. 3 as % of Col. 4 (6)
1961-2	700	1074	1846	37.9	58.2
1965-6	1244	1850	3689	33.7	50.1
1970-1	2048	3370	5958	34.4	56.6
1975-6	5120	7938	14344	35.7	55.3
1980-1	9881	16293	25591	38.6	63.7
1990-1	36330	62754	99282	36.6	63.2
1991-2	45784	77960	121619	37.7	64.10
1992-3	49518	87091	135422	36.6	64.3
1993-4	61993	105563	137446	45.1	76.8
1994-5	76161	123302	164931	46.2	74.8

SOURCES: 1. *Reserve Bank of India Bulletin*—various issues.
2. *Indian Economic Statistics*, Public Finance, Ministry of Finance, Govt. of India, New Delhi, 1991, 1994.

summarized in Table 1. It can be seen that the share of the states' own revenues as a percentage of the combined revenues of centre and states increased from 38 per cent in 1961-2 to 46 per cent in 1994-5. This suggests a decline in the level of revenue centralization. On the other hand it may be observed that the proportion of states' own revenues in some years was 35 per cent or even less. This suggests a high degree of centralization. Note too the high proportion of the centre's revenues in the combined revenues of centre and states—also the sign of a high degree of centralization.

Centralization of expenditure for select years during the period 1961-2 to 1994-5 can be seen in Table 2. There is no consistent trend, though the centralization of state expenditures as a proportion of combined expenditure has been declining. But in no single year was the states' revenue expenditure less than 50 per cent of the combined revenue expenditure. Comparatively, a greater degree of centralization of revenues can be noticed than centralization of expenditures. This indicates a situation of vertical fiscal imbalance, or fiscal dependence.

TABLE 2: EXPENDITURE CENTRALIZATION IN THE INDIAN FEDERATION 1961-95

(Rs. in crores)

Year (1)	States' Revenue Expenditure (2)	Combined Rev. Exp. of Centre & States (3)	Col. 2 as % of Col. 3 (4)
1961-2	1121	1769	63.4
1965-6	1892	3411	55.5
1970-1	3398	5812	58.3
1975-6	6966	12486	55.8
1980-1	14807	24882	59.5
1990-1	67860	122950	55.2
1991-2	83611	143532	58.3
1992-3	92150	159056	57.9
1993-4	109376	217545	50.3
1994-5 (R.E.)	1331014	253916	51.6

SOURCE: Reserve Bank of India Bulletins—various issues.

FISCAL TRANSFERS AND FISCAL DEPENDENCE

In order to reduce the level of vertical and horizontal federal fiscal imbalance and to enable the states to provide minimum standards of essential administrative and social services, the centre has been making fiscal transfers on the basis of the recommendations of the successive Finance Commissions and the Planning Commission for the last four-and-a-half decades. The fiscal transfers in the form of tax shares, grants-in-aid and loans made by the central government to the states during 1961-2 to 1994-5 may be seen in Table 3. It may be observed that the total fiscal transfers have increased substantially—from Rs. 825 crores in 1961-2 to Rs. 67016 crores in 1994-5. That represents an increase of almost 8223 per cent. Almost all the individual fiscal transfers—tax shares, grants and loans—have registered phenomenal growth during this period. The large-scale devolution of funds from the centre to the states indicates the dependence of the states and the dominance of the centre. Most scholars have measured fiscal dependence by the level of total transfers including loans. For instance, Bhargava calculated the ratio of tax shares, grants and loans to the states' total expenditure and

TABLE 3: FEDERAL FISCAL TRANSFERS DURING 1961-95 (Select Years)

(Rs. in crores)

Year (1)	Tax Shares (2)	Grants (3)	Loans (4)	Total Transfers (5)
1961-2	179	195	451	825
1965-6	276	330	816	1422
1970-1	756	566	1005	2327
1975-6	1599	1219	1294	4112
1980-1	3789	2623	3022	944
1990-1	14110	12384	14018	40512
1991-2	16849	15327	13123	45299
1992-3	19937	17636	13153	50726
1993-4	22395	21176	14410	57981
1994-5 (R.E.)	24850	22291	19875	67016

SOURCES: 1. Reserve Bank of India Bulletins—various issues.
2. Indian Economic Statistics, Public Finance, Ministry of Finance, Govt. of India, New Delhi, 1991, 1994.

found that states' fiscal dependence on the centre has been increasing during the period 1951-2 to 1980-1.[10] Studies by the World Bank,[11] NIPFP[12] and Chellaiah[13] have come to similar conclusions. The NIPFP concluded that the level of fiscal dependence increased up to 1972-3 and then declined. Ansari concluded that the financial dependence of the states on the centre also declined during the period 1950-1 to 1982-3.[14]

As the transfers in form of loans have to be repaid, they need to be excluded when measuring the level of fiscal dependence. In the present paper fiscal dependence has been taken as the ratio of tax shares and grants in the states' revenue expenditure. The percentage shares have been calculated during the period 1961-2 to 1994-5. As may be seen in Table 4, the ratio of fiscal transfers other than loans shows an increasing trend (from 33 per cent in 1961-2 to 40 per cent in 1993-4). Although the increase in the ratio is not consistent, it can be concluded that the states have been depending on tax shares and grants from the centre to finance almost 35 per cent to 40 per cent of their budgets (this proportion varies from state to state). Such dependence will surely lead to an erosion of the fiscal autonomy of the states.

TABLE 4: FISCAL DEPENDENCE OF STATES IN INDIA 1961-2 TO 1994-5

(Rs. in crores)

Year (1)	Tax Shares and Grants (2)	States Rev. Expenditure (3)	Col. 2 as % of Col. 3 (4)
1961-2	374	1121	33.4
1965-6	606	1892	32.0
1970-1	1322	3389	39.0
1975-6	2818	6966	40.4
1980-1	6212	14807	41.9
1990-1	26424	67860	38.9
1991-2	32176	83611	38.5
1992-3	37573	92150	40.8
1993-4	43571	109376	39.8
1994-5 (R.E)	47141	131014	36.0

SOURCE: Reserve Bank of India Bulletins—various issues.

Federal fiscal transfers are almost inevitable in any federation. The existence of this instrument of adjustment shows inherently the dependence of the governments receiving the fiscal transfers. However, fiscal transfers do not necessarily erode fiscal autonomy (though the very presence of transfers suggests a lack of independence). Fiscal transfers may be unconditional and automatic or conditional and the product bargaining. In other words, fiscal transfers may be statutory or non-statutory. Unconditional and statutory transfers of resources will not affect the fiscal autonomy while conditional and non-statutory transfers will do so. Thus, in India, all the fiscal transfers made through the Finance Conmission do not affect the fiscal autonomy of the states as those transfers are statutory. The tax shares and grants-in-aid recommended by the Finance Commission are of an unconditional nature and the states have the freedom to use those fiscal resources for whatever purposes they choose. However, the grants-in-aid recommended by the Planning Commission and the non-plan, nonstatutory grants do affect the autonomy of the states, as they must be utilized as per the conditions prescribed by the Planning Commission. The degree of fiscal autonomy of the states depends upon the relative proportion of these two types of transfers.

TABLE 5: STATES' FISCAL AUTONOMY 1961-2 TO 1994-5

(Rs. in crores)

Year (1)	States' own Revenues (2)	States' own Revenues and Finance Commission Transfers (3)	States' Revenue Expenditure (4)	Col. 3 as % of Col. 4 (5)
1961-2	700	934	1121	83.3
1965-6	1244	1607	1892	84.9
1970-1	2048	2974	3389	87.7
1975-6	5120	7238	6966	103.9
1980-1	9881	13967	14807	94.4
1990-1	36330	53834	67860	79.33
1991-2	45784	66079	83611	79.03
1992-3	49518	73308	92150	79.55
1993-4	61993	86457	109376	79.05
1994-5 (R.E.)	76161	103432	131014	78.95

SOURCE: Reserve Bank of India Bulletins—various issues.

In this study, the states' own revenues, together with the statutory transfers of tax shares and grants, as recommended by the Finance Commission, have been taken as a ratio of the states' revenue expenditure to measure the fiscal autonomy of the states. Table 5 shows that the states have been enjoying autonomy to the extent of 80 per cent as far as expenditure is concerned. However, it may be seen that the ratio shows a declining trend, implying deterioration in the fiscal autonomy of the states in recent years on the basis of this measure. In the early 1950s the statutory fiscal transfers were around 60 per cent while the non-statutory transfers constituted 40 per cent. The trend has been reversed over the period as the statutory transfers constitute only 40 per cent while the non-statutory transfers comprise 60 per cent of the total fiscal transfers. The situation is even worse when fiscal autonomy is viewed in terms of statutory and non-statutory grants. Table 6 shows that during 1993-4 and 1995-6 statutory grants constitute only 10 per cent and 11 per cent respectively while the non-statutory grants constituted 90 per cent and 89 per cent. These non-statutory grants have been given by the central government for state plan schemes,

TABLE 6: GRANTS FROM THE CENTRE TO STATES 1993-4

(Rs. in crores)

Type of Grant	1993-4	1994-5 (RE)
I. Plan Grant	18178 (86)	19343 (87)
1. State Plan Schemes	10770 (51)	9897 (44)
2. Central Plan Schemes	1066 (5)	1576 (7)
3. Centrally Sponsored Schemes	6272 (30)	6913 (31)
4. Special Plan Schemes	70 (0.33)	957 (4)
II. Statutory Grants	2069 (10)	2421 (11)
III. Non-Plan Non-Statutory Grants	929 (4)	527 (2)
IV. Total Non-Statutory Grants (I+III)	19107 (90)	22291 (10)
V. Total Grants (II+IV)	21176 (100)	22291 (100)

SOURCE: *RBI Bulletin*, December, 1995.
NOTE: Figures in parentheses represent percentages of the total.

central plan, schemes, centrally sponsored, and for special plan schemes as recommended by the Planning Commission. Fiscal redistribution in the form of grants will erode the autonomy of the states as they cannot spend on the things they want. They have to adhere to the conditions and stipulations made by the central government. If these grants were made through the Finance Commission instead, the states would enjoy more financial freedom and autonomy, though perhaps at the cost of more state fiscal irresponsibility.

FISCAL ASPECTS AFFECTING FISCAL AUTONOMY

In the last four-and-a-half decades, the decisions and laws relating to fiscal aspects made by the central government have affected the financial flexibility of the states by denying them their constitutional rights. What follows is a brief account of some of those fiscal aspects.

1. The Finance Act (Amendment Act of 1959) redefined shareable income tax as personal income tax and income tax paid by companies while excluding the income tax paid by companies from the divisible pool. Consequently, the states' share from the shareable income tax was reduced, depriving them of their legitimate share. Since then, states have been demanding either a share from the corporation tax or a restoration of the status

quo prior to 1959. It is pertinent to note that the rate of growth of revenues from corporation tax has been higher than that of income tax. For instance, the average annual growth rate of corporation tax was 16 per cent for the period 1970-1 to 1989-90 while that of income tax was 14 per cent.[15]

2. Under Article 271 of the Constitution, Parliament is empowered to impose a surcharge on income tax for a specific purpose of an emergency nature and on a temporary basis. Unfortunately, this became a regular levy. Although now obsolete, the surcharge yielded large dividends of revenue to the central government over several decades. Had the surcharge been merged with the basic rate of income tax, the states would have benefited.
3. The Government of India in May 1957 made an agreement with the states to levy additional excise duties on mill-made textiles, sugar and tobacco, in lieu of sales tax (a state tax). The centre would make good the loss of revenue that had been realized by the respective states in the financial year 1956-7. This Tax Rental Arrangement (TRA) was made only for a period of ten years. Yet the sales tax power on these three commodities of mass consumption was not restored despite protests from the states. This measure has deprived the states of huge revenues. It may be noted that the rates of union excise duties (central government) and sales tax have been increasing much faster than the rates of additional duties of excise (TRA). The states' fiscal dependence would have been reduced considerably, had the sales tax power been restored to them.
4. There has been vehement criticism that the central government has not fully exploited the taxes enumerated under Article 269 of the Constitution. Some taxes have not been imposed. Others have been abolished very shortly after their imposition. For instance, the tax on railway passenger fares was repealed after 4 years of its imposition in 1961. Again, the wealth tax on agricultural property was re-imposed in 1970-1 (after 20 years) and was then discontinued. Estate duty was kept very low until its abolition recently. As stated earlier, the net revenue of all these taxes should go to the states (though the legislation and administration power lies with the centre).
5. The states' right of raising market borrowings under Article 293(3) of the Constitution has become inoperative since 1961;

hence the states have to depend on the centre for loans. The constitutional right bestowed on the states to borrow funds within India has become a nominal power in practice.

Concluding Suggestions

Federal fiscal transfers are inevitable in any federation due to the existence of vertical and/or horizontal federal fiscal imbalances. The greater presence of fiscal transfers explains the fiscal dependence of the recipient governments on the other layer of the government. Here lies the importance of states' fiscal autonomy, one of the most important dimensions in fiscal federalism. In India there exist both vertical and horizontal fiscal imbalances as a result of the division of tax powers and functions between the centre and states and also due to the differences in the endowment position of certain resources of the states.

Fiscal dependence in a federation will lead to an erosion of fiscal autonomy. It has been found that the states have been enjoying substantial fiscal autonomy so far the revenue expenditure is concerned. However, there appears to be deterioration in this fiscal autonomy in recent years, in part because of the growing importance of non-statutory transfers including discretionary transfers. For instance, out of the total amount of grants currently received, about 90 per cent are non-statutory grants. The states' fiscal autonomy has been eroded also by decisions taken by the central government with regard to matters such as income tax, the tax rental arrangement relating to additional excise duties and exploitation of tax sources under Article 269.

The following changes would have the effect of injecting greater fiscal flexibility and reducing the fiscal dependence.

1. The divisible pool of income tax should be increased by including corporation tax (as was the case prior to 1958-9).
2. The surcharge on income tax should be imposed only with the consent of the states and that, too, for a limited period.
3. The states should have their powers of sales tax restored on textiles, sugar and tobacco, ending the TRA of 1957. Alternatively, the revenue growth from this source needs to be equated with the rate of growth of sales tax revenue of the respective states.

4. The tax powers enumerated under Article 269 of the Constitution need to be exploited to the maximum possible extent. Those taxes for which legislation has been made already should be imposed without further delay. Also, the revenue yield from the existing taxes under this category needs to be increased by better administration and by expanding the tax base.
5. The large part of the revenue resources distributed from the centre should be transferred through the Finance Commission rather than through the Planning Commission. The proportion of statutory grants should increase more than the proportion of non-statutory grants.

NOTES

1. W.E. Oates, *Fiscal Federalism* (New York, 1972), p. 17.
2. R.A. Musgrave, *Fiscal Systems* (New Haven, 1969), pp. 341-4.
3. Oates, pp. 195-213.
4. V. Pillai and G.S. Krishnan, 'Fiscal Centralisation in India: A Preliminary Analysis', *Margin*, January 1979, pp. 72-81.
5. M.M. Ansari, 'A Critique of the Developments in Indian Fiscal Federalism', *Margin*, October 1984, pp. 31-47.
6. NIPFP, *Trends and Issues in Indian Federal Finance* (Delhi, 1981), pp. 38-46.
7. R.J. Chellaiah, 'The Economic and Equity Aspects of Distribution of Financial Resources between the Centre and the States in India', paper presented at the Seminar on Centre-State Relations, Bangalore, Government of Karnataka, August 1983.
8. J.L. Bajaj, K.S. Sinha and O.R. Agarwal, *Finance Commission and Backward States* (Lucknow, 1985), pp. 29-40, 154-6.
9. C. Wallich, *State Finance in India, Revenue Sharing*, World Bank Staff Working Papers (Washington, DC, 1982), pp. 14-22.
10. P.K. Bhargava, *Centre-State Resource Transfers in India* (Gurgaon, 1982), p. 68.
11. Wallich, p. 22.
12. NIPFP, p. 42.
13. Chellaiah, pp. 16, 156.
14. Ansari, p. 43.
15. Government of India, *Interim Report of the Tax Reforms Committee*, Ministry of Finance, New Delhi, p. 24.

17

Federalism and Constitutional Processes in India

G. PARTHASARATHY

In 1996 over 300 million people, speaking over 15 distinct languages in over 350 dialects, turned out to elect 543 representatives to the Indian Parliament for the eleventh time since the people of India adopted their Constitution on 26 November 1949, constituting India into a Sovereign, Socialist, Secular, Democratic Republic, dedicated to promoting justice, liberty and equality of status and opportunity for all its citizens. Describing India's unique democratic practices, the person whom I regard as our most renowned constitutional expert, Mr Nani Palkhivala, observed in 1983: 'The largest experiment ever undertaken in human history in the art of democratic living has been carried on in India since 1950. Never before and nowhere else, has more than one-seventh of the human race lived together in freedom as a single political entity.'

In analysing the federal and other features of the Indian Constitution it is imperative to recall the traumatic circumstances that affected the country and its people in the period before and after India became independent on 15 August 1947. The immense sufferings that millions of people had to endure as they fled their hearths and homes to seek new and safe abodes following the Partition of the country, was compounded by the fact that under the Indian Independence Act passed by the British Parliament in 1947, 565 princely states technically became autonomous, raising fears of Balkanisation and chaos. Further, India's history was replete with instances where internal divisions and rivalries had made the country a fertile playground for foreign invaders and marauders. Alluding to the terms of the Independence Act, the Government of India White Paper of 1950 noted: 'The dangers inherent in the situation were underlined by the attitude of some of the Princes who were inclined to sacrifice national interests of the people on the altar of personal ambition. The events in certain states like Junagadh and Hyderabad had come as pointers in that direction.' More importantly, the Partition of the country on religious considerations made it imperative that secular principles be firmly embedded in the Constitution and the root causes of communal divisions like separate electorates be removed from the statute book.

It is primarily because of the country's historical experiences that the founding fathers of India's Constitution decided that Article 1 of the Constitution would describe India as a 'Union of States' and not as a 'Federation'. The main rationale for this was that, unlike the United States or Australia, the Indian Union was not constituted by any agreement between constituent units—which, therefore, should have no right of secession. Describing the reasons underlying the adoption of the term 'Union', the Chairman of the Constitutional Drafting Committee, Dr. B.R. Ambedkar said:

> Though India was to be a Federation, the Federation was not the result of an agreement by states to join in a Federation and the Federation not being the result of an agreement, no state had the right to secede from it. The Federation is a Union because it is indestructible. Though the country and the people can be divided into different States for convenience of administration, the country is an integral whole, its people, a single people living under a single imperium derived from a single source. The Americans had to wage a civil war to establish that the States have no right to secession and that their Federation was indestructible. The Drafting Committee thought that it was better to make this clear at the outset, rather than to leave it to speculation.

Given the fact that Constitution describes the country as a 'Union' and not as a 'Federation', and contains provisions empowering the Parliament to alter the territorial boundaries and names of the States even without their consent, can the Constitution of India actually be described as 'federal'? There has been much argument about this, but it can be stated that the normal attributes of a federal system are present in the Indian constitutional structure. First and foremost, the country is governed by a written Constitution which clearly spells out the distribution of powers between the Union and state governments. The provisions of this Constitution are supreme, with neither the states nor the Union having the power to override the provisions relating to the division of powers. Further, provisions having a bearing on the federal structure cannot be amended by Parliament alone, but would require ratification by the legislatures of not less than half the states. Finally, the judiciary in India has extensive powers in determining the constitutional validity of laws passed by Parliament and the state legislatures, with the Supreme Court having the authority to decide disputes between the Union and the states and to be the final authority in interpreting the provisions of the Constitution.

It is inevitable in any country with a written democratic Constitution that, with the passage of time, the judiciary will emerge as a powerful and independent element in interpreting the provisions pertaining to the separation of powers and the limitations in the powers of the executive and the legislature. The Supreme Court in India has emerged as an institution determined not only to protect the rights and freedoms of citizens, but also to preserve the sanctity and inviolability of the ideals and aspirations cherished by the Constitution's founding fathers. In a landmark judgment in 1973, in what is popularly known as the 'Keshavanada Bharati Case', the Supreme Court ruled that Parliament does not have the power to amend the Constitution so as to damage or destroy its essential or 'Basic Features'. The 'Basic Features' which have been identified by the Supreme Court include such issues as the supremacy of the Constitution, the rule of law, the separation of powers, federalism, secularism, freedom and dignity of the individual, free and fair elections and the unity and integrity of the nation. The inevitable impact of such judgments has been to strengthen the federal aspects of the Constitution.

While the powers of the Union and states have been clearly demarcated, constitutional experts in India have argued that in actual practice, the spirit of federalism has been eroded with the Union Government assuming and exercising larger powers and authority than the founding fathers had either envisaged, or desired. In the short time that I have been in Australia, I have heard similar arguments about the Federal Government and Parliament in Canberra likewise having acquired larger and wider powers than earlier envisaged, through legislation required to fulfil international obligations and treaties, including in the sphere of the environment. In India, the main criticism about what is claimed to be an excessive assumption of powers by the Union Government, stems from the vast powers now wielded by it in the regulation of commerce and industry, the imposition of what is termed 'President's Rule' in the states, the appointment of governors and the distribution of revenues between the Union and the states.

In a thought-provoking address entitled 'States Are Not Vassals of the Union', delivered in 1983, Mr Nani Palkhivala called for a national consensus under which the Union Government would have no moral authority to govern unless it showed a sense of constitutional morality, particularly a sense of justice and fairness towards the states. Mr Palkhivala noted that while the Constitution envisaged that trade, commerce, and the production and supply of goods were to be state subjects, a series of Parliamentary enactments had resulted in these virtually ceasing to be State subjects. He also noted that there had been a tendency to erode the democratic functioning of state governments by the imposition of 'President's Rule', often for partisan political considerations, under the provisions of Article 356 of the Constitution. Mr Palkhivala also argued for the states to be given a larger share in the tax revenues collected by the Union and a reduction in their reliance on discretionary financial allocations by the Union Government.

Given the rich ethnic, religious and linguistic diversity that constitutes the vigour and vitality of national life in India, there has naturally been a continuing and lively debate about what is termed 'Centre-State relations'. While, at the one extreme, there are those who argue that the Union's authority should be confined to essential subjects like Defence, Foreign Policy and Currency, there are also those who believe that, given the vast disparities that exist between the various states and regions in living standards and economic development, a measure of Union intervention and control is imperative and inevitable, if the goals of securing equality of opportunity and status enshrined in the Constitution are to be realized. It was largely with this objection in view, that the years following Independence saw the emergence of powerful institutions like the Planning Commission. Further, even though law and order is a state subject, there has been a substantial increase in the strength of central para-military police forces such as the Central Reserve Police, the Border Security Force and the Rapid Action Force, though these forces cannot be used in a state without the concurrence of the state government concerned. It must, however, be stressed that these central police forces have played a crucial role in helping state governments deal with difficult situations like externally aided insurgencies and terrorist activities and communal tensions, which state police forces lack the resources to deal with.

It was in response to calls for the need to review the working of existing constitutional and administrative arrangements governing relations between the centre and the states, that just a few months before Mr Palkhivala's address in 1983, the Union Government constituted a high level judicial commission headed by a distinguished judge of the Supreme Court, Justice R.S. Sarkaria. The 'Sarkaria Commission' was asked to recommend changes to existing arrangements which would enable centre-state relations to be conducted in a harmonious, just and fair manner, while ensuring that the goals of national unity, economic development and social justice envisaged by the founding fathers were fulfilled. The Sarkaria Commission submitted its report (of nearly 4900 pages) in January 1988. This voluminous document covered virtually all areas of centre-state relations. It dealt with the role of the governors, emergency provisions, deployment of the Union armed forces, reservation of Bills passed by state legislatures for assent by the president, financial relations, economic and social planning, interstate trade and commerce, inter-state river disputes, mines and minerals, forests and mass media. The report made a total of 247 recommendations on these matters.

While considerations of space make it impossible for me to cover in detail all the important recommendations of the Sarkaria Commission it is salutary to reflect briefly on some of the salient features of the Report. Most importantly, the Commission has held that the basic provisions of the Constitution are as valid and relevant today as they were when the founding fathers adopted them in 1949. The Commision has, therefore, ruled out any need for major changes in the structure of the Constitution. It did, however, make detailed suggestions on the functional and operational aspects of the implementation of the provisions of the Constitution. It also laid considerable emphasis on the need for evolving and devising healthy conventions and mechanisms for ensuring that these issues were tackled on the basis of a national consensus. Significantly, the Commission suggested the establishment of an Interstate Council as a permanent body under Article 263 of the Constitution to deal with subjects other than socio-economic planning.

It was suggested that the prime minister, cabinet ministers and all state chief ministers should be members of this Council. Other important suggestions of the Sarkaria Commission were:

- *Legislative Relations*: While some amendments to the Constitution have been suggested which would give the states more powers, the Commission has considered the existing provisions of the Constitution ensuring the supremacy of Parliament to be basically sound.
- *Executive Powers*: The Commission recommended that the state chief ministers should be consulted in the appointment of governors and made detailed recommendations on the norms to be observed in the selection of governors, so as to prevent that high office from becoming the subject of political controversy. The Commission also recommended broad guidelines to be observed by the governors in choosing chief ministers and urged that whenever there were doubts about a chief minister enjoying majority support in the legislature, rival claims should be tested on the floor of the assembly. The Commission looked with disfavour on the practice of prolonged periods of Presidential Rule in the states and made detailed suggestions as to the course of action governors should adopt when a state government lost majority support in the legislature. However, it rejected suggestions to curtail the discretionary powers of the governors.
- *Financial Relations*: Detailed recommendations were made by the Commission for amendment of the Constitution to permit Parliament to legislate on the sharing of Corporate Tax and for the sharing of revenues generated from advertisements in broadcasts. The Commission's recommendations are, however, such that the Union Government would retain considerable powers in respect of tax revenues.
- *Industry and Trade*: The Commission suggested that the Union Government should exercise greater restraint in administering industrial regulations and recommended a three-year mandatory review of Union control over an industry.
- *Interstate Council*: The Commission recommended the establishment of a permanent Interstate Council under Article 263 and suggested a number of measures to resolve contentious interstate river water disputes.

If implemennted, the Sarkaria Commission's recommendations should lead to the evolution of more healthy and transparent norms for the conduct of centre-state relations. Meanwhile recent judgments of the Supreme Court are also strengthening the federal characteristics of the Constitution. I have already referred to the Supreme Court's judgement on the inviolability of the 'Basic Features' of the Constitution. In a historic judgement in 1994, the Supreme Court ruled that even if a proclamation under Article 356 of the Constitution was approved by Parliament, the proclamation could not be excluded from judicial review. Thus, the Union Government is now accountable to the courts for actions of governors under Article 356. This judgement is particularly important in the context of the observations made by the Sarkaria Commission that the bulk imposition of President's Rule in a number of states between 1977 and 1980 was improper and violative of the spirit of the Constitution.

How will the federal structure in India be affected by recent political trends towards the formation of coalition governments at the centre? The last two elections have led to regional parties playing an important role federally as coalition partners. Under its 'Common Minimum Programme' the United Front government formed in 1996 committed itself to advancing 'the principles of political, administrative and economic federalism'. The BJP-led government formed in 1998 pledged to the implementation of the Sarkaria Commission's recommendations which enjoy a broad national consensus, to giving greater autonomy to the states in economic planning and to promptly granting assent to Bills passed by state legislatures.

In a populous country like India, does a two-tier federal set-up with constitutional powers divided between centre and states provide an adequate basis for dealing with the day-to-day problems of the people? Can an elected member of Parliament who represents 1.8 million people or a state legislator who represents around 300,000 people find enough time to address the immediate problems of their constituents? These are issues which have been exercising our minds in the recent past. And it was with the aim of promoting grass-roots democracy and decentralizing further the process of economic development that in 1993, Parliament enacted the Seventy-fourth Constitutional Amendment Act, establishing the framework for directly elected representatives for village councils and municipalities and for seeing that elected representatives at the intermediate and district level play their proper role in fulfilling the needs and aspirations of the people. The Constitution of India, therefore, today guarantees democratic functioning at the very grass-roots and not merely at the Union and state levels. What is more, in the municipal and district tiers of government in India, one-third of the seats are reserved for women. Further, the present government has pledged that it will take necessary action to see that one-third of the elected membership of Parliament and the State Legislatures will, likewise, be reserved for women. Empowerment of women, we are convinced, is the best way to ensure that values which have traditionally united Indian families are preserved and that women have a powerful voice in the community.

It is now nearly half a century since the Constitution of India was adopted by its people. In this period the country has had to deal with natural calamities, external aggression and externally inspired terrorism across its borders. It inherited an economy which was backward and stagnant and wholly dependent on the vagaries of the monsoon—an economy in which over two million people perished of hunger in the course of World War II. Barely five decades after Independence, India today is not merely self-sufficient in, but is a net exporter of foodgrains (despite life expectancy having dramatically increased and the country's population having grown from around 350 million when the Constitution came into force to over 900 million at present). Economic growth through the decade of the 1980s averaged over 5 per cent, with the growth levels reaching over 6 per cent in the past two years. Twelve general elections have been held since the Constitution came into force, with the people of India freely and peacefully casting their votes across the length and breadth of the country. Interestingly, apart from the judiciary, other constitutional institutions like the Election Commission are also now increasingly assertive about their role in safeguarding democratic freedoms.

For a civilization which derives its strength from an ancient heritage of tolerance, love and compassion, a half century is but a brief period. We in India can, however, derive legitimate satisfaction from the way our constitutional processes have retained a measure of flexibility to meet new challenges, as and when they emerge. We are now living in an era of global interdependence with revolutionary changes being brought about by technological innovations virtually on a daily basis.

India will naturally seek its rightful place in the comity of nations as we participate in this quest for peace, progress and prosperity. But, even as we do so, we would like to retain all that we cherish of our ancient values and traditions. We would like to remain committed to Mahatma Gandhi's vision when he said: 'I shall work for an India in which the poorest shall feel that it is their country in whose making they have an effective voice, an India in which there shall be no rich class and no poor class of people, an India in which all communities, shall live in perfect harmony. This is the India of my dreams.' We recognize that we still have to go a long way in fulfilling the dreams of the Father of our Nation. But we do owe a debt of gratitude to our founding fathers for their wisdom and sagacity in bequeathing to us a Constitution that gives us the democratic freedoms so essential for human fulfilment and progress.

Index